Praise for
*Glow in the F*cking Dark*

"Tara Schuster is a phenomenal stor̲ ̲, sisted on reclaiming her agency to shine in bleak circumstances. *Glow in the F*cking Dark* is a revealing and powerful book that lit me up from the inside out."

—Glennon Doyle, #1 *New York Times* bestselling author of *Untamed,* founder of Together Rising, and host of the podcast *We Can Do Hard Things*

"Healing takes effort—and we can't do it alone. In *Glow in the F*cking Dark,* Tara Schuster guides us along as she finds her way through her own pain and offers honest, often funny, and actionable advice for taking charge of your emotional health."

—Lori Gottlieb, *New York Times* bestselling author of *Maybe You Should Talk to Someone* and co-host of the podcast *Dear Therapists*

"Tara Schuster has done something remarkable: She's written a guide to facing the slings and arrows of life that's both delightfully irreverent and disarmingly earnest. You'll laugh, you'll cry, and you might just come away stronger and better."

—Adam Grant, #1 *New York Times* bestselling author of *Think Again* and host of the TED podcast *WorkLife*

"*Glow in the F★cking Dark* proves that Tara Schuster is a modern-day guru for people who really hate gurus. Ruthlessly authentic and bitingly hilarious, Schuster takes us on a roller coaster of self-discovery, revealing that we are all the student and the teacher on our own paths to growth and healing."
—Melissa Urban, co-founder of Whole30 and #1 *New York Times* bestselling author of *The Whole30* and *The Book of Boundaries*

"Former Comedy Central exec Schuster follows up *Buy the F★cking Lilies* with an upbeat plan for readers to become more confident versions of themselves. Blending witty personal anecdotes and ample doses of wisdom, Schuster urges readers to surpass their 'good-enough plateau' and 'unleash [their] inner glow.' . . . Her stories are candid and funny, and her chatty tone keeps the narrative moving. Readers will be charmed by Schuster's honesty and humor."
—*Publishers Weekly*

"Schuster organizes her ideas into easy-to-follow steps (each chapter ends with a bite-sized 'Little Thing That Helps') and also provides funny, self-deprecating anecdotes—e.g., the time she gave herself an allergic reaction eating a self-imposed raw-beet-and-kale diet during an online meditation retreat. The author doesn't shy away from her darkest moments, writing about her troubled relationship with her father or her struggle with suicidal thoughts, which can 'make you feel full-body sick, like your insides are going to leap out of your skin or, sometimes, like every muscle is paralyzed. It's an excruciating kind of agony that you want to end at all costs.' . . . An approachable, exuberant combination of memoir and self-help."

—*Kirkus Reviews*

BY TARA SCHUSTER

Buy Yourself the F*cking Lilies
Glow in the F*cking Dark

Glow
in the
F*cking
Dark

GLOW
IN THE
F*CKING
DARK

*Simple Practices
to Heal Your Soul, from Someone
Who Learned the Hard Way*

TARA SCHUSTER

THE DIAL PRESS

NEW YORK

LIBRARY OF CONGRESS CATALOGING-IN-PUBLICATION DATA
Names: Schuster, Tara, author.
Title: Glow in the f *cking dark: simple practices to heal your soul,
from someone who learned the hard way / by Tara Schuster.
Other titles: Glow in the fucking dark
Description: First edition. | New York: The Dial Press, [2022]
Identifiers: LCCN 2022043873 (print) | LCCN 2022043874 (ebook) |
ISBN 9780593243114 (trade paperback) | ISBN 9780593243107 (ebook)
Subjects: LCSH: Self-actualization (Psychology) | Self-acceptance.
Classification: LCC BF637.S4 (print) | LCC BF637.S4 (ebook) |
DDC 158.1—dc23/eng/20220922
LC record available at https://lccn.loc.gov/2022043873
LC ebook record available at https://lccn.loc.gov/2022043874

Printed in the United States of America on acid-free paper

randomhousebooks.com

2 4 6 8 9 7 5 3 1

Design by Diane Hobbing

AUTHOR'S NOTE

I AM THE last person you want to calculate the tip at a restaurant, or track the expenses of a group trip (ask my friends), or tell you what time to arrive at the airport unless you want to play a thrilling game of *Is There Any Chance in Hell I Will Make This Flight?* This is to say that I am terrible with numbers, dates, and time to the extent that within one journal, covering one month, I have listed my entries as having taken place in different *years* despite the fact that I am no time traveler. So, to deal with my "imaginative" sense of time and with the fact that healing, sadly, isn't the linear pursuit I have always hoped it would be, I have rearranged and compressed the timeline when it served the narrative or when I just couldn't fucking remember. I have also changed most names and identifying characteristics of the people who appear in this book, because I'm not trying to go after anyone (*yet*—I reserve the right to do so when I'm ready) and I don't want people worrying that by interacting with me they will end up in a book. They will. But with a new name, and that makes all the difference, right?

I've tried to show myself, fully. In all things, I let truth, courage, and compassion guide me.

For you,
well on your way,
illuminating the path for us all

We are stars wrapped in skin. The light you are seeking has always been within.

—Rumi

CONTENTS

PULL OVER

I'M CAREENING DOWN Highway 40 in the Mojave Desert as night threatens to engulf the day. Blistering wind floods through my car's open windows, whipping my unwashed hair around my face in stinging lashes. Through the strands, I clock my surroundings: nothing but gnarled Joshua trees and never-ending sand melting into a blur, and the world looks alien, like Dr. Seuss's version of the moon. I need to get out of here, to launch off the road and break through the atmosphere and into outer space, because Earth is not tolerable right now. I jam my right foot on the accelerator and watch the car's speedometer push from eight-five to ninety, and now ninety-five, as I feel less and less in control.

"WHAT IS HAPPENING TO ME?" I scream to no one as I bang my hands on the steering wheel. But, my hands? They don't appear to be *my* hands. Though I recognize my beloved rings and my shoddy, self-done manicure, my hands appear to be hovering a few inches off of the steering wheel, in no way connected to my body, which is—to say the least—freaking me the fuck out. And actually, my *whole body* feels like it's floating above me like a morbid kite, making me nauseous. But I've barely eaten in the past two days, so what would come up? All of my insides? I sure hope so, because that seems a whole lot better than what I'm experiencing now.

How can I feel this sick, this out of control, this soul-level bad? I wonder. Because in some pretty fundamental ways, my life is damn good. In fact, for the past decade, I have worked like hell to heal the emotional wounds inflicted on me by my parents during my neglected-shit-show-psychologically-abusive-mess-wreck-disaster of a childhood. I might have grown up in a house where things came to die, in a din of my parents' never-ending screaming, chaos, stress, and money troubles, but I have *worked* to bring radical self-care, healing rituals, and self-love into my life, and it has changed me. It really has! I re-parented myself into a flourishing adult who is, most days, *not* having an out-of-body-panic-attack-doom-spiral experience. I've even written a book about it. So why, oh why does every cell in my body, every single tissue, feel like it is being wrung dry? *And why can't I feel my hands?*

Well. Here's the thing. I just lost my job. My executive position at Comedy Central, where I have worked for over a decade. One-third of my life. It was my happily-ever-after job. The thing at which I pointed to show that, *Yes, I was a neglected child who had to overcome my ingrained beliefs that I was worthless, that I could never give up my addictions to weed, booze, and boys, that I could never stop treating life like a series of crises to be endured, but LOOK—it turned out all right—I'm a successful adult, I'm living the dream!* People introduced me as "Tara Schuster, Comedy Central" like it was my married last name. But it's gone now. The financial fallout from the pandemic shut down our whole department. I'm remarkably lucky to have savings, no kids to support, no mortgage to pay, and to not be in any *real* danger. But I have to tell you, it's been hard.

The toughest part has been figuring out how to structure my days without someone else telling me what to do. I went from showing friends with pride how many overlapping, brightly colored meeting boxes made up my Outlook calendar to *maybe* having one Zoom every few weeks *if* I could coerce friends to "hang out." I went from waking up thinking about what I had to accomplish at the office and how I would strategically zigzag my way from task to task with MAX efficiency, to lying in bed, wondering if I had the stamina to go to the grocery store. I have been working since high school, taking summer jobs, weird internships that were more like indentured servitude (one was billed as an opportunity to learn about playwriting but turned out to be a master class in removing filthy storm windows from the walls of a decrepit theater, which, by the way, I did gladly), so it feels disorienting to have no schedule. And, if I'm real with you, my job was my entire life; I hung most of my self-worth on it. And now, for the first time, I'm completely alone. Cooped up in my one-bedroom apartment during a global pandemic with my fractured identity, my raging anxiety, and about one ton of dried black beans that I had to fight for.

And so, two days ago, because my life is a petit disaster, and because the way I deal with distress is by DOING—by going, moving, fixing, by "KEEP ON ACHIEVING, *WOMAN*"—I googled "How can I help in the 2020 election?" and clicked the first result: "You can help in Arizona!" So just like that, I decided to move to Flagstaff, way up in the mountains, where the Internet tells me I am needed. Light research revealed that it *snows* in Flagstaff, which I can barely believe, because it does not fit in my mind's eye of Arizona (i.e., orange earth, cacti, Wile E. Coyote). Flagstaff allegedly has a pinewood forest, too, and it's the world's first "International Dark Sky Community," which, I learned, means that the government and citizens have agreed to work together to keep the night sky as dark as possible so that you can see the stars shine. Can you believe that in 2020, an entire city has agreed on *anything,* much less night sky stewardship? Something about being in a place known for darkness feels like it matches my current mood perfectly.

Which brings us to now, flying down the highway as the sun sets on yet another grim, *why-God-why* day. *I know that day follows night but right now it feels like every day is a new night, somehow bleaker, more horrible than the previous. When is light going to break through? How long can we live in obscurity?* I think. My spiraling is interrupted by the ringing of my cellphone. It's my new therapist, Dr. Candace. I called her before getting in the car to (1) have a meltdown on her voicemail because, well, it's kind of a classic move for me and really, if you can't melt down to your therapist, who *can* you melt down to, and (2) let her know I had the excellent idea to fix all my problems by moving to Arizona.

I pick up and her voice floods through the car speakers. "Hi. I just got your message. Are you safe right now?" *What a stupid question,* I think. "Yeah, of course I'm safe. I'm just . . . driving . . . to Arizona," I defensively explain. "Tara. Driving from Los Angeles to Arizona in your condition is *not* safe. From what you described in your message, you're somewhere between a dissociative episode and a panic attack." Dr. Candace and I have been talking a lot about these "dissociative episodes," instances when a traumatic memory is so overwhelming that my brain effectively tries to escape reality to protect me. It makes me feel like I'm living outside of myself, which gives me some momentary relief, but it also makes me sick to my stomach and question basic things like if my hands are actually *my* hands and if I should cut my own bangs. (Obviously not. There is never a reason to cut your own bangs.) "You can't drive right now." Dr. Candace is stern. "What I need you to do right now is *pull over.* Can you safely pull over?"

"Pull over." The words ring in my head like a cymbal— surprising, piercing, sharp. It has never *once* in my life occurred to me to pull over. Since I was a child, when confronted with any discomfort, my gut reaction has been to hustle—to get good grades, to make teachers like me, to show my boss I am the best, to *do,* to achieve every marker of external success, to make it *somewhere.* But where exactly? I'm not so sure anymore, but I've been in constant motion for the past thirty-four years, hurtling forward with no regard for how it *feels*. And how it feels, by the way, is like sandpaper on the soul: rough and raw and *wrong*. My friends often tell me that I have a "productivity illness"—this means that even when I am in the throes of a depressive episode, I can, say, send out a newsletter, take a meeting, or volunteer at the Covid vaccination clinic.* It has always felt to me that if I am not *doing,* I am not existing. But lately it all just feels . . . useless. Whenever I get "there," "there" immediately disintegrates and I turn to some new, impossible task that singularly grabs my attention as I shove and press and race for it not only to work but for it to be THE BEST. I have to be the best, there is no alternative.

As I hurtle down this remote highway in my Prius of Doom, my legs sticky with sweat on the pleather seat, I finally see the obvious: I no longer have a choice. I actually *can't* keep moving forward. Even if I think I should be fine, even if I have it "pretty good," I've forced my mind and body into overdrive one too many times and they have justifiably revolted against me. Something deep within me seeks liberation, from my thoughts, from my anxieties, from my past, from my voracious need for outside achievement to give me my worth. I've got to figure out who remains when everything is taken away, because many things *have* been taken away. I urgently need to stop producing, stop fixing, stop spinning, just stop, stop, STOP.

I pull over. For the first time in my life, I pull over.

* * *

So . . . here's the thing. What I said before? About losing my job? And *that* being the catalyst for my panic drive to Arizona? It wasn't the *whole* thing. Losing my job was not what had me so unteth-

---

* This is true. If you came to Kedren Health to get your vaccine and saw a woman in a lily-print mask asking for your driver's license, she was crying on the inside as she made friendly small talk with you.

ered, even though for a long time I thought (and maybe wished) it
was. The job had simply been a levee, keeping the surging—at
times, unrelenting—deluge of my deepest storms at bay. Because
as much as I write about how I didn't have "the worst childhood
ever"—and I really didn't—there are things that happened that
were . . . truly disturbing. Things that maybe someone else, someone stronger, someone *better*, could have just walked away from,
unscathed, or at least less fucked-up, but I'm not someone else. I'm
me, and that shit still hurts.

If you've read my first book, *Buy Yourself the F*cking Lilies*,* then
you know that after a minimally parented, emotionally abusive
upbringing, I hit rock bottom on my twenty-fifth birthday when
I drunk-dialed my therapist, threatening to kill myself. COOL,
NON-EMBARRASSING STORY. The morning after, I felt so
ashamed that I decided that if I didn't do *something* to save my life,
I wouldn't have much more of a life to live. I didn't have parents
around to teach me how to take care of myself, so I spent the next
five years creating a Google Document called "A Curriculum of
Self-Care/Re-Parenting Myself," in which I noted any idea that I
thought might heal me. I read memoirs *as* self-help, I gave up my
Great Love and trusted crutch, marijuana, altogether, I asked
adults I admired how they lived, I put paying for therapy above
every other expense in my life, I tried every single solution in a
~~desperate~~ courageous attempt to grow myself up. *And it worked*.
BY GOD, IT WORKED! By thirty, I found that I was no longer
thinking of ending my life, I was eager to *live it*.

And living it I was. My rituals gave me the stability and the opportunity to love myself and build the life I so desperately wanted.
I enjoyed my days, I felt content for the first time ever, a feat that,
before I re-parented myself, seemed impossible. But how great

* And if you haven't . . . I don't know what you're doing later today but I have a pretty good idea
for you . . .

could things be if I had just been on the highway in the middle of a desert, going dangerously fast, experiencing what felt like the unwanted love child of a panic attack and a dissociative episode? It didn't exactly scream "picture of mental health and stability."

The truth is, for years, even though I kinda, sorta knew I had more work to do, I had been too afraid to face my soul bruises simply because I didn't know how. And! My life was good! It was kind of awesome and glamorous, and fun—FUN! Life was fun for the first time . . . ever! What would happen if I dug deeper? Would I mess with my hard-won stability? Would I ruin everything I had so PAINSTAKINGLY built? I couldn't even *think* about risking that. Losing my job made the decision for me. Isolated at home with nothing to distract me, the things I didn't want to face finally had the space to face me, to present themselves like furious, feral monsters I had banished to living under my bed. Once free, the monsters would not go back to sleep. I had no choice but to see them in all their hideous glory.

I don't think I'm alone in this. I think there are a lot of us who carry emotional hurts, big and small, but ignore them because we have never been taught to do otherwise and we don't want to muddle up our lives with what we assume will be an overwhelming experience. I mean, I remember taking geometry and learning what the Pythagorean theorem was,* but I have zero recollection of a teacher explaining how to mindfully navigate anxiety. Or how to quiet negative self-chatter. Or HOW TO BREATHE DEEPLY. Like, for real, HOW ARE YOU SUPPOSED TO BREATHE?! I STILL DON'T KNOW.

What we do know is the fact that we live with the fear that the rug is always on the verge of being yanked out from under us and that it is probably, in *some way,* related to our alcoholic mom whom

---

* But ACTUALLY, I have no recollection of what it meant. DO I NEED THIS KNOWLEDGE NOW? Please send help.

we had to walk on eggshells around. But! We don't deal with that lasting hurt because we "don't have time." We know that the reason we feel like we'll never be good enough is probably, in *some way,* related to our father, who criticized every single thing we did growing up and, well, frankly, still does. Buuuut! There is laundry to do and family obligations, and isn't it self-indulgent to focus so much on "healing"? Or, we're not at all sure why we wake up in the morning fully panicked, hyper-vigilant for threats, living in a constant state of vague worry. We'll handle it later, someday, after our kid turns five, after we make partner at our law firm, maybe, "when things are less hectic." But you know as well as I do—if you're not dealing with the thing you know you need to deal with, it's dealing with you. And it's likely that the people around you are dealing with it too.

I'm reluctant to talk about "trauma" here. I'll be honest, I always thought trauma was reserved for people who suffered BIG-TIME, that it had to be utterly appalling to be real, or that maybe trauma was actually fake and that people just needed to move on, and that my pain—the anguish and turmoil living just under my skin—was unjustified and maybe even normal. But as my therapist likes to remind me when I go on a rant questioning if I have the right to feel as bad as I do, there is an easy answer. First off: Every human has the right and worth to feel however they feel. Full stop. It doesn't help ANYONE for ANY OF US to deny what is real or to insist upon a hierarchy of pain* in which some people are entitled to feel heartache and the rest of us "need to move on." Second, simply ask yourself: Did an emotional laceration from way back cause lasting distress that haunts your present in a pattern you

---

* This is from the psychotherapist Lori Gottlieb. Just one of her beautiful, smart insights from her super-entertaining AND helpful book *Maybe You Should Talk to Someone* (Houghton Mifflin Harcourt, 2019). I learned a lot about the process of therapy, how healing actually occurs, and myself through her funny and insightful storytelling.

can't seem to change? Does your past bleed over your present? Yes? *Welp*. Then you are allowed to claim your own suffering. It's actually that simple.

For me, with the dimness of the world, with the loss of my job, and with my most shadowy memories blasting to the surface (*ugh, we will certainly get to those later*), I knew I had to dig deeper and heal that *something* that was so troubled at the bottom of my soul. I could hear this pained little voice calling out, but her message was muffled and scattered. What was I supposed to do with that? Like, *at least* speak clearly into the soul-phone, little voice, this is hard enough. I wondered: Could I actually, for real, heal my bedrock wounds, the things that happened so early in my childhood that they, in very large part, formed who I was and how I thought and how I behaved? Could I heal the things in my adulthood that felt insurmountable?

Honestly, I doubted I could, and even if it was possible, JESUS, was that going to take a lot of work. Work that in my current condition, I was in no state to take on. Instead, I decided my life could get to a certain level of satisfying, but that I would never be able to transcend my "Good Enough Plateau": a place where I had an almost-right job, in which I felt mostly happy, like a modern Little Miss Muffet chilling contentedly with her curds and whatever the fuck "whey" is.* Don't get me wrong: I was grateful for the plateau, at times I CLUNG to the plateau, the plateau was miles and miles above where I had started. But . . . become a person who utterly trusted herself? One of those super-annoying people who, starry-eyed, leaps into their wildest dreams? Build internal safety so that external forces could never destroy my peace? Become one of those people who can hear their own instincts and have the

---

* Parents! Is Little Miss Muffet still an acceptable children's rhyme or did someone do the BARE MINIMUM of research and realize it was highly problematic? I feel like that's super possible here.

bravery to follow through with them while looking chic as hell in just jeans and a white T-shirt? No, I wasn't one of them. I wasn't Kristen Stewart.

So. I settled. I settled on something that while awesome and better than where I began didn't feel entirely true or entirely *me*. And the more I made "good enough" decisions about my life, the more lost I felt. Because now that I loved and respected myself, it felt much worse to ignore my damage. The self-care gave me the perspective, self-awareness, and self-respect to see that there was more work to do, but I wasn't ready.

* * *

Back alongside the exit ramp off the highway, I park on a dirt road, somewhere between Los Angeles and Arizona, with Dr. Candace's words "pull over" resounding in my head. There are no cars, people, or buildings for as far as I can see. I gingerly open the door, and put one foot out after the other, slowly, onto the ground beneath me. I take one step, then another, and feel the sand crunch beneath my weight. I notice how good the solid earth feels, how it immediately steadies and supports me. I breathe in the hot desert air and feel it warm my lungs, my throat, my blood.

Scanning the horizon, I see that the blue of the sky is varied, an ombre shade that moves from navy to cornflower blue, to purple, then to white as the last rays of the sun fade away into astronomical twilight, that singularly spectacular moment the sun submits to the moon. *It's not that bad to be on the side of the road,* I think. Tearing down the highway at ninety-five miles an hour, so overwhelmed by my panic, I hadn't noticed that the real-life view in the present was actually spectacular.

I continue to walk in the sand, regaining my composure, coming back to my body. I look up and the sky is morphing, turning darker and deeper navy, until all around me I am surrounded by a vast . . . fucking . . . *star field*. I don't know how else to describe it. In the desert, with no light pollution, all I can see are pinpoints of luminescence, a screen of glitter enveloping me. These stars don't just glimmer, they *glow;* they cast off an almost protective aura of light. My skin breaks into the good chills and I wonder aloud, "How do you do that? Can I do that?" Now that we all know how quickly the external circumstances of our lives can go to utter shit, can I create my own light, a light that I can take anywhere, a light that sustains me even when things get profoundly dark?

I climb back into my Prius and start googling the fuck out of stars.* According to my extensive and highly scientific Internet research, the reason stars glitter is *because* they have been through so much. Stars are born when clouds of gas and dust are pushed together by the unrelenting force of gravity. All of the motion, the pushing, the prodding, the exertion of forces beyond the gas and dust's control, heats up the nebula, making the star smaller and smaller and hotter and hotter until the center becomes so blistering that the hydrogen gas in the star goes nuclear. At the moment when the vapor couldn't feel more squeezed, it becomes a star that has the power to glow for *billions* of years. It's the pressure, the process, all of the bullshit the star has endured, that gives it its resiliency. And as we know, the stars don't just shine for themselves, they shine for all of us here on planet Earth looking up to the sky, in our pulled-over cars, asking *what the fuck* of life.

We are stars. I mean that quite literally. Most of the elements that make up our bodies *came* from the Big Bang, from the very things that make up stars. I think you've probably heard that before and it isn't a fable, it's true. Isn't that just about the most enchanting thing to think about? That you *are made of stars*? I also mean this figuratively. We arrive here as unique clusters of DNA that only our parents could create, and we have our very own per-

---

* Do I think it was divine intervention that I had service in this remote area? I sure do!

sonalities from the jump (if you've met *any* toddler, you know this to be true). Then, our parents, our teachers, our society, our obligations, history, power structures, other people's expectations, push and push on us, but rather than make us implode or explode or throw our hands up and give up or settle down, I've learned that we can be just like stars, taking all of that pressure and turning it into our eternal glow.

What does it even mean to glow? you very rightly ask. That word has been pretty diluted by the beauty industry lately. Please allow me to reclaim it. The dictionary definition of "glow" is "to give out a steady light without flame" or to give off a "a steady radiance of light or heat." Notice how the flame is *not* a part of glow? Flames burn out. Instead, glow is an inner light that luminates on its own. It's inextinguishable and can both fuel and sustain you. It's *hard* to be a person, really, it is, and the fact that you're here at all, the fact that you've survived everything you've been through and you're with this book now, questioning how to heal your soul, that tells me everything I need to know. You are ready, you are capable, you are worthy, and you are going to do this work wearing the dopest sneakers of all time because that's just you. And I am going to give you every ounce of myself and every (highly embarrassing and painful) lesson I've learned, because I want you to know that you are allowed to lead the mystical, magical, and safe life that you dream of.

To be very clear with you, I am no expert. I'm not a therapist, nor have I gone to theological school, nor am I claiming to have all of the answers. I VERY MUCH DO NOT HAVE ALL OF THE ANSWERS. I am someone who ignored her mail for so long that by the time I *did* bother to open it, I found out my car insurance had been canceled, a hospital had put me into debt collections for a twenty-five-dollar bill, and *all* of my friends were getting married. That was last week, by the way. I certainly do not have it all together. I'm just a person who went through some shit, continues to go through shit, and is endlessly curious about *how* we can make the process of living enjoyable and meaningful. This is probably because I was straight-up miserable the first twenty-five years of my life and vowed not to waste another second hating myself or feeling like a burden. While I don't have the answers, I know I'm asking the right questions. I know I'm making progress when I look at my journals through the years and read how much more I both know and *trust* myself. I know my worth, and that is just about the biggest goddamn shock of all.

I'm not saying it's going to be easy. *Oh man, I am not saying that.* There's no sheet mask to cure your deepest emotional damage. If there were, you know I'd own the world's supply. I'd make my own brand #GlowMask #Influencer (#Gross). Still, there is a little shortcut I can offer you: I know you have the power to glow because *you already do.* The human body *is* bioluminescent. It glows on its own. Ultrasensitive cameras can photograph our natural radiance. So, you glow already, whether you like it or not. Now is the time to clear off the dirt, the cobwebs, and the ghosts that are obscuring the shine within you and set that glow free.

This book is a guide to healing your past, getting off your Good Enough Plateau, finding a safe home within yourself, developing habits that will give you true resilience, and creating the life that *you* want. You are allowed to have your own experience, a life that has never been lived before. Because it hasn't.

It's a practical handbook to reclaiming your soul. No big deal. It's for people who are ready to heal their innermost wounds and discover their purpose. It's for anyone who is tired, hurting, and feeling like their shine is gone. I am not going to advocate that you quit your job, move to Arizona, or start your own crystal healing center. Though, if you do, please invite me. I love shiny things and I am down to learn your mystical craft. But neither am I going to suggest that you can do this work "later," when you have "time," or "money," or your "life has calmed down." That time WILL

NEVER COME and this work will end up like your last scrap-book project in the cupboard—a nice thought, never to be tackled again.* Instead, I am going to share with you the practical, free, *joyful* baby steps you can take today to unleash your inner glow, to make it so luminescent, so fucking bright, that it lights the way not just for you but for everyone around you. Because, as we know too well, shit can be grim, and it would benefit us all to share whatever glimmers of hope we can find, in an attempt to internal-ize the reality that we are not alone, even when it feels that way. Together we make up a constellation of the most exquisite, be-loved, glittering stars in the night sky. We desperately need to light the way for one another. Or, I'll just speak for myself: I need you to glow for me so that when I get lost, I can find my way back home.

I'm not fishing for a compliment here, but I want you to know something: There is nothing particularly special about me other than that I show up for myself again and again. I *try*. I fall down. I *try* again. I try so hard every day to stay curious, to remain open to possibility and growth, because if I had a fixed mindset, then I would still be convinced that I was just as worthless as my parents made me feel, believing that it would be easier to die than to take responsibility for my life, and probably still be wearing an outfit from Forever 21 that was so synthetic I could burst into flames at any minute. And if *I* did it—the six-year-old with dirty tights fall-ing down her legs and a rat's nest of hair because her parents ne-glected her; if *I* did it—the high school student who felt such emotional turmoil and pain that she perma-smoked weed to blunt and escape all of her feelings; if *I* did it—the twenty-five-year-old drunk-dialing her therapist threatening to take her own life, you can *absolutely* do it. I know it sounds impossible, but I once thought becoming a morning person was impossible and I now get up at six-thirty A.M. every day. Even weekends. It's disgusting.

* Sorry, high school scrapbook project! I'll get to you . . . one day.

The life you want is already here, waiting for you. The person you want to be, that dynamic spark that while sometimes dimmed is always lit within you, it's all already here. We just need to crack you open a little and let those rays out. Out of the gloom and into the light, I promise life is easier, more enjoyable, and full of fucking glitter, but not the kind you can't get out of your rug.

So what do you say, my darling friend? Are you ready to take all your disappointments, defeats, and damage and pull them in so closely, hold them so dearly, treat them so lovingly, that you fuse them into a star that can't burn out? Are you ready to plant yourself firmly in the night sky so that you can be a beacon for everyone around you and for yourself when you inevitably get a little lost? Are you ready to claim your ancient birthright, to embrace that you are already made of stars, you are already miraculous, and that you are allowed to shine however you damn well please? Are you ready to glow in the *fucking* dark?

Grab my hand. Let's go so deep into the night and glow so outrageously brightly that we become our own sun and make our own day, our collective light pushing back against the seemingly endless night.

I'm in if you're in.

With tears in my eyes and love for your soul,

Tara Schuster

A.K.A.

THE ARTIST FORMERLY KNOWN AS T$ (THANK YOU FOR MAKING THAT A THING)

I.

HEAL

Tro-mah
If It's Hysterical, It's Historical

THE FIRST TIME I HEARD someone earnestly use the word "trauma," I was on a date with a guy I met on the Internet. I had sneaked my way into an invite-only celebrity dating app where I had options for potential dates like, "DJ slash Instagram influencer slash model" and "████████████████"* Not only had I tricked the app into thinking I was worthy of people who listed their profession as "founder,"† I had even secured my first date and found myself sitting across a wooden bistro table from a bona fide Hot Person: an actor who was *professionally* attractive. As someone who usually dates "interesting" to "sickly looking" people,‡ this was a revelation. *A verified, blue-checked Hot Person!* A tall Australian with a tousle of strawberry blond bangs swooping over his glasses and an accent that could melt the artisanal butter right off your gluten-free bread.

---

* Please know that I tried to tell you EXACTLY who was on this app at the time, but Matthew Martin in the legal department of Penguin Random House prohibited me from doing so and thus ruined my fun. He also is very nice and probably protected me, *BUT STILL.*
† Can we talk about the SHEER VOLUME of "founders," "CEOs," and "photographers" on dating apps? Are ALL of the CEOs on dating apps? Haven't some of them been married off yet? And what qualifies as a "founder"? Am I a founder of books? Can I put THAT on my profile? Also, who knew there were so many photographers on planet Earth! I have yet to meet ONE in real life, but on a dating app, your odds of matching with a photographer in Los Angeles are four out of five.
‡ My friends' words. And my sister's. And mine.

As we discussed the menu, I felt those *I wanna get close to your skin* butterflies. Flustered by his attractiveness, I hastily ordered the first item, a cold kale salad with dried cranberries (???). I tried to recover from my incredibly lame, not-enough-food order by asking for the dressing on the side and a cup of water with no ice (again: ???), as if complicating the order made it better. Nothing says romance like cold kale (that was for sure going to end up stuck in my teeth), dressing on the side, and lukewarm tap water.

As we exchanged our getting-to-know-you questions ("Where are you from? Who do you hate?"), I asked him what he was currently working on. He explained that he was in between seasons of his hit biker/zombie/apocalypse TV show and was taking this hiatus to work on a documentary. "I'm looking into how tro-mah affects every single part of our lives. You look at the root causes of war, you look at how people mistreat one another, and usually, all our issues stem from tro-mah. Mom who has severe anxiety and gives it to her children? Tro-mah. Dad who is abusive to his kids and was abused himself? Tro-mah. And then there is cultural tro-mah! The Holocaust, the political system, discrimination and oppression. We soak in that tro-mah every day."

Eh . . . Did I miss something here? What was "tro-mah"? I wondered as I looked into his unreasonably blue eyes. (*HOW WERE HIS EYES THAT BLUE? HOW DO SOME PEOPLE GET BORN LIKE THIS?!*) It took me a minute to come out of my swoon and realize that the word "tro-mah," without a bewitching Australian accent, was English for "trauma." *Trauma*.

Oh God. No. I felt a full-body revulsion as if my eyes might roll so hard into the back of my skull that they would come loose and drop down my throat like errant pinballs, only to land somewhere in the pit of my stomach. *We all have our shit, but do we really need to dwell on it? Is EVERYTHING really "trauma"? This feels indulgent.* Just moments ago, I had been thinking about how to ask this gorgeous specimen to come over to my place for a post-salad snuggle. Now I just wanted to get the fuck away from him.

I wrapped up the date as quickly as possible, oddly insisting that I had an early meeting the next day (I did not—it was Saturday), and that this, in some ways, was a work dinner (it definitely was not and framing it that way was highly problematic). I flagged down our waitress and, without waiting for the bill, reached for my credit card so that we could expedite the process. My wallet, however, had other ideas. I was so flustered that I ripped the tab off the zipper and was now unable to open it. I grasped at the brass nub, but it wouldn't budge. I picked up a butter knife and jammed it into the track, trying to jimmy it loose. With pity in his eyes, the hot Australian looked at me, the wallet with a knife in it, and said sweetly, "I can cover your salad."

Back home, I had two major realizations. The first was that kale salad is not dinner. If I order a kale salad without any protein for dinner, then I will be inhaling an entire frozen pizza two hours later. The second, and *marginally* more important, realization was that I had clearly been set off by the word "trauma."

As is my custom when I have an intense and inexplicable reaction to something, I sat down on my aggressively floral duvet, picked up my journal with a cover illustration of the Trevi Fountain depicted in delicate detail, and let my favorite white-and-gold pen investigate. As I wrote, I found myself proclaiming, "I didn't have it that bad! I have no right to trauma. Trauma is for other people who have really SUFFERED. I just had a kinda consistently bad childhood. Why is everyone so sensitive? Why does everyone have 'issues'? AND, let's say that some things, for me, *were* a little on the 'traumatic' scale, well fuck that! I have already done SO MUCH WORK. THERE CAN'T BE ANYTHING LEFT TO DO. IT WOULDN'T BE FAIR!!"

Wow, I thought, reading my scribbled temper tantrum. *The lady* *doth protest too much, methinks.*[*] If the mere suggestion that trauma could play an unconscious role in *people's* lives—the dude had never said anything specific about *me*—forced me to skip a potential make-out sesh with a legitimately paid-to-be-handsome person, then I knew there was definitely something to unpack.

Even though I had been in therapy off and on for ~~ten, fifteen,~~ twenty years, there were certainly some feelings and memories that lingered that I wished didn't exist. At some level, I understood that they affected my present life, but mostly, I ignored them, thinking that they weren't "important" or "big" enough to be addressed. They played like a program I neglected to shut down, running in the background of my computer screen, invisible behind all of the windows and tabs I had open, but sucking down my emotional battery nonetheless.[†] I called this cluster of bad feelings and memories "the Thing." It was like a cloud, a sequence of hard-to-swallow moments from my early childhood that I had absolutely no interest in revisiting. But every now and then, they would visit me, unannounced and certainly unwelcomed. Rude.

Recently, they found me on my first "post-Covid" outing, when I attended a reading for a new poetry book about how love is an act of resistance in late-stage capitalism. Or something like that. In any event, I *think* that's what they were talking about because I know NOTHING about "late-stage capitalism," and I have to confess, I am barely interested in the topic. But the guy I was dating knew the author, and a poetry reading seemed like a pretty soft launch into the post-quarantine world.

We were on the back "patio" (converted parking lot) of a dive

---

[*] Shakespeare reference, what-what, yes, I DID go to college, and yes, I did have to take most of my classes pass-fail because I was too burned-out from my childhood and high school and life to soak up new knowledge. What-whaaaaat!

[†] At this very moment, BTW, my Internet window has ten open tabs that have accumulated over the week, one of the tabs is my email where there are 4,180 unread messages, and my laptop screen currently has twelve open windows. Which is to say nothing of the mosaic of files that makes up my desktop. It is a very upsetting way to live and I do not recommend it.

bar. Everyone's outfits seemed strange, like people were deciding what fashion was for the first time and the decision was chunky sneakers, giant flood-leg pants, and crop tops. After a pandemic, what you wear on your first outing is a *statement,* and I was not here for these statements. And honestly, why are crop tops a thing? How can you charge me for a full shirt when a quarter of it is missing? *OH GOD, WRITING THIS MAKES ME FEEL SO OLD.* To be fair, however, I have always hated crop tops, even when I was young enough to wear them. Though I did partake in the Baby-T Movement of the 1990s, my chubby little belly spilling out from under a T-shirt that read DA BRAT, in giant block letters. But I digress . . .*

The plastic tables and chairs had, in my estimation, been set up incorrectly—way too close together, not socially distanced at all. The stage was wrong, too, directly adjacent to the sidewalk and street, so the author had to compete with the loud conversation of a family trying to decide if they were parking in a legal space. "Well, what does the sign read?" a man barked, totally unaware that on the other side of the wooden fence, an audience of seventy was straining to hear the poet passionately discuss "social contractions." "I don't know, it's confusing, 'No Parking Anytime,' but two-hour parking seven A.M. to six P.M.? What does that mean? Is it *no* parking or *some* parking?" A woman tried to decipher this Rosetta stone of municipal regulations. I had no idea what the fuck anyone was talking about, either with the parking or the *poetry about* post-sovereign precepts. It did not help that the speaker was also, tragically, stationed directly next to the open-air "kitchen" of a hot dog roller and French fry stand. Every time an order was ready, a waiter had to walk across the stage with trays of fried food. It was a *shit show.*

---

* Confession: As of the printing of this book, I now own and wear so many crop tops that I am for sure having a quarter-life crisis. I even have a winter sweater that is a crop top, how does this make sense?

As I sat there envisioning how superior my version of this reading would have been, I was hit by a feeling of sadness, and panic. *Why wasn't the guy I was here with holding my hand?* And not only that, why had he not introduced me to his friends? Instead, when we arrived, he'd gone to mingle and left me on my own, with nothing to do but ask random strangers about their outfits. "Tell me about your belly chain! Where did you get it?" I asked a girl with a thick, metal belt of interconnecting circles lying across her hips. "I made it," she said, laughing. "Too much alone time in Covid and I picked up welding." *Wow.* She had mastered an actual skill while I still couldn't bake the goddamn bread that apparently every self-satisfied person on earth had perfected. (*I still don't know what a "starter" is, nor do I care to.*)* I'm good at making friends, so it wasn't a huge deal, but it didn't feel great to not be included. I tried to look cool and act like I didn't care, but I did care. *Why was he ignoring me? Was he not as into me as I was into him?*

I began a familiar spiral of *DOES THIS BOY LIKE ME? Have I misread all the signs? Does the fact that he won't hold my hand mean this relationship is doomed?* A creeping sensation spread across my skin, sharp and tingly, as if my whole body yearned to be pulled into his orbit and soothed by his touch. Once we were seated, I inched closer to him, letting my hand graze his, almost begging for him to grab onto me. But he WOULDN'T GRAB MY HAND, no matter how much I coyly grazed his.† I bit down as hard as I could, feeling my jaw tighten with pinpricks of fear as my stomach swelled with the churning acid of anxiety. I felt dizzy, and like I was miles away from the incomprehensible poetry reading.

---

* Obviously, I care to. If I didn't care, if I wasn't deeply, unwaveringly JEALOUS of everyone who can now make bread, I would not be on this tear at all. So, if you make particularly amazing bread, please just send it to me. It is my favorite food. And that is where the similarities between me and Saint Oprah end.

† I suppose I could have grabbed his hand. But, no.

Suddenly, I remembered the threat of inflation to the U.S. economy. I had spent my entire adult life saving money and kept it in cash because I was too risk averse to put it in the stock market.* As the threat of inflation loomed, would I be wiped out? Images from my AP European history textbook of children carting wheelbarrows full of money in Weimar Germany flashed in my mind and now caused a full-blown stress migraine, the kind that pushes from the back of your brain to the front wall of your skull. The panic and fear of inflation triggered a new thought—with everything going on in the world, with Covid, with the fact that this boy was going to abandon me, and the reality that soon, children would be playing with my valueless money, and since everything was going to ruin anyhow—*maybe it would be better to be dead?* Or at least unconscious for the next five years . . . minimum? Maybe that would be easier?

At this point in my life, I had done enough therapy, had touched suicidal thoughts often enough to know—this *probably* wasn't rational. And like the good patient I am, I got through that reading without revealing my panic, and the next day, took my thought loop to my psychologist for investigation. In my most "serious" voice, I described the scene to Dr. Candace in excruciating detail. How I didn't feel seen by the boy I was with. I described how his lack of touch and the possibility of abandonment triggered an unbearable thought loop of loss. I lamented how I just couldn't get on board with crop tops. I knew Dr. Candace would validate all of my feelings with profound compassion. But. She burst out laughing. Not a chuckle. An uncontrollable fit, to the point where she threw her head down and then back up again, flipping her hair. She had a *huge* smile on her red face, tears coming to her eyes,

* Smart finance friends: I KNOW WHAT YOU'RE GOING TO SAY, "Keeping a stash under your mattress is not an investment strategy," AND I KNOW THAT NOW, okay? We'll get to that later!

and—maybe it's revisionist history, but—I feel like she even slapped her knee? This was all on Zoom so in speaker view, her laughing face took up my entire computer monitor.

At first, I was taken aback, *THIS WAS SERIOUS!* I was having thoughts of *dying*. But then I laughed too. It suddenly struck me how wildly off base from reality these thoughts were. "I'm so sorry to laugh that much, really I am," Dr. Candace managed to get out as she recovered. "But what you just described is a *textbook* trauma reaction. When you are at ten out of ten, i.e., 'This is so unbearable that it would be easier to be dead,' but the situation is a lame poetry reading—it doesn't get more on the nose than that. You were hysterical (and I'm sorry to use that word) about something *historical*. Reacting to the mundane present as if you were living in the past as a neglected child. If you are actually safe, but it feels hysterical, it's historical."

If it's hysterical, it's historical. That framing hit me like a shock wave. I could instantly think of times when I responded to something with panic that wasn't warranted by the situation. Please don't judge me, but I have reacted to leasing a new apartment as if it is life or death, *for real.* Lost between excruciating, multiday depressive episodes about how I can't afford *any* apartment and that one wrong decision will trap me in a lifetime of financial ruin and that someone else, someone better and smarter than me, needs to make this choice for me, I wear myself (and everyone I know) down to exhaustion. By the time I *do* move, it's a relief because I no longer have to live inside my tempestuous head about the decision. And when it comes to professional feedback? *Oh lord.* If my former boss, who trusted me and rarely criticized my work, gave me *any* feedback, I would launch into a full-blown internal civil war—cannons, muskets, and threats of secession—the part of me that trusted myself violently clashing with the part of me that thought I was an incompetent, unworthy fraud. Dear former boss: Although I appeared to be placid as a lake and really *ingesting* your helpful pointers, please know that when I excused myself from your office it was to go to the parking lot, lie in the backseat of my car in the fetal position, turn on calming sounds of the ocean meant for lulling babies to sleep, and weep.

I grudgingly decided to start a new kind of therapy with Dr. Candace, one directly aimed at healing "complex trauma," a label for people who have been chronically exposed to severe events—usually early in their lives—like abuse or neglect. Trauma therapy is different from traditional therapy. Instead of telling stories about the past and looking for insights and patterns like you do in "talk therapy," you go back to the wound, to the traumatic event, and "re-process" it so that it no longer causes you distress in the present. You don't delete the painful memories, this is not *Eternal Sunshine of the Spotless Mind* and I am not Kate Winslet as much as I want to get close to Mark Ruffalo; rather, with the help of a psychotherapist, you convert the memory into something that no longer causes you suffering. Does that all sound fake and vague? Because at first, it sounded like pure make-believe to me.

It didn't help that the techniques for this type of rehabilitation sounded even more bizarre. Dr. Candace explained that through the use of mindfulness, intentional breathing (finally, I was going to learn how to breathe!), Internal Family Systems (a type of therapy that postulates that all parts within you, even the parts that are totally destructive, actually want to help you), and EMDR* (a treatment that uses rhythmic eye movement to alleviate emotional distress), we would encourage my brain to heal itself.

All I had to do was sit down and sweep my eyes from side to side to the sound of a ticking metronome (as you do in EMDR) and then I wouldn't be thinking suicidal thoughts at a poetry reading anymore? That couldn't be real. But as I researched the technique,

---

* Eye Movement Desensitization and Reprocessing—if you don't know what that could possibly mean, you're not alone. I still don't know and I have been *doing it* for three years.

I learned it was indeed scientific and it was *recommended* by both the Department of Defense and the Department of Veterans Affairs to heal PTSD in soldiers returning from war. That sounded legit. Who was I to question something that worked for veterans who had *really* been in life-or-death situations? Besides, if it was as fake as I thought it was going to be, who would even know? I had nothing to lose and many non-doom-spiral poetry readings to gain.*

With the help of this treatment, I could look back at my abandonment-economic-ruin-maybe-it-would-be-better-to-not-exist thought loop at the poetry reading and understand what provoked it. I know for a fact that I was rarely held in a loving way as a child. My mother often pinned me to the carpet of her bathroom floor in order to "examine" everything that was "wrong" with my body. I remember it feeling excruciating. I would thrash and scream, but I was little and powerless. That rage transformed into an instinct to flee from my mother whenever she was nearby. My father has confirmed that he rarely touched me because he was afraid. "I thought your mother would accuse me of being a pervert or doing something wrong if I held you, so I just . . . didn't. I would get scared if we hugged, so I kept my distance." My father and I have hugged so rarely that when we do now, it's awkward. It lands somewhere between a side hug and a pat on the back.

So, I have this five-year-old in me who, after having been deprived for so long, is desperate for touch, from just about *anyone*—babysitters, playmates, and, as I've gotten older, men. So even if a dude was treating me badly, even if my date was, say, not paying attention to me at an obscure poetry reading, that five-year-old doesn't understand that I don't need to freak out. All she wants is physical comfort and she will keep me in relationships I don't want

---

* Sidebar confession: I don't really "get" poetry. My mind wants to move too quickly and understand what it all MEANS immediately, so I often give up, frustrated after the first few lines. I wish I was intellectually rigorous enough to appreciate poetry but I don't. And now you know.

to be in, she will direct me toward decisions I don't want to make, and ultimately, she will drive me out of my mind if she doesn't get what she wants. And all she wants is her fucking hand held.

We all have trauma. The hot Aussie was right—we get it from our parents, our teachers, our culture. Trauma occurs across all races and all socio-economic classes. It's nothing remarkable, special, or new, it's the common denominator of being alive. It's been here as long as we have! I mean, in the creation story, God makes the world in six days but then is so stressed by how hard it all was that the Great Almighty had to take a mental health day. We couldn't even go a *week* without trauma.

If you kinda gag at the word "trauma" like I once did and need a more grounded term, we could also call this what the Buddha referred to as "suffering." We all suffer. Terrible things happen to us—death, robberies, pain, abuse. And less serious instances of suffering happen every day—injuring ourselves, a friend betraying our trust, having a phone conversation with a representative at United Healthcare as we try to get at least *some* of these goddamn therapy bills reimbursed.

When I talk about trauma, I am using the definition of Gabor Maté, the renowned Hungarian-Canadian psychologist, physician, and bestselling author who is seen by many as the "father" of trauma research. Maté, who suffered excruciating trauma as an infant in Nazi Germany, said in an interview with the Skoll Foundation that "Trauma is not what happens *to you,* it's what happens *inside* you . . . the wound that you sustained, the meaning you made of it, the way you then came to believe certain things about yourself."* He also points out something that is often missed: "Trauma can also be inflicted not by what happens to you but what *doesn't happen* that should happen. . . . Even if you weren't overtly

* This is from Gabor Maté, "Trauma Is Not What Happens to You, It Is What Happens Inside You," Skoll.org, July 22, 2021, YouTube video, 1:54, https://www.youtube.com/watch?v=nmJOuTAk09g.

hurt, you're still wounded by not having your essential human needs met."* What makes something *traumatic,* then, is not the event itself but being totally overwhelmed in that moment, finding a coping mechanism to get you through it, and then using that coping mechanism in similar situations forevermore, regardless of the reality of the situation. Unless we are shown or taught that there *might be* another way to deal with our feelings, we can become grown adults living in a five-year-old's mind. I'm totally down to live in my five-year-old's mind of loving feather boas and singing everywhere and anywhere, but little girlfriend is probably not to be trusted when dealing with work criticism, romantic relationships, or anything beyond delight and wonder. However, most of us don't even know this is happening because our coping mechanism, whether from childhood or later in our lives, is just the way we experience the world.

"Sure, sure, sure, whatever, why can't we just push this down and move forward with our lives? Why do we need to endlessly rehash the past? I've gotten this far already, haven't I?" you justifiably quiz me as you look at your watch, wondering how much longer I am going to ramble about the lasting effects of trauma and now the Book of Genesis for some reason. The problem is, just because something is buried doesn't mean it's dead. We act as if trauma is so intimate that it only affects the person who suffers directly from it. But as you know, most people have terrible poker faces. Our children feel our trauma when we tell them not to cry because we ourselves grew up thinking our emotions were unsafe and wrong. Our partners feel it when we are so ashamed of ourselves that we can't be fully vulnerable with them. Our colleagues feel it when we put them down or undermine them because we grew up in a household where we had to be tough and fight for

---

* BTW: Gabor Maté didn't italicize these words, because he spoke them. I italicized them because I am going overboard trying to tell you exactly what his words meant to me. Going overboard is my modus operandi.

limited resources. I'm very sorry to tell you this, but your trauma isn't just *yours*. If you aren't dealing with it, you might very well be forcing the people you love the most to deal with it instead. Call these unresolved feelings trauma, suffering, pain, emotional wounds, call them whatever the fuck you want, maybe the Great ICK would be better, all that matters is that we deal with these things so that they don't deal with us—and with others.

If you've built your calm, stable, beautiful home on a graveyard of memories, emotions, and thoughts that you don't want to deal with, if you've settled on a life that is feeling increasingly unsettling and at odds with a profound force within you, then I just want to remind you that no one said you had to build your house on top of a graveyard. No one said you had to be haunted. There are other places to live. The address for your safety, your okayness, is inside of you. And best of all, you, right this second, *already* have the strength, the wisdom, the courage, to deal with your own "Thing."

One of my favorite thinkers and spiritual leaders, the late Rabbi Alan Lew, wrote, "[W]e are terrified of the truth. But this is a needless terror. What is there is already so . . . Owning up to it doesn't make it worse. Not being open about it doesn't make it go away. And we know we can stand the truth. It is already here and we are already enduring it."* *WE KNOW WE CAN STAND THE TRUTH. IT IS ALREADY HERE AND WE ARE ALREADY ENDURING IT.* That makes me want to leap up off my sofa, raise the roof with my hands, and shout, "AMEN, ALAN LEW, AMEN!" The worst things you've ever been through, you have *already* been through. *Congratulations, you made it!* But if you remain hostage to your past reactions to hardships, you become a

* This is from page 150 of my favorite spiritual book of all time, Alan Lew's *This Is Real and You Are Completely Unprepared* (Little, Brown, 2003). It's supposed to be a guide to the High Holy Days in Judaism but I heard his words as if they were an alarm clock waking me up to my life. So yeah. I recommend it.

prisoner with no hope of escape. I hate to be a dick here, but it's true. Even if someone did something extremely awful to you when you were young, if you keep reacting to it, *you* are adding torment to your life. So maybe . . . just a thought here . . . it's time to deal with the truth in a way that doesn't feel *horrendous* and might actually heal and free you? And maybe it will heal and free the world? IDK. Just a thought.

So, my fellow traveler, are you ready to get on the road with me? Are you ready to sit in the driver's seat of your life and let your hair go wild? Are you ready to ditch being a passenger to your emotions and thoughts? Are you ready to feel the wind on your skin as you experience how exhilarating your present life can be?

I brought the snacks, why don't you pick the music?

Ways I Distract Myself from How Un-Fun Healing Is

Um. So. Don't hate me but this work is not necessarily going to be "pleasant." I'M SO, SO SORRY. If you've been living in a trauma reaction for the past two years, we can't undo it with one hot bubble bath, no matter how luxurious it is. Trust me, I've tried. We are going to have to revisit the hurts of our soul, and like you've probably guessed, this shit ain't easy. But we don't need to push through it and overwhelm ourselves either. There is no pain-endurance prize for who went the hardest at healing. Instead, we need go-to distractions to lighten up when things feel too heavy. It's easier to heal when you have the mental capacity to do so. These are mine, what are yours?

1. I use the "good bowls," the ones I bought in Japan from a discount restaurant supplier that I treasure like fine china inherited from my imaginary aristocratic grandmother. According to me, they can only be hand-washed and *lord help you* if you attempt to put them in the dishwasher. You

will know my displeasure immediately. They usually sit on a high shelf above my kitchen sink to be admired by on-lookers (just me) from afar. I eat my Greek yogurt out of them. Or hummus and carrots. One time I used a "good bowl" as a soy-sauce receptacle. Using them for little things feels like a tiny, delicious rebellion.

2. I stress-research "best pants for one's shape" on the Internet. I have become obsessed with what kinds of pants I should wear not because I want to look younger (which I do) but because I want to experiment with my style. I know jeans should no longer be skinny but I'm not into a flood leg either. Thank you for trying to convince me that "they look good on you!" sweet saleswoman, but you can't tell me that they are flattering because I, too, can see my reflection in the mirror. What would a cross between Audrey Hepburn and Billie Eilish in pant form be? That feels like my vibe. A classic, gorgeous cropped jean that tells you to go fuck yourself.

3. I look at my face in the mirror about once every hour and wonder, *Do I want Botox?* I stretch out the lines etched between my eyes with my thumb and pointer finger to simulate what I think Botox would do for me. I spend hours online looking at before and after pictures of people with Botox and then at the "worst Botox accidents." I make an appointment to get Botox myself then worry for the next few weeks that it's too pricey, that it will hurt (needles in your face?!), and that getting it makes me a shallow, vain, bad person. I cancel the appointment.

4. I cycle between LOVING, NEEDING, SAVORING salty snacks and then banishing all salty snacks. This is not about

an eating disorder, this is not about my weight, this I now recognize is an *important* part of my healing journey. The yin to the yang. All things go in waves, in cycles. The only constant snack in my overcrowded kitchen cupboard (read: a shelf) is popcorn. I, for real, don't think I could have confronted so many soul wounds without the comfort of a hot bowl of microwavable popcorn. *Why are you so good, my popped princess?*

5. I make a new Botox appointment, keep it, get actual Botox put into my frown lines, and fall instantly in love with Botox. It doesn't hurt at all, it takes under a minute to perform the procedure, and it makes my face look like I'm not constantly scowling. And! In the most surprising and important news, it cures my chronic morning headaches. Cures! WHO KNEW? I schedule a new appointment for more Botox and quickly see how I could be one of those people who becomes addicted to plastic surgery and ends up looking like a bloated plastic cat. I might be vain, but I no longer have headaches!

6. I make utter nonsense lists to distract myself from how unfun healing is. Why don't you give it a try?

A Little Thing That Helps

When working with an overwhelming tro-mahtic memory, sometimes I imagine I have a big plastic storage container. I take the memory and the thoughts and emotions associated with it, tie a leaded weight to them, place them in the box, and close the lid. I will come back to the box later, when I'm ready.

The Citadel

Your Journal Is Your Safe Place

I STARTED MY HEALING ON the side of that road in the Mojave Desert, so struck by the stars that I sat for an hour basking in them, letting their brilliant rays light me up with celestial power. By the time I arrived in Flagstaff, I was no longer having a panic, dissociative, *why-God-why* episode. Still, I had the shaky sense that I had only narrowly escaped drowning. I felt like I had been sucked down into the undertow, where I'd been thrown and spun, only to be spat out, my mouth full of seawater, onto the Arizona desert sand. I decided that this was exactly what I needed—to dry out. To rest. To regain my composure before I began my volunteer work on two local congressional races.

I was renting the last available place in the whole town because, pandemic. At that point, every inconvenience seemed to be caused by the global nightmare and its "supply chain issues," which I think was a hopeful euphemism for "looming Armageddon." I found a condo on a golf course that was decorated like a ski lodge's dream of Thanksgiving. There were gourds everywhere. So. Many. Gourds. Ceramic gourds, wooden gourds with feathers attached to them, gourds with hand-painted children who looked like ghosts, real gourds (Were they going to rot? Was I supposed to do something with them, or do gourds stay intact forever?). While this was *for sure* not my style, it was surrounded by pine trees and opened onto a giant red wooden deck overlooking Mount Elden and a vast expanse of sky. After months of being cooped up in my apartment, this was a huge improvement.

My first morning in Flagstaff, I found a cute café for a little breakfast and journaling. As I waited for my burrito to arrive, I ~~eavesdropped~~ overheard a mom, dad, and two sons, roughly eleven and eight (Though I am very bad at ages. It's also possible they were both five. Or fifteen?) having a conversation. They were smiling and laughing and, as a Californian, I would say they gave off "good vibes." When a waiter came, the father exclaimed, "We'll start these guys with the mac-and-cheese fries!" prompting a cheer from both boys. "We're carbo-loading because these dudes have a big day tomorrow—we're going canyoneering!" I had never heard of "canyoneering" before, so my ~~eavesdropping~~ listening intensified. The waiter left and the dad explained, "Now, boys, I've never done this myself, so I don't know what to expect, but if you get scared, I just want you to know, we've got a guide with us who's done this hundreds of times before and whose *job* it is to keep us safe. So even if it's scary, you're gonna be safe." *You're gonna be safe.* His words landed on me like warm morning sunshine after a cold night, clarifying something I hadn't realized before: I had *never* felt safe growing up.

In fact, my parents regularly told me how *unsafe* I was. From as early as I can remember, my mom cautioned me that "Sickos are out to get you. Kidnapping is up in the country and you're the perfect target! You could be raped, tortured, and murdered, or *worse*! You have to be very, very careful." *What was worse than raped, tortured, and murdered?* I didn't want to find out. I recollect one time when I was nine years old and sitting in a restaurant on the Third Street Promenade (one of the most popular outdoor shopping malls in Los Angeles) needing to go to the bathroom. When I asked my mom to be excused, she barked at me, "Pay attention, you never know who might snatch you." With the threat of "snatching" in the air, I decided that it would be best if I stayed put, even though we were in one of the safest neighborhoods in all of human history.* I decided to wait until we got home.†

While my mom constantly warned me that the outside world was perilous, my dad ceaselessly told me that we had exactly zero financial safety. One day while driving me to middle school, he started shouting, "We're ruined! If this deal doesn't go through, I don't know what we're going to do. We're in so much credit card debt, we're DOOMED." Just your typical Schuster Monday morning pep talk. What was most confusing to me was that he was saying all of this while driving a custom-made Mercedes-Benz. How could my dad have such an expensive car and at the same time insist that we were in financial dire straits? I'm still not totally sure what my dad did for a living (Entrepreneur? Whatever that means?) but whatever it was, he was *on the daily* worried about how a lack of money was going to ravage our lives. As he continued his diatribe, I peered out the window and fantasized about swinging the door open and rolling out onto the black asphalt. *What would that feel like on my skin?* When I returned from my escape fantasy, I reassured him, "You'll land on your feet, Dad, you always do," but I had no confidence that was the case.

Despite my parents' extreme paranoia, the truth was that, as a child, I was often not safe—physically or emotionally. My house was literally built on an unstable foundation that necessitated constant fixing. But my parents often resorted to lazy work-arounds that didn't hold up, and our home devolved into a haphazard construction zone. When I was six, for instance, my mom initiated a

---

* Eh, well . . . minus the O. J. Simpson murders.
† Maybe this is TMI, but because of this I developed a fear of bathrooms and always tried to "hold it" until I got home. This lasted well into my late twenties when I realized—"WAIT, I AM ALLOWED TO GO THE BATHROOM!" Now, I drink tons of water and go *frequently*. It feels kinda baller to me. Like I'm showing off. Like I'm a big deal who is allowed to go to the bathroom *whenever I fucking want*.

completely disorganized remodeling project for the house that would take place while we were out of town. When we arrived back home, we were aghast to find the innards of the structure exposed—the insulation, the piping, the plywood. If you brushed by a wall too closely, you might catch a nail or a nasty splinter. It remained this way for SIX YEARS, with our various pets defecating on the carpets with no consequence because *who cares,* the house was already a nightmare shithole.

Before my dad asked my mom for a separation (which, by the way, he did by taking me, my sister, and my mom to dinner, and breaking the news to *all of us at the same time*), he decided that he would finally fix the house. *He,* with absolutely no construction experience and no training. Why did he do this? Because he wanted his family to finally live somewhere safe? Because he thought we deserved better than to live in a pile of plywood and cat piss? Nope! He knew "the surprise divorce dinner" was imminent and he wanted to get the house in better selling shape.* But like my mom, he didn't file permits or make the proper "plans." He simply hired some dudes from the parking lot of a Home Depot and got to work. I have to admit, the house did look a lot better after his crew plastered the exposed walls, replaced the disgusting carpet, and patched up the unexplained holes in the ceiling.

My dad was so thrilled with his (the Home Depot crew's) handiwork that he decided to build a big deck for himself. Radolpho, the leader of the Home Depot crew, constructed a wooden deck off the second floor of our house. It overlooked the canyon, giving an expansive city view of the west side of Los Angeles, the office buildings at night twinkling like urban stars. But. There was no

---

* So that you know, I recently asked my dad if he had, in fact, only fixed the house to sell it and he looked at me, taken aback. "No, of course not, I wanted us to have a nice home." I think in my little-kid mind, the fact that the time was so short between the house being fixed and my dad's leaving led me to believe there was a connection, whether or not it was my dad's intention. I also think my little-kid mind might have been damn right.

railing. Nothing resembling a railing! My dad was making a bold bet, considering the fact that an eleven- and five-year-old could wander out there at any moment. Moreover, the deck was built on thin beams, so thin that when you stepped on them, they creaked and groaned, shifting under your weight.* The thing was fucking terrifying. I couldn't go out there without imagining falling off and hitting the brick patio twenty-five feet below with a thud. But this was my dad's pride, something he (the Home Depot crew) had built. "Girls, come out here and sit on the deck," he'd coax. When I resisted, saying, "Dad, I'm scared of it, it shakes so much," he'd take offense. "Of course, you don't want to come on the deck, because I can't do anything right! I should have never married your mother, it ruined my life!"

While the house itself was not to be trusted, the people who came in and out of it felt even more dangerous. There was a re-volving door of babysitters, handymen, (never paid) "chefs," as-sistants, and sycophants obsessed with my mom.† There was Oona, the Danish horse breeder who practically lived at our house, doing what, I don't know. And of course you remember Barry, right? Who I detailed at great length in *Buy Yourself the F*cking Lilies*? The handyman who lived in the garage apartment of our house for no reason, with his white van that signaled child abduction, who popped his dentures in and out of his mouth to terrify me? Who had a wayward, Satan-worshipping youth named Dan living in the sauna of said apartment, who collected rattlesnake tails to affix to the ends of pencils? You remember them, right?? And then there

---

* My dad denies this. "The deck was solidly built and had rails all around it. The construction problem was that it was attached to the house. That was not kosher in California, because having wood attached to the house could rot the whole thing." The truth of the deck is probably some-where in between my memories of being terrified and my dad's memories of being proud of something he built.

† She had long been a women's healthcare advocate and attracted patients who had been abused by the healthcare system. She took them seriously and worked tirelessly on their behalf. They then sort of just hung around.

were men who drifted in and out of my mom's life. One of them, Jason, who could not have been more than twenty-five at the time, actually lived with us for a stint, and I'm pretty sure was straight up having an affair with my mom. (Is it an "affair," though, if your lover lives with you and your husband?) My strongest memory of Jason is of him lying on my parents' bed with his shirt off, face-down, while my mom straddled his back to pop his pimples. Like . . . the fuck?

Add to that I have a bunch of random early flashes of memories and moments that have no context. I remember being maybe three or four and brushing my teeth when WHAM—a babysitter slapped me so hard across the face that I was knocked off my pink step stool. I have another flash of sitting in a closet when someone, I don't know who, grabbed my wrist so tightly that they left bruises as I screamed for them to let go. I can't recall the context for either of these instances, but they live in my physiological memory. All of the chaos and disorder in my house made me feel that, fundamentally, there was no safety net, no one to protect me.

Since I didn't grow up feeling safe, it's not something that's really on my radar. My friends have often remarked that it's "brave" that I travel around the world on solo expeditions, taking on twelve-mile hikes through slot canyons with no other person in sight, wandering cities alone at all hours of the day and night. But I'm not brave, I'm oblivious. I think I just learned to disregard safety altogether. This doesn't mean I don't feel scared *all* the time; it means I've learned that that's how life is and there's nothing you can do about it. Feeling terrified, like I have no control over my body, like at any moment anything could happen to me, jumping at the sound of a trash can lid closing, that is just how I live in the world. I never tried to "fix" it because I wasn't aware that feeling safe was important.

Early in the pandemic, a friend set me up with a guy he knew who lived in Paso Robles, an idyllic slice of California known for its vineyards and olive groves just north of Los Angeles. His name was Charles.* Since I lived in LA, our first date would have to be on Zoom, as was the case with so many other single folks in the global garbage, shit-fuck pandemic. Zoom was a new thing, no one quite knew what background you should use (A city? A kitchen that is not your own?), or how to make the lighting not look like a proof-of-life video in a hostage situation. Charles was my seventh Zoom date, and given the six previous people I had met, I had low expectations. Lucas, the Brazilian VR tech guy who seemed sensitive and sweet and was a *very* active member of Goodreads, had immediately ghosted me and then ghosted me a *second* time after apologizing for ghosting me the first time. Then there was Jon, a "crypto" investor guy,† who told me, "There's something biological that makes women want to own their houses," and also said, "Maybe this whole Covid thing is a hoax." So, as long as Charles didn't immediately bail or turn out to be verging on an incel, I figured we'd be fine.

I sat in my dining room, which I had converted into a WFH office, as he sat on the patio of a vineyard (his?!) with acres of grapevines and rolling green hills behind him. It was stupid nice. "Hi there, I'm Charles. I'm so happy to meet you," he introduced himself. "Hi, I'm Tara, it's nice to meet you too. Your Zoom background is so much more awesome than mine, you're already winning," I joked to him. "Yeah, but you're so much more beautiful than I am, I have to make up for it somehow," he sweetly bantered. He was playful, light. Over the next month we talked every few days at a pace so chill and calming in an otherwise not chill and

---

* BTW, Charles was not his real name. The only Charles I know is my cousin Charlie and he is awesome. Hi, Charlie.

† Whatever "crypto" is. The blockchain has been explained to me AT LEAST ten times, by experts in some cases, and either I just *can't* understand it or I *refuse* to understand it, which yields the same result: When you start talking NFTs and Ethereum, I start thinking about what I'm going to get at Trader Joe's, or observing any blemish on your face.

not calming world that I started referring to him affectionately as "Slow Burn Charles." I learned that he was super into meditation and that he loved taking personal development classes. "I want to know myself really well. I don't want to waste my time on earth living a life that isn't mine," he confided. *Yeah, Charles! Super down with that!*

A month in, on a Zoom date to learn how Alice Waters shopped a farmers market (unrealistically elegantly and easily), he changed the subject. "Hey, so. I have a question for you. My brother and I are going to do a big Southwest camping trip. We're going all over Utah. The camper van I'm renting is pretty close to Los Angeles, so . . . I thought you could join me for the first few days in Bryce Canyon?" We had only been "dating" for a month. But without a moment's hesitation, I agreed. It was an adventure! And I'm always down for adventure.

The next week, Charles picked me up in a *psychedelic,* FAR-OUT camper van. Geometric stripes of yellow and orange were painted across the sides that were also decorated with decals aplenty—a heart, a peace sign, a "hang loose" hand gesture, and a message to "respect the locals." It looked like something perfectly nostalgic for a past that never existed—a 1970s of the imagination—with a dash of self-conscious irony, like when people use disposable cameras or sport mom-style fanny packs across their chests. It was an Instagram thirst trap on wheels.

I had waited for him in my apartment for three hours as he repeatedly texted that he was "just an hour away." At first, I wondered if I was being catfished. By the time Charles did pull up to my curb, he was sweaty and nervous, seemingly verging on some kind of hissy fit. "I've had a *very* frustrating day!" That was the first thing he said before launching into a list of complaints. "First, the van place was running late, and then I took off to stock it at Whole Foods for the trip, but then I realized, I had no idea how to use the refrigerator, and what if the cheese melts? So I spent an hour in a parking lot watching YouTube videos, and then I thought, *Fuck it, I've got to get Tara.*" He was acting like it would be a total tragedy if his Whole Foods brie went bad. Which, I kinda get because WHY IS WHOLE FOODS THE MOST EXPENSIVE PLACE ON EARTH? If I go there to buy apples, I will walk out with Epsom salts, rare olives, and a new nut-based milk that, when combined, cost somewhere around seventy dollars. *Always.* But to have somewhat of a meltdown with someone you were just meeting?

When we finally left, I tried to steer us toward a conversation unrelated to the problems of the morning. "What's your love language?" I coyly asked. "Um. Acts of service," he curtly replied. I waited for him to expand or ask me a follow-up question, a softball, like, oh, I don't know, "What's *your* love language?" but he did not. And when we somehow got to the topic of family and my strained relationship with my dad, he cut me off mid-sentence and said, "You should mend whatever is wrong with that relationship. You really only get one dad and you should fix it." I wanted to reply, "Oh my God, *thank you, Charles, WOW,* I had never thought of that until you brought it up just now. It's not something I have been thinking about essentially every day of my entire life. What a revelation!"

When we finally arrived at Bryce Canyon, nine hours later, without having eaten anything more substantial than brie and Red Vines and weird Whole Foods "healthy snacks" (a truly unpleasant combination), I was tired, disappointed, and already ready to leave. I realized that Charles's "slow burn" affect was actually a lack of curiosity about other people. The only good news was that as we drove through the park, I was awestruck by Bryce Canyon. If you have not been, GO! It is one of the most astounding places on earth. Orange-and-white spires of compacted sand, called hoodoos, rise from the deep canyons, surging toward the sky, some as tall as ten stories, as if the Earth has crafted its own totem poles. It looks alien and almost unnatural, like a set for a movie about a different planet, like there is no possible way something like this could exist—except it does! And you are lucky enough to bear witness. Charles was not living up to expectations, but Bryce Canyon was blowing my damn mind.

As we pulled up to our campsite, Charles's brother, Jared, ran to the car, yelling "Charlie boy!" before reaching in through the open driver's side window to wrap Charles in a giant torso hug. They were sweet and warm with each other and made me think about my own sister and how I might shower her with explosive affection if I hadn't seen her in a while (three days). I felt a little bad for being so judgmental about Charles. Maybe he was, as I had said, just a slower burn?

Jared asked me if I wanted to take a quick walk while Charles set up camp. As we wove our way through hoodoos on the Queen's Garden Trail, taking in our magical surroundings, Jared blurted out-of-fucking-nowhere, "You know what's crazy? I recently escaped a sex cult!" *Wait. What?* "Yeah, it was crazy. At first, we thought it was a leadership training, like a personal development course, though a little weird because we had to earn sashes and everyone was *super* into this one guy, and kind of idolized him, but then . . . it sorta went sideways and I went through some things in Mexico City that I really regret." HE WENT THROUGH SOME THINGS HE REALLY REGRETTED IN MEXICO CITY? AS A PART OF A SEX CULT? What is the appropriate response to an admission like that from a stranger? "Oh"? "Tell me more"? I was off-balance, spinning from the what-the-fuck-ness of this hike that somehow managed to be worse than the car ride. But then he hit me with the coup de grace: "You know, Charles was in the cult too." He seemed surprised by the shock on my face. "Didn't he tell you?" *No, Jared. Charles had somehow skipped that one.*

When Jared and I arrived back at the campsite, I ~~calmly walked~~ ran up to Charles and burst out with my question, "Hey, so, this is strange, but . . . Jared just said you were in a sex cult? That you had to escape? Care to elaborate?" Charles looked unbothered. "Oh, Nex-i-um? I wasn't a part of the sex stuff." It took me a second for the information to register. WAIT. *NXIVM?* NXIVM of branding women's bodies and sexual slavery NXIVM? The NXIVM featured in a terrifying documentary that I had to stop watching because it was too upsetting? "Yeah, that NXIVM," he replied.

"Don't worry, it really wasn't as bad as the media made it out to be and I only did it for a little bit, and *never* the sex stuff." Okay, this was better, I thought. "Also, it's super odd that Jared told you that." I was a little more reassured that he wasn't a part of the sex stuff and that he, too, thought it was bizarre that Jared had shared this with me. *Maybe this wasn't SO terrible. Maybe he just got sucked in and that's something that could happen to any of us? Like, maybe I could accidentally end up in a sex cult?* I wanted to know that this was all a short-lived mistake to him, so I asked, "So you were only in it for a little bit. How long was that?" praying he would say something like, "A week and then I realized it was BS." "I don't know," he reflected, "maybe a year?"

My. God. The "personal development" courses he described had been part of a cult. Now, YOU, at this very moment might be crying out at the pages of this book, "Run! Escape! Get out of there ten minutes ago!" But I was unable to move or think, standing perfectly still as the sun set on the hoodoos of Bryce Canyon. Before I could process anything, Charles slung a camera bag onto his back and started to walk away, without saying *a word*. "Uh . . . where are you going?" I asked. "I'm gonna take some night photos as the sun sets!" he yelled, practically running away. "But what about dinner?" I asked. "When will you be back?" He turned around and shouted, "Why don't you make dinner on the camper stove and when I'm back from shooting, we can eat." *Why don't you make dinner on the camper stove?* WHAT CAMPER STOVE AND WHERE MIGHT I FIND IT, CHARLES?

Jared had been sitting at the campfire this entire time, listening to his brother ditch me for "night photos." As soon as Charles was out of earshot, Jared yelled over, "You want to know something funny?" I wanted to scream back, "NO, JARED, NO MORE FUNNY OR CRAZY THINGS." But he began laughing. "You know those photos Charles is taking? He's never gonna get them developed. He has hundreds and hundreds of rolls of film, from like ten years, from all of our family vacations, and he has yet to get a single one developed." I'm not quite sure why I found this detail to be more disturbing than the cult, but it seemed like the final, ultimate red flag.

Looking back, I now see that I had options in this situation, I didn't have to stay there. In that moment, though, my mind was blank, I couldn't think or move, I knew my life was not in danger, I didn't think Charles would hurt me in any way (aside from emotionally), and yet I felt frozen with panic. So do you know what I did? I decided I'd go for a "night run."

One of the ways in which I deal with anxiety is through running, a.k.a. nature's Xanax. As soon as I hit the road, I get into my body, and the rhythm of my feet bouncing off the ground always calms me down. Now, I'm no athlete. Part of the reason I love running is that it's so hard for me that it forces me to focus exclusively on how much running sucks as opposed to whatever storm is in my mind. That said, in the hundreds of miles I've run over the past few years, NOT ONE has been in the dark.* In that moment, though, as adrenaline caused my heart to beat faster, I convinced myself that a night run was not only good self-care, but the only reasonable option. I didn't need to deal with the fact that I wanted to leave this camping trip, I just had to quell my anxiety. I didn't have cold-weather running gear, but I *did* have a bottle of whiskey.

---

* TOTAL BRAG! I AM BRAGGING TO YOU! I RAN 1,176 MILES BETWEEN 2020 AND 2022! BOOOOM! This makes me feel just as baller as regularly excusing myself to go to the bathroom. #Progress.

So I did a VERY not-me thing, since at this point I barely drank at all, and took two shots of Bulleit Bourbon to give myself an internal warm blanket. It didn't cross my in-shock mind that a night run with only brie, Red Vines, seaweed chips, and two shots of liquor in my stomach was probably not my best idea.

I set off. Charles could have his night photography and I would take an epic run as the sun set spectacularly on the canyon. As I ran, I became increasingly angry. *Fuck Charles,* I thought. *Fuck him and his weird brother.* Distracted, I ended up going farther than I had wanted until I didn't know where I was anymore. *That's okay, I'm on the rim of the canyon, I can easily trace my way back,* I told myself.

But night had fallen, and I couldn't find a single marker to show me where I was supposed to turn. I now saw that it was potentially not a good idea to be running on the side of a cliff with a multi-hundred-foot drop. I had gotten myself lost, in the dark, with no supplies—no food, no headlamp, nothing to keep me warm—next to the mouth of a canyon. I invite you to shake your head at me right now. I'm certainly shaking mine.

Gingerly, I backed away from the canyon, figuring I would hit a road at some point? Finally, I came across one but still didn't know where I was. For the next hour I wandered along the road and down paths, trying to find the campsite, leaving little rocks so that I could find my way back to the road, like a sad, semi-tipsy Gretel shivering with cold, until I saw a giant dumpster I recognized from when we drove into the campsite. God, I wanted to kiss that dumpster.

I made it out of Bryce Canyon alive. Later, when I mustered the courage to tell friends what became of "Slow Burn Charles," their number one question was, "WAIT, *that* NXIVM?" followed quickly by, "But why didn't you just leave?" I didn't know the answer. I didn't know why, when, in a somewhat unsafe—or at the very least, uncomfortable—situation, I only made things worse for myself. I only knew how I felt in the moment—trapped, paralyzed, my brain scrambled, with no good ideas about how I could protect myself or leave or even just tell anyone that I didn't like how I was being treated.

And so, at the café in Flagstaff, listening to a father who had thought about his children's safety and had taken actions to ensure their protection, I breathed in the crisp October air and felt the truth land on me: I had never felt safe as a kid and that feeling of insecurity was how I thought life was supposed to be. My mind flashed from the terrifying home I grew up in to the strangers who slapped and disregarded me to my parents screaming to that fucking deck to Bryce Canyon. I never learned to value my safety or understand that I deserve it.

Back at Gourd Central, I called my BFF-soulmate, Fisch. She is an early childhood development specialist and the mother of three girls—a job that requires such superhuman strength that I really do ask constantly, and I swear not patronizingly, "How *does* she do it?" She picked up and I launched in, "When you were younger did your parents tell you explicitly that you were safe? And now, do you tell your kids that they are safe?" Silence. "Wait, are you serious?" she responded. My eyes filled with tears. "I am," I mumbled. "Yes, of course. I would say that's my number one job as a parent and as a teacher, to make sure my kids are physically and emotionally safe—they just don't have the skills to feel safe on their own. They need adults for that. And when they don't feel safe? They act out or freeze or run away. They're in survival mode and it's hard to do *anything* when you don't feel safe."

It's hard to do anything when you don't feel safe. Huh.

What I have come to understand is that we all deserve a base level of safety. If we don't have it, we are robbed of our ability to make rational choices that are free from fear. And yet, many of us have apprehension instilled in our brains and bodies at a young age. From teachers who make us feel bad for our natural behaviors, from babysitters who ignore us, from bosses who explode on us, from romantic partners who threaten us, from the very real systematic ways in which people are threatened physically, mentally, emotionally, all of the ways, from THE ACTUAL REAL-WORLD EVENTS AROUND US WHICH HAVE BECOME TERRIFYINGLY UNSAFE ON ALL LEVELS. In a time when the Earth has spun off its axis and appears to be rapidly free-falling into a black hole, is it any wonder so many of us feel untethered?

So the question becomes: If we can't control the external, how can we create our own safety? Is it possible to build an internal zone where we have a little security for ourselves? Cultivating this place is, in fact, the very first step in unearthing ourselves. It's the precondition for creating a life you love and for turning your imagination back on, because as I am sure you know from your lived experience, when we are panicked and in fight-flight-freeze mode, it's hard to dream or see possibility and opportunities. It's difficult to set boundaries with someone destructive in your life when you're afraid of what might happen if you stand up for yourself; it's tough to pursue a new job; it's challenging to open ourselves to love; it's impossible to choose what we want to make for dinner on night 9,897,456 of "shelter in place." When we don't feel safe, we are the tiniest little figurine in a Russian nesting doll, protected but a prisoner at the heart of all of the shells we have built around ourselves.

But we are not born afraid. We are born free, open, and loving; you only need to look at a baby's smile to know that. And since fear and insecurity are not inherent to who we are, we sure as shit can do something about it. For me, the *best* tool for building my internal safety zone is journaling. It provides me a safe place, an actual location where I can always express how I feel. I've written before about how journaling allows you to "DM with your soul" by getting sneaky messages from your authentic self. It also helps you to see patterns in your life and discover long forgotten or suppressed dreams. But I've come to see journaling as even more powerful and fundamental. Journaling is my emotional safety valve, a place where I am truly free to be vulnerable without judgment or consequence. And it has opened me up in five truly magical ways.

The Power of Journaling

1. **We learn to feel again.** We're so used to being "good," "bad," "fine," or "stressed," and we've been told for so long how we should and shouldn't feel, that many of us have simply lost the vocabulary for our emotions. Since we can't identify them, they stew within us, and erupt often in the most unproductive of ways. To help me better understand myself, every morning I ask my journal, "How do I feel?" and then refer to an "emotion wheel" (I'm going to give you mine shortly). Do I only feel "bad"? Or am I "busy" and "pressured"? If that's the case, what can I do to relieve some pressure? Am I "good," or more specifically feeling "powerful" and "creative"? If that's true then I know I have to seize this moment to work on a project. In either case I have more information for how to best proceed. And once you are aware of how you actually feel, YOU CAN DO SOMETHING ABOUT IT!

2. **As soon as we are able to label an emotion for what it is, we feel physical relief, as if our soul is crying out, "THANK GOD YOU SEE ME! IT'S BEEN A MIN-UTE!"** I then say to myself, "I notice my [name of emotion] and I take good care of my [name of emotion]." This is based on the teachings of Vietnamese Buddhist priest

Thich Nhat Hanh. This framing welcomes the emotion instead of rejecting it. I may not be a Zen Buddhist but I sure feel like one when I do this!

3. **Journaling is a free, quick, self-soothing ritual that builds reliability in an unreliable world.** And! If we treat our journaling as a sacred pause, if we use a boldly floral notebook with our favorite white-and-gold pen, light a candle, and sip an oat milk latte, we create a habit that is, in and of itself, TRANQUIL AF. Not only does journaling give you a window of time for yourself, but that window can look out on a vista of the life you want.

4. **Over time, we realize that our emotions won't leap off the pages and hurt us.** Your emotions aren't dangerous. Just as they can peacefully live on the page, so, too, can they peacefully live within you. If you are afraid (like I was) that if you write down the truth of how you feel it will overwhelm and destroy you, just try it once, and tell me if it ruined your ENTIRE LIFE FOREVER. Maybe you cried, maybe you cursed my name, but did the experience lead you to something like, maybe the question, *Why am I crying right now?* And did that reveal something to you? Maybe your journaling took twenty uneasy minutes, but maybe it saved you years of living without self-awareness.

5. **The best consequence of keeping a journal is that it gives us a sense of power.** Every time you sit down to write, you are saying, "I am worth time," "I have a voice," "I matter," "My story is important," "This time is for me." Keeping a journal gives you a refuge where you can have

some order and autonomy no matter your circumstances. If you are feeling unsure of yourself, or shaky in a totally precarious world, a daily proclamation of your importance is a potent elixir that, with time, shows you that you have a unique voice that can't be taken away and can never be stifled. Even if you are in unsafe situations, natural disasters, perilous family life, or just a job you *hate,* in your journal you can see that you take up space, that your experience is valid, and that you might have more ability to change your circumstances than you ever thought possible.

If what you are trying to do is to heal, to dig back to your most authentic self, then having a sense of safety is the very first step because you create a place you are in control of, a space for all of you to exist, not just the parts you are proud of or want others to see. Journaling is a free form of therapy in which you can have a conversation with the person who knows you best: you. And, whether you realize it or not, you are also the person who knows exactly what you need.

We search and search and search for external things that we think will make us secure. We think a partner will at last make us feel protected, or that having children will soothe the chaotic emotions we harbor, or that there is a certain amount of money in the bank that will make us safe. I love you an unreasonable amount, but there is nothing on planet Earth outside of yourself that can give you complete security, except maybe The Rock. (For some reason, I really trust that dude.) You are your own safe house. Inside of you is the peace, comfort, freedom, and security that will help you weather any storm, that will be a citadel to protect and nurture you when the world is at its worst, or even when it's just not that great.

You already have the key, are you willing to unlock the door?

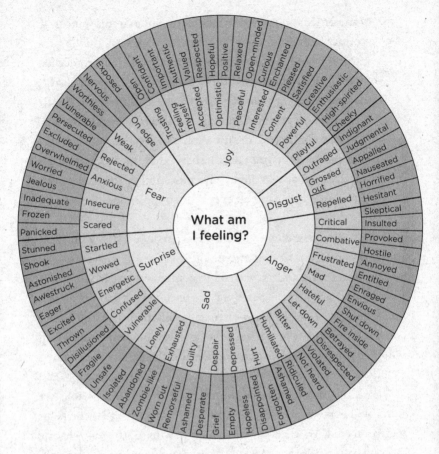

The Emotion Wheel That Convinced Me I Have Emotions Other Than "Fine," "Good," and "Bad," and That Feeling Those Emotions Would Not Ruin My Life

* NOTE: You can look at the wheel starting inward going outward OR outward going inward. So, for example: If you can't start from a place of "joy" (and who can, really?) look at the outer ring and see if any of *those* words resonate. You might not feel FULL-ON JOY! But, maybe you feel "curious," "valued," or "open"? Go with that.

Don't overthink this, my straight "A" darling. Just go with the words that feel "good enough," not that perfectly describe the whole of you. Nothing bad will happen if you don't NAIL this emotion wheel. I promise.

Often, I feel many emotions at once. I might feel joy, optimism, and hope about a piece of good news I just received. AND AT THE SAME TIME feel fear, insecurity, and inadequacy about a work project. By identifying and writing out how I feel, I see the truth, that I am a larger whole, capable of feeling multiple emotions at once and thus don't need to solely focus on my feelings of inadequacy. And, by labeling my more negative feelings, by giving them a name and the dignity to exist, they usually lose a little bit of their charge.

A Little Thing That Helps

If you are afraid of your journal being stolen, HIDE IT somewhere obscure, somewhere no one will ever look, maybe even get a box with a lock, and don't tell people you have a journal! This is for you, not for anyone else.

Doing, My Undoing
An Un-horrible Approach to Meditation

DO YOU THINK MEDITATION IS annoying? That people who tout it as a cure-all are full of shit and should get off their cushions and DO something instead of "being with" themselves (*whatever that means, are we not ALWAYS with ourselves?*) and stop telling the rest of us what to do from the entitled, detached, patchouli-scented clouds on which they float, totally ignoring the REAL, HARD conditions on planet Earth? Are you enraged when you read in a self-help book that to find inner calm all you need to do is "simply allow the experience of life to come in and pass through your being"?* Or even worse, that to stop endlessly ruminating on your problems, all you need to do is "let go"? Do you say to yourself, *OF COURSE I WANT TO LET GO, BUT HOW, FOR THE LOVE OF GOD, HOW? How about I let go of my fist into your stupid, tranquil face? HMM?*

That's exactly, quite specifically, how I felt about meditation.

I have been trying to meditate for a miserable, frustrating slog of twenty-five years. I first discovered the concept when I was eleven and my dad took me to our local bookstore† to choose some

---

* Maybe you liked this book but I found Michael Singer's *The Untethered Soul* (New Harbinger Publications, 2007) to be largely unreadable because I was so angry at the sweeping statements. I have no doubt the author feels these states but can he back up and take me to step one?

† I'd like to pour one out for our beloved Dutton's bookstore. A magical, sprawling complex

beach reading for an upcoming family vacation to Hawaii. First, I should define "vacation" in the Schuster family: a week of my parents screaming at each other, which was, of course, nothing new but *this time* the subject was how much they couldn't afford the vacation they were on. My dad would yell at my mom, "Carol, you're driving us bankrupt! BANKRUPT," and my mom would scream back, "I'm a *doctor,* I worked for this! THIS IS MY MONEY!" as the hotel staff awkwardly looked away, because this fight had, of course, been in the middle of the lobby. Anyway, in the bookstore, instead of choosing, I don't know, *The Baby-Sitters Club,* or *Goosebumps,*[*] I picked up Che Guevara's *Guerilla Warfare,* Noam Chomsky's *Class Warfare,* and Sylvia Boorstein's *That's Funny, You Don't Look Buddhist: On Being a Faithful Jew and a Passionate Buddhist.* As you can tell, I had many friends and was exceedingly cool.

In Hawaii, I splayed out my body on top of my pink terry-cloth hotel towel and held the book about Jewish Buddhism high above my head, utterly transfixed. The author, Sylvia Boorstein, wrote, "[I]n the middle of a Buddhist meditation retreat, my mind filled with a peace I had not known before—completely restful, balanced, alert, joyous peace . . ."[†] *Her mind filled with a JOYOUS PEACE? HOW?!?!?!* I scrawled in the margins "I WANT

---

with knowledgeable and kind booksellers that was unceremoniously shut down to (allegedly) make room for a parking lot, which never actually materialized, so the building has stood there empty, to this day, twenty-five years later. Thank you, capitalism, and thank you, Joni Mitchell, for being an oracle and the coolest person ever.

[*] I will now admit that even though I wore *Goosebumps* branded T-shirts (which, at the time, were curiously sold by Best Buy right alongside the Grateful Dead tie-dyed shirts), even though I had a *Goosebumps* lunch bag and claimed I was obsessed with the series, in reality, I never read a single one. Scary stories were and remain my least favorite genre, so if you knew me at eleven and I told you how much I LOVED *Goosebumps,* I was lying to your face. I only tried to pass as a *Goosebumps* aficionado because I thought that would make me popular. Which shows you how on the money I was for things that make kids popular.

[†] Sylvia Boorstein, *That's Funny, You Don't Look Buddhist: On Being a Faithful Jew and a Passionate Buddhist* (Harper San Francisco, 1998), p. 1.

PEACE!" even though I had little conception of what that actually meant. TBH, if it just meant "not chaos," it would be a major improvement.

You see, at the age of eleven, I felt pretty shitty and doomed to feel shitty forever, given all of the shitty things that had happened (see: definition of "vacation," previous chapters, last book, etc.). I lived in a house consumed by pandemonium where I felt like I was being buffeted from one emotion to the next with no help to steady myself. My parents never—and I mean that literally—comforted me, so the idea of finding something called "peace" was intriguing to say the least.

Unfortunately, I was eleven and my meditation infatuation was fleeting because I quickly got sidetracked by the movement Free Tibet. My fave band, the Beastie Boys, was WAY into freeing Tibet and I thought that by joining their beloved cause it might bring me closer to meeting Ad-Rock and that once he met eleven-year-old me, we FOR SURE would elope, on the spot. Which would not have been weird at all given my advanced reading level. I WAS BASICALLY AN ADULT.

Though I did not free Tibet, meditation crossed my path again in my mid-twenties as I desperately worked to re-parent myself. I read over and over again in self-help books or on random Internet searches for "how to feel better" that just about everyone I admired—the Dalai Lama, Elizabeth Gilbert, and, most important, RuPaul—meditated. Apparently, the practice could help regulate your emotions, which in all seriousness I did not know was a thing that was possible until I by chance read the phrase on some blog. Perhaps that's what Sylvia Boorstein meant all those years ago by "peace," maybe it was simply a life where you weren't in one extreme state or another.

To me, it had always seemed normal for one's moods to change drastically throughout the day, driving you from anguish to a manic kind of joy. After all, that's exactly how my parents lived their lives, and "mood regulation" was not something they taught in school. (AGAIN, we need to have a serious talk about substituting real-life skills for at least some of the trigonometry.) By my mid-twenties I had assumed that my emotional life would emulate the stock market, sometimes at record highs, bringing temporary joy, and at other times plummeting, triggering debilitating depression.

Of all of my emotions, I was most often dominated by the feeling of being totally overwhelmed, like I was underwater, flailing in the Mariana Trench, the deepest part of the ocean, where I could only wince in terror as unseen sea creatures brushed up against my skin. I was drowning under my work obligations, my fears of financial instability, all of the social plans I had made (few of which I actually looked forward to), politics, the news, my family drama—I was drowning under EVERYTHING. I didn't know how to live a life that wasn't completely overwhelming.

I wasn't hesitant to try meditation. I usually try things because I think they are bullshit and won't work and I want to spitefully prove that I knew better than everyone else all along. *Now you know. I never said I was a nice person.* But meditation was different, it was the one thing, aside from heavy tranquilizers, that I had consistently read could help people calm down, and oh my God did I want to calm down. But when I earnestly, sincerely, put everything I had into trying to meditate, using the apps, going to classes, reading endlessly about different practices, I found it HARD, like impossible, demoralizing, *am-I-the-only-person-who-can't-do-this?* hard. If I was having a panic attack and tried to meditate, it only amplified the already hellacious storm of feelings swirling within my body. If I was depressed, I would end up doom spiraling and chewing myself out for how bad I was at meditating as my mind wandered. I needed help if I was ever going to find mindfulness, and by my mid-thirties, I finally found a person who could guide me toward "winning" meditation: my dear friend Sarah.

Can I go off about Sarah for a moment? She was a senior speech-writer for President Barack Obama before becoming Michelle Obama's *head speechwriter* (Um, WHAT??? SHE *knows* Michelle Obama?!), writing speeches for the 2008, 2012, and 2016 Democratic National Conventions ("They go low, we go high," anyone?!)[*] but at the height of her career, when she could have written for just about anyone (though how much higher can you get than Michelle Obama—God?), she decided to explore her curiosity in Judaism and to embark on a more spiritual life[†] (So . . . yes! I guess the only being on a higher plane of existence than Michelle Obama is God). I knew she had found meditation hugely beneficial in her life, and had even written about its transformative power, and so I called her up to ask, "What am I doing wrong? Why does meditation make me so panicked? How can it possibly calm you down when all it seems to do is rev me up?" "Well, my friend," Sarah replied, "first off, meditation isn't about getting rid of anxious or panicky thoughts, it's about noticing them." She continued, "And I still struggle with it. It's so hard! It's more like going to the gym than going to the beach. But meditation helps me get some space from those thoughts and touch into the actual *feelings* beneath them—like sadness, shame, loneliness. And when I can do that, then I'm no longer held hostage by anxiety. Also, some of the moments in my life when I've felt closest to divinity, they've happened while meditating."

Um. Fuck, I thought. I found this take to be personally offensive in how appealing it was. Not only had meditation helped Sarah regulate her emotions, but it helped her get CLOSER TO *DIVINITY*? That seemed more beneficial than my current medita-

---

[*] Sarah, because she is one of the most humble, non-credit-grabby people I know, insisted that I tell you that she did not come up with that specific phrase and that it was all Mrs. Obama.
[†] Sarah wrote a wildly beautiful and easy to understand book about Judaism titled *Here All Along*. If you are interested in learning about the life-transforming wisdom this ancient tradition offers about how to be a human being today, I think her book is just about the best out there.

tion substitute, online shopping, which only left me closer to a closet full of the same Zara shoes in multiple sizes that I desperately needed to return. From there it only got worse as she told me that her favorite meditation retreat was coming up in two weeks. "Just try it! What's the worst that could happen?" *Agony, Sarah, complete and utter agony.*

The silent retreat was led by a Rabbi James Jacobson-Maisels* and was to be held on Zoom because of the totally normal plague that was ravaging the earth's people, but as I scanned the website, I saw that the teachers were still going to adhere to the same horrifying schedule of a classic retreat. The agenda described how I would wake up at five-thirty A.M. every day and spend the next eight hours and thirty minutes in a combination of meditation, "blessing practice," chanting, walking, and mindfully eating. For six days. In silence. OH! And I wasn't allowed to read, write, listen to music, or look at my phone. I didn't hesitate. I love extreme things—the harder, the more intense, the more I'm attracted.

I decided that the hardcore schedule demanded a hardcore effort. I wasn't going to just dip my toe into meditation. *Non, non, non, ma chère.* I was going to fully do this (even though I had never successfully meditated for more than ten minutes in my life) so help me GOD, so that I could get "credit" for having done it "right." Who was this credit coming from? Good question. I rented a little cabin in Ojai, California, which is just about my favorite place. There really is something in the air, and it isn't just the smog; it's a combination of eucalyptus trees and blue skies and sunlight the color of honey, and just, *my God,* Ojai is a truly blessed

---

* I have now attended many of Rabbi James's retreats, both in-person and virtual, and I can say he is one of the best teachers of *anything* I have ever encountered. The word "brilliant" gets tossed about a lot but Rabbi James's knowledge, wisdom, and compassion have shown me the true meaning of the word. If you are interested in a retreat like I went on, or want to try a class if you're not quite ready for that yet, check out his organization, Or HaLev ("Light of the Heart" in Hebrew!) online. But don't do his retreat how I did it. Please.

little pocket of earth located conveniently off the 101 Freeway. I prepared a week's worth of food in advance (Because I thought we were barred from cooking during the retreat. But guess what? I found out that advance meal prep was only highly recommended! Why, God, why didn't I read the rules more carefully!), which I ALSO decided should be vegetarian even though nowhere on the website did it say I needed to eat vegetarian. I felt like that choice would give me extra credit. I threw my never-used yoga mat into my Prius and set off for battle.

My cottage in Ojai looked like it was straight out of Mr. Toad's Wild Ride in Disneyland—a cross between what Hollywood thought "English Tudor style" meant and what chain restaurants thought "medieval times" looked like. I walked under an archway with the words THE RAVEN painted on it in the kind of font that you might see at a Renaissance fair, fanciful and of a different, fetishized, indeterminate era.* As I walked through, I imagined how perfect this retreat was going to be. I could picture myself sitting at the cozy kitchen table, contemplating the mysteries of life as I ate my delicious, healing kale chips. I envisioned peacefully sitting on the patio that opened off my bedroom's French doors surrounded by magenta bougainvillea and listening to the gurgling of the water fountain, feeling utterly calm and maybe even attaining enlightenment? At a *minimum,* once the retreat was over I FOR SURE could see myself taking some tasteful bikini selfies for my dating apps.

But of course, you know how the best laid plans of mice and men go—to utter shit. The next morning, I woke up exhausted. Even though I usually get out of bed at six-thirty, I find five-thirty to be an ugly hour. The only living creatures that should be allowed to be up at five-thirty are newborn babies and bats, neither

---

* OF COURSE I was obsessed with Renaissance fairs growing up. My sister was once crowned the Princess of the Faire in a joust we attended. Again, we were very popular. If you'd like to go with me to one now, I'm not above it.

of which I identify as. I went to grab my phone to (what else) scroll through Instagram but remembered that I wasn't allowed to use it. Bleary-eyed and already in a kind of crummy mood, I made my way to my laptop (ironically the only way to do the technology-free retreat was through a pretty major piece of technology) and opened up Zoom, to see a "room" full of boxes with the faces of people I didn't know. There were all kinds of people: young, old, people with babies, coupled-up people. It was kind of touching. In the midst of a harrowing pandemic, there were people just like me, willing to do anything to feel better. Including self-isolate in an already isolated time.

I barely made it through the morning meditations. And by barely, I mean I didn't. Maybe it was the early wake-up time, or maybe it was years of accumulated exhaustion that were finally given the space to exist, but I fell asleep sitting straight up, my head jerking forward with my mouth agape. In the rare moments when I was conscious, my mind was all over the place, jumping from one inane, useless thought to the next. *Good job getting this cabin. . . . You are bad at meditation. . . . Holy shit I am tired. . . . How long has it been so far? . . . Can I get eyelash extensions when I'm back home, or is that a faux pas in a pandemic?* At no point did my mind feel any measure of the peace Sylvia Boorstein had written about.

After the morning meditation we were supposed to do a "walking meditation." What is that, you ask? Imagine walking but it's unbearable and makes you want to die. You're supposed to pick up your right foot slowly—first your toes, then your arch, then your heel, as if your legs were planted in tar, and repeat this process, leg by leg, step by tortured step, at your slowest possible speed, so that within fifteen minutes, you have only walked a FEW steps in any one direction. It. Was. Painful. The only thing I could think to do to make this walking meditation bearable was to go outside and soak in the glorious Ojai sun. I swung open the front door to the enchanted cottage, ready to be flooded with warmth and sunshine, only to be met with a GIANT fucking spider right in front of me, humanlike in its deliberate movement as it slowly paced, clearly succeeding in its own walking meditation.

I want to be clear: I am not one of those people who freaks out when confronted with a spider. I sometimes pretend I don't see a spider just because I don't want to deal with it,* and on the rare occasion when a spider looks like it might bite me, I have no problem killing it. I once found a small, black spider in my kale Caesar salad at work, and rather than throw the salad away, I took it out, squished it with a napkin, and finished my salad. Later, when I polled the office about what they would have done in my position, a colleague pointed out that the reason she wouldn't have continued eating was because "where there is one spider, there must be more." I had not thought of that AT ALL. Spiders simply are not one of my manifold problems. But this one, *oh my lord*. It was the size of a golf ball and so thick it looked like it might have a human spine. I froze. I couldn't step on it because what if it made a screechy cry like a small animal dying, like, "EEEEEEE"? And how *not* Zen would it be to kill a spider on a meditation retreat? I was in a tough position: I couldn't kill the spider, but I also couldn't get past it because WHAT IF THE SPIDER GOT AIRBORNE? I shut the door just as quickly as I had opened it.

At lunchtime, I sat down to eat my "good meditation student" meal, a feast of raw kale and beets. The food itself was exactly what you'd expect—not good, not filling—but since one of the rules of the meditation retreat was that I couldn't speak to anyone, I couldn't call in takeout or risk the interactions of going to the grocery store, beet-and-kale slaw it would be. The mixture immediately didn't sit well with me, but I chalked it up to not eating

---

* Sidenote: How ARE we supposed to deal with spiders? Do you just cohabitate? Take them all outside? What is a reasonable number of spiders to have in your house?

enough vegetables in my non—meditation retreat life and gulped it down.

The rest of the week went just as well as the start—terribly. I aggressively tried to stay present and let my mind open up to the universe or whatever stupid bullshit I was supposed to be doing but I wasn't even able to stay awake, much less achieve nirvana, and I was unraveling into an anxious wreck. On the third night, I lay in bed, frustrated that I couldn't do better, seriously hungry, with no distractions to soothe me. Quickly, I spiraled into my favorite subject of all:

A List of All the Things That Are Wrong with Me

1. I am unemployed.

2. I am unmarried.

3. People are supposed to have met their person by now but I have not.

4. Or had I met them and fucked it up and now could never go back in time?

5. I don't talk to my mom. Sure, I have my reasons, but are they valid?

6. I haven't really accomplished anything if you thought about it.

7. And now I can't even relax? Like, I am getting relaxing wrong?

AND ON AND ON AND ON to infinity. After relentlessly beating myself up, I finally fell asleep at four A.M., an hour and a half before my alarm went off to start the whole cycle again. I was unhinged. The kale-and-beet diet was causing my stomach to bloat up in pain, and I kid you not, every time I opened the front door to go outside, that fucking spider was there, staring straight at me. HOW WAS IT THERE EVERY TIME? Was it a new high-tech surveillance device, watching my every move? Because that's how it felt. And I quickly realized my colleague was right; there were more. The cottage was *infested* with spiders. Tiny ones that moved quickly, like little ants on a hill. My skin started to feel itchy and I became paranoid that they were crawling on me every time I felt my hair graze my neck. Now, you might have taken all of the above as a sign to stop, to maybe slow down—break a rule and get a real meal, or at least contact management about the spider scourge. But I barreled on. Because didn't it mean something if this experience was hard and terrible and stressful? My childhood, my education, my career, my whole life, shouted back at me a resounding "YES." Anything worth doing was *supposed* to be hard.

It was in this exhausted, self-pitying, hungry state that, on the fourth day, I sat down for a session, just praying that night would come soon so that at least I would be closer to the end of the retreat. I tried to breathe in and out on a count of two. Meaning, could I just count one-two without becoming distracted? No, I could not. Somewhere between one and two I thought about needing to file my taxes. I just wanted this whole forsaken mess to be over. With my eyes closed I began to plead with Sarah's divine universe. *Okay, if there is a God, can you just tell me what to do? I want to feel close to divinity, I really do, but I am so lost and uncomfortable, and just not good enough to do this right. Can you help me? Can you at least do something about the mutant spider?* As my pleading took over my concentration, I started saying, "Please help me, please help me, please help me," like a mantra, focusing my entire attention on these words. I'm not sure how long I sat there repeating that phrase—it felt like hours—but at some point, I felt the good chills break out all over my body, and I heard the words, "I am right here with you. You trust in me so you can trust in yourself." *AHHHHHHH!* Had I just heard the voice of GOD? My whole body felt like it was cracking as the tears poured out. I opened my eyes to find myself uncontrollably sobbing, my face red and slick with snot. But *I had done it!* My suffering had been worth it. FUCK YOU, MEDITATION!

My first thought was that I needed to tell the rabbi in charge of the retreat, Rabbi James, about my REVELATION. I mean, of all people, he had to know that God had *spoken* to me. I had pushed myself to misery, but now I had been rewarded with the ultimate experience—communion with the sacred. Luckily, we had our fifteen-minute one-on-one right after the session. When I logged in to speak to Rabbi James, I could barely get out a "hi" before I burst into tears describing my experience. "It's the craziest thing, I was sitting there, so anxious, PRAYING for help, when (heaving) GAAAAWD (hyperventilating), GOD (crying) SPOKE (crying) TO (hiccupping) ME (crying)!" And then, I let it all out, crying not only from exhaustion and whatever weird state I had worked myself into but also tears of grief for losing my job, for losing the one place that had been my safe home for ten years. My ten years at Comedy Central were the closest I had ever felt to living in a "functioning home," my colleagues the only "family" that reliably checked in on me or genuinely wanted to know me. It had been a refuge, a place where I was valued, and now it was gone. I was too exhausted to continue pretending that losing my job had not been devastating.

I'm not sure how long I was totally losing my shit before Rabbi James could get a word in. "Hmm . . ." He closed his eyes. "It seems like you've had a powerful experience." *DUH, RABBI! I SPOKE TO GOD, KEEP UP!* He opened his eyes and continued, "That's certainly something we can explore, but for now, you seem flooded by emotion, perhaps we could work with that?" I didn't want to work with *that*. Being overwhelmed was just how I led my life; honestly, it was how most people I knew led their lives. *I was having a breakthrough, there was no need to talk about this normal breakdown!*

"What about the God thing?" I probed, hoping he had misheard me through my tears or perhaps he didn't realize what an incredible miracle had occurred.

"Yes, that does sound powerful, but you seem overtaken right now. Part of the wisdom of this practice is that we want to work gently and expansively with ourselves, with a sense of safety and support so that we can feel the emotions that are present within us without getting lost in them." As he spoke, I defaulted to my usual boredom and hatred toward meditation teachers, and the language I so detested: words like "wisdom," "practice," and "expansively" that meant nothing and gave me no helpful hints as to how one might achieve anything other than hatred of meditation jargon. "If you'll allow it, I'd like to try a practice with you," he offered. *Blech, gah, fine, but if God disappeared while we were "expansive," it would be on the rabbi, not me.*

"Take a moment to bring your attention to your feet, to your legs, to whatever part of you is in contact with your chair. Can you feel the weight of your body on the chair? Do you feel contact with the ground? Can you sense that even if you are lost in your emotions, you are actually *supported* by the ground?" Weirdly, I could feel that I was supported. While my mind felt like it was a million miles away, I felt weighted in my body in the comfy armchair. "Yes, I can," I mumbled, surprised at the almost immediate sense of grounding. "Now, in your line of sight, can you notice three things that are pleasant? No need to overthink it," he coaxed. I scanned the room and found a tree outside the living room window, a candle on the coffee table, and a tube of hand cream with pretty, pink lettering. "Now, I want you to bring your focus to one of those objects, and notice it for thirty seconds. We don't often pause to take in the good things around us," he explained. I looked through the window to my left and realized that even though I had been in this cabin for almost a week, I hadn't even noticed how incredible and grand the tree outside the window was, its branches extending from the trunk almost like an outstretched hand toward the sky.

"Through attuning ourselves to what is pleasant in our lives, by seeing that even within a distressing moment, we have the capacity to take in delight, we more easily unhook ourselves from flooding emotions." He then finished with words that have now influenced every facet of my life: "We don't need to overwhelm our way through meditation."

Up until this point, I had been facing meditation like it was an impenetrable brick wall that I was supposed to smash my way through. I now saw that muscling through the least muscly thing in the world—meditation—was not only *not* necessary, it was actually stopping me from progressing. I was so fixated on needing to attain some level of perfection that I was never able to enjoy or benefit from having the most basic blessing that meditation had to offer—at least half an hour of quiet time to myself. That alone was a gift, but I had been experiencing it as a nightmare.

And just as I couldn't white-knuckle my way through meditation, I realized that I couldn't push myself through the process of grieving my job loss and healing my soul. For more than a decade I had treated the work of nurturing myself like it was a full-time job, taking constant notes and tracking my progress. I mean, I even compiled it all into a book. I literally turned healing into a career! This zeal had truly served me; my life was infinitely better than it had been. But the new kind of soul work I was doing could not be graded, could never be perfected, and—oof—I knew it would never be finished. Beating myself into healing just wasn't going to fly, unfortch.

Like most of us, I had been sold the creed of Hustle—if you

wanted your life to have meaning, you had to achieve and pro-duce. If you found that constant forward motion overwhelming and unpleasant, get in line with the rest of us, sweetie, discomfort means you're doing it right. Dogged efficiency had become a moral imperative. In work, we were told, we would find ourselves, our passions, our value, and so, wasn't it just obvious that you should grind as hard as possible in your nine-to-five and start a side-hustle and be the best friend to everyone you knew, and agree to do things you absolutely did not want to, and spend most of your hard-earned money keeping up with everyone's awesome social media lives, and be up on the latest health-food trend, and have an extreme workout regimen, and have the right, hip luggage, and know the best restaurants, all while looking like a wrinkle-free "boss" who could handle everything with your perfectly shaded eyes closed? The more you did, the better you were as a person, even if the doing was your undoing.

In this context, life for me (and maybe you?) became a series of *if/then* statements. *If* I worked my ass off in high school to the ex-tent that I developed chronic migraines, *then* I would get into col-lege and find happiness. *If* in college I met the "right" people and fought for the "perfect" internships, *then* I would set myself up for a better job and, in turn, a better life. *If* I put my career above every other consideration, forgoing time with the people I loved and hobbies that brought me joy, *then* I would find my most powerful self. But all of those statements had led me to now—crying hys-terically to a rabbi, in physical pain because it turned out I was al-lergic to raw beets and a simple Google search would have alerted me to that had I not been too proud to break the rules, exhausted, frustrated, potentially having hallucinations of God, and allowing myself to be ruled by a kingdom of spiders. I had often heard the hacky saying, "The journey is the destination," but now it made sense to me. I saw that if I approached *everything* as a means to make it somewhere else, I wouldn't enjoy a goddamn thing. I would always miss the trees outside my window.

Through the practice of meditation, I have come to understand four essential life truths.

The Artist Formerly Known As T$'s Four Life Truths

1. **You shouldn't eat a salad with a spider in it.** One spider in your food is one too many spiders and it won't make you bankrupt or a bad person to buy another salad.

2. **When we find ourselves in distress, there are still other emotions and sensations available to us.** "Nothing is solid," as Rabbi James would say. At any one moment we hold so many feelings and can recognize so much more of reality. With a ton of practice, if you can ground yourself and find a little bit of the pleasant in an unpleasant situation, you can give yourself enough space to be the driver of your emotions, not the hapless passenger. This is not toxic positivity, because we aren't denying how bad anything is. We're just embracing that whatever challenge we are facing is real and adding an acknowledgment that the pleasant *is real too*.

3. **When we try to fight reality, we lose.** The more we reject how we actually feel, and the real circumstances of our lives, the more pain we put ourselves in. I've come to realize that the distance between how things are and how I want them to be is the exact measure of my suffering.

4. **It feels bad to overwhelm our way through life.** We don't need to and if anyone asks that of you, it's too much.

That doesn't mean we shouldn't work hard to achieve our dreams, take care of our loved ones, and create a more equitable world. It just means there is a certain wisdom in leading a life that doesn't kill you.

Do I live up to these standards all of the time? NO FUCKING WAY. I *regularly* get overtaken with one emotion and can't see that there's *any* pleasantness available. I can be myopic as fuck. I also fight with reality. Right this very second, I am writing in a friend's house, wishing I owned my own house, and getting a little obsessed with what milestones I should have achieved by this point in my life. And I most certainly have not given up my addiction to overwhelm; I can get sober for long stretches of time (one week) only to have a relapse when a shiny new project comes along. But through the practice of meditation, there is a huge difference in how I relate to all of this. I don't judge myself about any of it and I kinda don't care about the results. I'm just trying my best to lead a life that has some amount of peace in it and to bring that peace to my friends and family and, well, hopefully you.

Now I see that getting lost in meditation is not a problem. The point of meditation is not to clear your mind, or even to find joy; it's simply to have enough mental space to keep some control over your emotions and beliefs so that you can live life in the present. And those annoying thoughts that feel like they are getting you lost? They are helpful because every time you unhook from one, you learn how to come back to focus. Getting lost is equally important to getting found.

Still with me? Or did all this talk of meditation force you into a nap situation? I'm getting close myself. I know that nothing I am saying is new. Not one piece of it. My only hope is that I've said it in language that is at least 25 percent less irritating than how many meditation people talk about it and, as a result, that you are either

SLIGHTLY more curious to try it out for yourself, or that you come back to your own practice having had a little LOL because basically anyone who meditates knows that there is no perfection in meditation. As I've become less obsessed with needing my life to be perfect *now,* my emotions seem to have eased up, too, and let me go a little. As the author John Steinbeck wrote in *East of Eden,* "And now that you don't have to be perfect, you can be good." I never really understood that until I started meditating.

I am devastated that meditation is the thing that finally helped me regulate my emotional life and, now, with every ounce of my being, I wish that devastation upon you. *Namaste.*

Meditation Translations

Urgently needed translations for the truly implacable, often maddening phrases you might encounter when meditating.

"Focus on your anchor."

Pick one thing to concentrate on. Your breath, the feeling of air coming in through your nose, city sounds around you, the sensation of your feet on the floor, anything that is easy for you to focus on. It's hard for me to use my breath, so even tho that's the most common anchor, it's rarely mine.

"Find your seat."

"Seat" is a fancy word for "butt." Find your butt, feel what you're sitting on.

"Clear your mind."

A lie. A fraud. A discouraging phrase none of us needs to hear. Nobody's mind is a blank unless they are dead.

"Cultivate beginner's mind."

"You don't know shit." And that's good. If you come at meditation like a beginner, then every new thing you learn delights you, and ignorant of the "rules," you can play with whatever might work for you.

"Mantra"

A phrase that you can keep your attention on and also use to cultivate some characteristic in yourself. I love "I am free" and just the word "soul," over and over again.

"Walking meditation"

Torture.

"Toilet Zen"

Something I made up. This is how I meditate each day. Every time I sit on the toilet, I don't look at my phone (We can be honest that that's what we're all usually doing, right? And that it's super gross?). I say, "I am here," and remind myself that I am actually here and present. Bathroom time is me time and since I'm going more often, I'm really balling out on this.

"Close your eyes."

You can keep your eyes open. Sometimes closing our eyes is scary. You can keep your eyes open or partway open, just keep a soft focus on what you are looking at.

A Little Thing That Helps

To get the benefit of a meditation retreat, you don't need to take off to the woods. Try a session that's online and only a half day (Tara Brach and Jack Kornfield have great free ones). That's my reset button.

The Scarlet Letter
Find What's Under Your Anxiety

> "I can teach my little Pearl what I have learned from this!" answered Hester Prynne, laying her finger on the red token.
> "Woman, it is thy badge of shame!" replied the stern magistrate.
>
> —Nathaniel Hawthorne, *The Scarlet Letter*

I FEEL YOU, HESTER PRYNNE, I really do. I, too, wore a damning "A" as my primary label for many years. And I suspect I'm not alone. There are a whole hell of a lot of us who wear a flaming, red-hot "A" on our chests as a badge of honor, an ID card, a life sentence, or, in some cases, as an eye-catching accessory that boldly displays our personality to the outside world much like a strong red lip or one of those handbags that is so mini you just wonder—*Why? What can you fit in there?* It's the modern scarlet letter: the indelibly branded "A" of Anxiety.* It goes so well

---

* To my English class nerds: You didn't see a Nathaniel Hawthorne reference coming, did ya? To my non–English class nerds who probably had a chance to sit at the popular table with your shell-top Adidas, or at least not be publicly mocked for raising your hand to annoyingly answer every damn question in class: In the book *The Scarlet Letter,* Hester Prynne (a pretty badass independent woman condemned to live in 1600—can you imagine?) is forced to wear an "A" on her chest to show she was an adulterer. How kind of cute is that? That in colonial times being an adulterer could RUIN your standing in the community for the rest of your life. Now I feel like you can cheat, fly a hate flag in your front yard, and cook salmon in the office microwave and no one even bats an eye.

with all of my outfits that on a typical day, I forget I'm even wearing it.

A Typical, Shitty Anxiety Day, in Which, Even Though I Thought I Had Conquered This Disturbing Way of Thinking, I Slip Back into Bad Old Habits and Am So Overwhelmed by Worry That It's All I Can See

Los Angeles, August 8, 2021

1. Wake up in a panic, drenched in sweat, heart racing and busting through my pink pajama top that's decorated with illustrations of bows and lipsticks. I'm worried that I will not be able to meet my writing deadlines, that everyone is going to be mad at me, and all of my opportunities will vanish, and even though I have plenty of resources *now* to support myself, the fact that I want to embrace a creative career will surely lead to poverty and then to my death. I am fucked.

2. Brush teeth.

3. Go get an oat milk latte as a balm for the crappy feeling of waking up worried. Realize the latte is going to cost seven dollars, feel alarm that coffee now costs seven dollars. IT'S OATS AND NOT EVEN REAL MILK! *WHAT IS HAPPENING IN THE WORLD?* Stand in line debating if I can afford a seven-dollar latte, remember the poverty I will endure someday soon, exit the line, and walk back home uncaffeinated, which is the true crisis of the morning because I don't even want to be around myself without coffee.

4. Go to lunch with a friend and worry that this person is not my friend at all. What are friends even? How do you know?

Maybe this person hates me? Maybe I hate them? Maybe I have chosen all the wrong friends and now *no one* in the world understands me and I need to meet new people ASAP and fast-track them to intimacy. How will I do that? Rapid-fire texting? Get seven-dollar lattes together and act like someone who is comfortable getting a seven-dollar latte? SPIN INTO A BLACK HOLE OF ALL THE MISTAKES I HAVE MADE IN FRIENDSHIPS.

5.   Pick up the mail.

6.   Look at my phone to see that my boyfriend has once again turned the "read receipts" function on in its settings without my knowledge. *Cool.* That means he took my phone when I wasn't looking and changed the preferences to make sure he knows the time at which I read his text message versus the time I respond to him. How do I know he did this? Because two months ago I noticed that in the hundreds of contacts I have in my phone,* of the millions of text messages I have ever sent, never *once* have I turned on read receipts because *WHY DOES THAT SETTING EVEN EXIST? WHO WANTS THAT? NO ONE!*† but it was mysteriously on for him. So, I turned it off. Now it is on again. There is only one thing I can conclude.

7.   Call a psychiatrist and make an appointment to be evaluated.

---

* Most of which, BTW, are "Josh, Actor, Dating App" or a similar permutation for a similar first date that went nowhere.
† "Read receipts" are like the atomic bomb of cellphones: Even though we have the power to create it, does that mean we should use it? You Apple engineers are playing God and I don't like it one bit.

8. Burn pile of mail.

9. Repeat.

So. Yeah. The way I deal with anxiety is I don't.

The lens through which I have historically seen life is a pair of transfixing, spinning anxiety glasses, the kind they sell at the circus to "hypnotize" you, but that no one actually wants to buy. I have been WORRIED since time immemorial. As a child, I fretted that robbers were going to smash in through the glass sliding doors to a patio off my bedroom and "rape, torture, or murder me." (*Remember that one? Thanks, Mom!*) Around age six, my anxiety got so bad that my parents (rather than assuaging my fears about rapists, torturers, and murderers) bought me a television for my room so that I always had noise to distract me. Who needs a bedtime story when you can binge-watch *Matlock* or even better—*Murder, She Wrote*?

By the time I was thirty and had successfully re-parented myself, my anxiety was at an ALL-TIME LOW. Hallelujah! But going from a perpetual, eleven-out-of-ten, "*oh sweet mother of God,* the entire world is unsafe and I am helpless" style of worry to a five-out-of-ten, "my skin is regularly itchy and my body is uncomfortable and I can't stand being still in this chair with how anxious I feel" was not what I would deem "ideal."

With work, many of my more irrational and low self-worth anxieties were lifted off my shoulders, but now that I had a little more clarity of mind, I noticed, as I grew older, that there was *a lot* to legitimately be worried about. Did my youth spent in the California sun damage my skin so much that I am 100 percent going to get cancer? Speaking of cancer, has the aluminum in my deodorant been building up in my armpits, preparing to spread to my entire body? And what about the very real climate emergency we are facing that politicians seem hell-bent on avoiding even as their states drown in floods and go up in flames? What about systematic oppression? What about the loss of voting rights in America? What about ALL OF IT?

So, in 2020, while I was in the midst of trying to heal/take back/find whatever my soul was, I decided I really needed to do *something* for my anxiety beyond my self-care habits. I was just *tired* of waking up fully anxious, hyper-vigilant, scanning the world for threats as my body flooded with cortisol. I reluctantly made (and kept—big win) an appointment to see a psychiatrist.

I had a long history with pharmaceuticals. Since the age of eighteen, I had experimented with amitriptyline, Cymbalta, Effexor, lamotrigine, Lexapro, Prozac, trazodone, and for sure others that I can no longer recall. I know there's a joke somewhere in there about having been on "the ABCs of medications," but I am too anxious to write it. I really tried to find a medical solution, but *none* of these drugs ever seemed to actually help, no matter how many I tried or in what combination. Prozac, for example, made me incredibly tired to the point where I could not stay awake in the afternoon.* The only pill that worked was clonazepam in an emergency panic-attack situation. But, like all the things I love, it turned out clonazepam can become addictive over time, so it wasn't a long-term solution.

Because the pills never seemed to help, I decided to taper off them in 2018, right after I had completed the manuscript for *Buy Yourself the F*cking Lilies*. I was in a DRASTICALLY better headspace than I had ever been in and felt like I no longer needed to be medicated. And . . . if I'm being honest, which, why wouldn't I be at this point, because you know *far* worse about me than this and yet you appear to *still* be reading (hi!), there was still a part of me that thought that even if I could find the right drug, it would be

---

* This is an exceedingly RARE reaction to Prozac; for most people, it's a stimulant. While I appreciate that I am a unique, special individual, when it comes to medications and health, I would really prefer to be average.

better if I managed my mental health without the aid of pills. I know. I *know* that "I know better." But I took pride in the fact that since 2018 I had been medication-free and could handle my mental health "on my own"; I felt like I should get some self-satisfied-smug-bougie award, like a campfire-scented candle in the shape of a box of oat milk? But by the time I was hit by the shit-storm-nightmare-is-this-for-real? apocalypse otherwise referred to as 2020, my anxiety had become unmanageable (see page 61) and at the ~~constant, unrelenting, ANNOYING, peer pressure~~ suggestion of my two best friends, Fisch, who you'll remember taught me that safety is a prerequisite for doing anything, and Julia, one of the steadiest, most caring, and just *best people* I have ever met,[*] I went to a new psychiatrist, Dr. Wallace, open to the prospect of prescription solutions, but still not entirely convinced.[†]

Dr. Wallace asked me about my mental health history so I gave her the highlights—or lowlights—reel: neglect; psychological abuse; scary, unsafe childhood; blah, blah, blah; recurrent suicidal ideation; blah, blah, blah; overcoming a weed addiction; trying every single solution known to man to heal myself except for acupuncture, because for some reason I have a real mental block on that one; and FINALLY finding stability, contentment, and even spells of joy after I re-parented myself (although I knew that was a process that would never end). I had been off medications since 2018, but now was suffering from morning anxiety attacks that I couldn't understand.

"I mostly don't even feel bad about my childhood anymore!" I proclaimed. "I've done so much work, healed so many wounds

---

[*] OG *Lilies* readers: Yes, this is "Fucking Julia" who taught me that running could significantly alleviate my anxiety. If you're irritated that she's always so dead-on for what I need to do to gain my stability, so am I. *Fucking Julia.*

[†] I know I've talked about multiple doctors here so let me break it down: Dr. Candace is a psychologist who works on mental health through words and exercises, and Dr. Wallace is a psychiatrist who can prescribe medication. Why aren't they just the same person? Because that would be too easy.

from the past that the PAST IS FINALLY IN THE PAST! And even when it's not—I can recognize that and help myself! You know? It doesn't overtake my life like it used to. That's why this anxiety doesn't make any sense! I know we are in really trying times, but the facts of my life are actually *awesome*! I'm living my dreams, I have amazing friends, there's no financial stress [*yet*, knocks on wood, apologizes to the evil eye], I'm healthy in a time when our health is at risk, I mean . . . what more could I ask for?" I asked her, but also myself. "The only thing I can think of is my boyfriend might be stressing me out a little. I don't know. He's . . . eclectic?"

"Tell me more," Dr. Wallace probed.

Liam* and I had been dating for about six months. He was classically handsome like a modern Cary Grant, most often sporting brown Gucci loafers, the kind with golden buckles, which he wore, of course, with no socks. He had the cheekiest smile, and when he beamed it at you, you knew he was up to some kind-hearted mischief like ordering you almost everything on the menu when you were in the bathroom. And his laugh—*oh my word*—his laugh. It was big and boisterous with almost an echo to it that hung in the air. It was the kind of laugh that makes you proud that you have the ability to invoke such a pure and joyful sound.

On our first date I learned that he was not from Kansas City as his Hinge profile described, but was instead from New York City, which, as far as I knew, had not been relocated to Missouri. "How does that work?" I asked. "You're Upper West Side by way of Missouri? Midwest values in a prep school suit?" I needled. "Go on and laugh but I'm very tied to Kansas City. It's where my brood has roots. We're just another one of those Midwest old piles, a dime a dozen. We go back generations really. I might have grown

---

* Liam's real name is not Liam. BUT! Liam is obviously a very hot name, and I have not ruled out dating you, future Liam.

up in New York but my heart belongs to the Show Me State." I didn't know what "old pile" meant, but I pretended to because he said it so offhandedly, like for sure I should know that term. As the night went on, between A LOT of jokes and laughing and finding we loved all the same things—adventure, reading, judging other couples—he revealed that he was the descendant of a storied American family. The kind who used "summered" as a verb and who swore croquet was a legitimate sport.

When I asked him what he did for a living he explained. "I help fund nonprofits," he vaguely demurred. Clearly not wanting to get into the specifics of his career. "So your job is to help charities?" I asked, a little impressed. "It's not just my job, it's my life. I was born to privilege, I know that, and I know it's not mine. I didn't earn it, I shouldn't keep it. It's one of the greatest pleasures and responsibilities of my life to give back, just a ghost in the background with a checkbook. I vanish the second the project is complete," he finished, brushing his hands one against the other and then lifting them up, his palms facing me, the international sign for "it's done and I'm outta here."

I excused myself to go to the bathroom to have a CAN THIS BE FOR REAL? moment. I was being scammed, right? There was no way I happened to swipe on an incredibly handsome descendant of magnates who gave his money to charities and talked in an accent that was part Jimmy Stewart and part LA dude? And even if I had—this guy had to be running *some kind* of con. I looked at my red-lipped reflection in the bathroom mirror, wondering if he could possibly be real, when I realized that "old pile" meant "old pile of money." Either he was a gentleman from a bygone era transported to Los Angeles to help in any way he could, or he had *Talented Mr. Ripley*–ed someone. Either way, I was fascinated.

Liam lived in a mid-century architectural gem, high up in the rolling Hollywood Hills. From that vantage point, you looked out onto otherworldly views of Los Angeles. I could see the ocean to downtown from the front door. "It's rumored to be one of John Barrymore's old haunts but according to Los Angeles real estate agents, *every* house was once John Barrymore's or Lucille Ball's," he said, laughing as he took off my coat. I was immediately struck by how stylish the place was. Bachelors are not known for having the greatest interior decoration, but Liam had impeccable taste. There was a rare Noguchi lamp next to the inviting, soft, brown leather sofa; the pristine, all-white kitchen had no visible cabinets, nor did it have any visible handles or seams, you simply pressed the wall and suddenly it sprung into a pantry; and up against the windowsill that looked out onto a lush green hillside, a photo of his family stood casually next to a mason jar of wildflowers. Everything looked perfectly curated, but perfectly rumpled and broken in. Like someone had bought all the finest things but just couldn't be bothered with them.

The walls were *covered* in art. But not prints or what I might fall in love with and buy at the flea market. This was ART from names I'd seen in museums. "Is that a David Hockney?" I asked, recognizing the distinct style of the pop-art painter. "Oh sure," he offhandedly confirmed. "I'll probably give it to the Hammer this season." And by that he meant he would just "give" this painting to the internationally acclaimed Hammer Museum in Los Angeles. Ya know, like we all do from time to time.

But I didn't care (~~too much~~ exclusively) about the obscene wealth. The thing that really got me? He lavished me with compliments *constantly*. When he couldn't reach me to tell me, "I'm toast, sweetheart, your eyes, they've got me," he instead would text my friends things like, "Isn't our little Schustey bear the most beautiful girl you've ever seen?" Every day he'd almost sing, "Brown eyes, you are the most gorgeous girl in the world, and that ass . . . oohhhh . . . girl! That ass is what a boy dreams about." I had never once considered my ass before and was glad someone was taking on that responsibility.* One morning he *did* sing about me. I heard "Schustey, Schustey, Schustey, Schuuuustey" coming from the shower. When I peeped my head into the steam-filled bathroom, he drew a giant heart in the condensation on the glass. I hadn't been praised for my physical beauty to this extent before. I'd been called smart, ambitious, cute, funny . . . but beautiful? Never. Not by my dad, not by Mom, not by a previous partner. I was intoxicated by his compliments, obsessed with his obsession with me, and through Liam's eyes† I started to see that I *was* actually beautiful, every ounce of flesh the exact right amount of flesh and every curve as perfect as a sculpture.

Let's check in, shall we? What would you think if the smart, funny, handsome, interesting scion of a super-wealthy, old-money family had two passions in life—giving back and . . . *you*? You would be suspicious, right? I, too, thought it was too good to be true. Liam had no online presence (Red flag? Or cool flag?), but when I googled his family, I saw pictures of him at hoity-toity events, the captions and Wikipedia entries confirming that he was very much a descendant of a magnate. I kept waiting for the other shoe to drop, but I couldn't find anything wrong with him. Except for one thing that started to feel like that pebble in your hiking boot that you try to ignore because you don't want to stop and miss any of the vistas.

Liam exaggerated or spoke in half-truths, *a lot*. Always about small, seemingly innocuous things, but the frequency was off-

* Can we talk about this for a moment? I know that "asses" are a thing. That we should have "good" ones and that people get implants to achieve this. BUT WHY? I WILL NEVER SEE MY BUTT! Ya know? Of all the things about me, this is very much on the backside and I just can't see myself being concerned with something I myself won't see and can't enjoy. I've wanted to tell this to someone for ten years, so thank you for bearing witness to my IMPORTANT butt thoughts.
† Please don't neg on this. I know the male gaze ain't great, but it CAN feel incredible to be praised purely for the physical, especially when you haven't had that kind of attention. I imagine it is the same for guys. Sometimes you just want your hotness confirmed. If this makes me "bad," okay. I'm bad. And hot.

putting. I once overheard him tell a gallery owner that he owned his house, when I knew he rented. And then there were things that weren't quite lies but just very *off*. He said he attended a year of high school in Denmark but couldn't remember the name of the high school or what town it was in. Odd. And I mean, on his dating profile he had twisted the truth about where he was from.

I let these little fibs slide because who were they hurting? I figured Liam was insecure and that with time he'd get more comfortable with me and they would stop. But as we grew closer, they only ramped up in frequency, and eventually, they were directed toward me. It started small: "Brown eyes, I signed up for your newsletter!" he proclaimed one night in the car. "Oh, you don't have to do that—in fact, don't. Please don't," I joked back. "The newsletter is just a weird part of my brain, it's really . . . personal," I explained. "Too late, I want to hear what my Schustey bear is thinking." (*Please don't cringe too hard right now with the nicknames.*) When I got home, just because I had an inkling that something was off, I checked to see if Liam was on my subscriber list. He was not. I didn't care one way or the other, but why had he gone out of his way to lie about it?*

And then, Liam proclaimed, *many times over,* that he was a multi-millionaire. The Internet had confirmed that he was heir to a billion-dollar family fortune, but one day he called me sounding a little desperate. "Little fox, I hate to do this but I'm in a pickle. I'm stranded. I was driving my old Thunderbird in the desert and it broke down." *Of course it had broken down!* I thought. Liam had a vintage red Thunderbird with no seatbelts, no airbags, not *one* modern safety feature, that he had basically driven into the ground. It looked chic until on closer inspection you realized all of the interior hazard lights were on and parts of the floor seemed to be

---

* But while we're here . . . are you signed up? It would make my day if you did! Taraschuster .com/newsletter end of plug.

rusting away. When you got in the driver's seat, you didn't so much "drive" the car as point it in the general direction you wanted, then pray as the steering wheel, of its own volition, seemed to pull you from left to right. "I'm in a tight spot, honey, can you lend me thirteen hundred dollars?"

Now, I don't know a ton about multimillionaires, but I found it odd that someone who went out of his way to make wealth a defining characteristic of his personality would need to borrow cash from *me,* a not-millionaire. Maybe none of his assets were "liquid"? Whatever that means? But, from my non-millionaire viewpoint I knew I would never-ever-in-a-thousand-years ask someone I had only been dating for a few months for money. In fact, I would rather sell my eggs than ask *anyone,* but unfortunately, at this point in time, my eggs are considered geriatric (something which we will get into in painful detail later, you have a lot to look forward to!). But, I liked Liam. I really did. So I nervously Venmo'd the tow truck company anyway, only later wondering, *What kind of towing costs thirteen hundred dollars?*

But the thing that was really, I don't know, *irritating* to me happened at a soiree he threw at his house. There was no reason for this party, no birthday, no holiday to celebrate. One day he simply proclaimed, "I'm feeling jaunty, let's throw a little get-together!" I was game for a small dinner, maybe I could invite some friends to meet the guy whom I'd started to call (very much behind his back) "the Great Gatsby IRL," but he had much grander plans in mind. He hired a team of chefs and servers, a famous DJ, he arranged the best-stocked bar I had ever seen even though he did not drink, and he had his house cleaned and decorated until it *sparkled*—I mean, really glittered in the glow of hundreds of candles mixing with the city lights of Los Angeles visible from his rooftop deck.

At this point we had been dating for five months and his constant, almost unrelenting question to me was "Can we have babies? I really want to settle down with you, little fox, and start a family.

You're the one, my darling." In fact, on our second date in March, mid-make-out session on my too-small sofa, he playfully asked, "Wouldn't it be a lark if we could give my mom a grandchild by Christmas?" I don't typically refer to bringing a human soul into the world as a "lark," but I figured he was joking and laughed. But as we went on dates three, four, and five, his jokes revealed a major frustration in his life. "I'm forty and I don't have the one thing I want: kids! And now here you are with *so much* going on, and your crazy career, and in no rush to start a family, and where does that leave me? With nothing!" While I was flattered at first, it was too fucking much. Every time I gently protested he would counter, "Schustey, I know you think you don't want to get married right now, but you're going to fall so deeply in love with me that it's going to be brutal. We'll have a little clan of kids and I'll support us while you write. You're going to hate this so much. It's going to be the *beeest*." His words, while I'm sure meant to feel reassuring, felt kinda like a threat. Should love be brutal? And after having survived serious financial instability as a kid, there was no way on Earth, the moon, Mars, or some yet-to-be-discovered planet that I would ever want another person to support me, not because I am a good person and "above money" (I am not! And we'll spend time on money later) but because given my past, I could never trust anyone else to be in charge of my finances.

Back at his house, preparing for his party, Liam zipped up the back of my Target dress styled to be fancy because you know I love a good Target find. He turned me around by the shoulders, leaned in close to my neck and cheek as if to kiss me, and whispered, "Let's not tell anyone we're dating, all right? I would hate for this to become some kind of 'coming out' party. People are terrible gossips." I was surprised. I hadn't even thought about what he would call me except for "Tara," but the same man who was on the daily insisting that I was going to fall in love with him and have his children didn't want to call me his girlfriend? What could I say except "Okay"?

He could tell I was a little disappointed and made an attempt to comfort me. "Now, my Schustey, don't be cross with me. I got you a gift to celebrate how fantastic your book is." I was even more surprised by this since, up until this point, he had refused to read one chapter of my book because he didn't want to "cross [my] boundaries," even though I, the person whose boundaries we were discussing, was the one who asked him to read one chapter, just so he could, I don't know, feel a little proud of my work? He pulled a bag out of his closet and put it behind his back. I expected it would be something "writerly," like a nice pen or a bag of salty, crunchy, stress-eating-worthy chips, but instead, as I opened the sack and reached in, I pulled out something familiar, a copy of my book.

Why was he giving me back my book? He immediately explained that this was HIS edition of the book. "I turned your book into something really special to me and it would mean a lot to me for you to have it, I think it will make you smile." He beamed with pride as I took the book out of the gift bag. I leafed through it and the dedication page fell out. It had been written over with the word "FIRE" in big red crayon letters with a stapled picture of flames affixed to it. As I continued to skim through, I saw that on some of the pages after I had written a point, or a takeaway, he had written on the page "correct," or "perfect," as if he had the authority to judge how I thought about the world. On additional pages he had pasted *other* people's writing, cut out of *their* books, *on top* of my words, most notably a long Chekhov passage obscuring the final paragraph on dating. The whole book was falling apart, stuffed with so many cutouts from magazines, drawn all over in his handwriting that could only be described as "the work of a drunk toddler," and finally, on the back cover he had stapled leaves and feathers. "I want you to keep this, it means so much to me," he told me, his eyes slightly squinted, as he put his hands over my hands holding my book. I did not find it "nice" at all that he had painted over my words. I felt violated. But a swarm of partygoers was beginning to descend upon the house and maybe I was over-reacting? Maybe this *was* nice? I forced a smile and said, "Thank you."

As we left his room the first guests arrived and one man in a three-piece suit, and glasses that verged on being a monocle situation, shouted out to Liam as he descended the stairs into the living room, "Liam! You old dog, you're moving to Africa?! You couldn't give LA two full years?!" "Yes, that's right, I go where I am needed," Liam confirmed. I would have been surprised and dismayed had I suddenly learned from Mr. Monopoly that my boyfriend was moving to Africa, but I knew, at this point, not to trust anything Liam said. If he was going to move at all it was ten miles away to Echo Park. In that moment, as I thought about the book, about the laundry list of distortions, and now that he was telling people he was moving to Africa to do charity work, my heart started pounding uncontrollably, tiny little knives of worry striking at every cell in my body.

* * *

As I finished rattling off my list of foibles and mixed feelings about Liam to Dr. Wallace, I concluded, "So, I don't know why I'm ten-out-of-ten anxious every single morning, ya know? Even if Liam isn't my match, I'm not in REAL danger, there's nothing totally wrong. Liam's not going to kill me. And the rest of my life is so good. So why do I feel so anxious??" Dr. Wallace, with her chin in her right hand, looked at me through the lenses of her rimless glasses and said something I never expected, "I don't think you're anxious. I think you're furious."

Have you ever seen the Maxell tape commercial? Where a man in a leather jacket and sunglasses, sitting in an armchair, has his butler put a Maxell tape* into the stereo and the sound of the tape blows back the leather jacket guy, his hair, his glass of wine, where everything is pushed back by the power of the sound? I felt like that man, only it wasn't my hair being blown back, it was my whole conception of my interior life. I felt like I had been thrust into an empty room where there was only one thing to face—the truth. I *was* furious. As soon as she said it, I knew it was true. Furious at how my boyfriend's never-ending truth-stretching made me feel persistently on edge. What was true? What wasn't?

The guy had borrowed money from me, he pressured me about having kids almost daily, and the primary way I felt when I was around him was unsafe. In all of those instances, my reaction was to freeze, feeling panic creep from my belly into my heart and chest, taking my beautiful, flirtatious butterflies and transforming them into moths that eat your clothing. I would find myself unable to say anything or do anything, like a deer in the Rolls-Royce headlights.

Dearest reader, do you recall in the second chapter (the one about journaling, oh you forget so easily!) how I said that many people do not even know how they feel inside? I am those people. I hate to keep going back to my childhood, but I think that you might be able to relate to this, or just part of it?

I remember being in college and returning home for Thanksgiving break. My dad and I were meeting for dinner, and I rushed into the restaurant a few minutes late, needing to use the bathroom. "Hi, Dad, be right back, have to use the ladies' room," I said to him as I made a beeline to the loo. As I returned to the table, I

* I wrote this chapter in 2021. In whatever future year you are living in—I only have one essential question: Have tapes make it back "in" again? I feel like they need to have their nostalgic moment, like vinyl records, butterfly clips, and those bucket hats, but up to the printing of this book they have not.

saw my dad sitting there, in the middle of the restaurant, smoking weed from a vape pen. Now maybe to you this is what a "cool" dad would do, but a couple weeks earlier, I had confessed to him that I was struggling with my own addiction to weed. I was looking for support or encouragement to quit, but he had said *nothing*. Also, ever since I was a teenager I had begged, pleaded, and cried to him to do me the courtesy of not being high around me. Every time he was high at dinner (which eventually became every time we had dinner) it made me feel like I wasn't worth being sober around. My brain started pounding, and I walked up to him and said, "If this is how you're going to act, then I have to leave. I told you I don't want to be around you when you're high." This was the first time I drew a clear boundary. I walked out of the restaurant and pleaded with the valet to give me a deal on the parking— after all, my car was still at the curb.

The next morning, I awoke to find a note from my dad slipped under my bedroom door. "You humiliated me last night. I would have never done to my parents what you did to me. What you did to me was terrible. —Dad." I felt perhaps the most worthless I had ever felt. I started to question reality. Was I a terrible person who had embarrassed my dad? Was I fundamentally bad? Or had my dad's actions embarrassed himself? Either way, it yielded the same result—my dad punished me with harsh words and the silent treatment for telling him how I felt. I think this is part of the reason, or *the* reason, I am so bad at telling *anyone,* even friends, how I feel, because for so long my feelings were muzzled and rebuked. In time I learned to stop telling anyone how I felt. Including myself.

Dr. Wallace paused as she watched me reel with newfound understanding. "I think you're right," I confessed, "I've never felt angry before. I think maybe there are a lot of things I haven't felt before." Dr. Wallace took her hand from under her chin and set it on the arm of her chair. "Many people use anxiety as a blanket emotion for all of the things they can't, won't, or don't know how to feel. Anger is one of them. You might be pushing other feelings down, and that denial, that pushing down how we genuinely feel, *that* feels like anxiety." My mind totally and utterly blown, she prescribed me Wellbutrin, not for anxiety, but for depression. "I think it's more likely that you're depressed. You have a lot to be depressed about. Maybe with a little space, a little pick-me-up, it will be easier to deal with the things you have inside of you but have not had the ability to feel or articulate before." I thanked Dr. Wallace and grabbed my bag to leave but she stopped me at the door. "I don't usually give advice but . . . you should also think about breaking up with Liam." *Already on it, Dr. Wallace. Already on it.*

With the help of Wellbutrin to elevate me (which, HALLELU-JAH, FINALLY seems to work for me), to give me enough space from my emotions that I can see them instead of *become* them, with daily work with my emotion wheel and journal, with a safe home now firmly within me, I have come to recognize that when I feel "anxious" it's often a cover for "full of rage," "disappointed," or "holding contempt." I know I'm not a doctor, but I do visit WebMD and Psychology Today a lot—*like every day a lot*—so that has to count for something, right? But in my experience, I recognize that having labels like "anxiety" and "depression" can be LIFE-GIVING. They can point the way toward proper treatment, solutions, and a basic understanding of ourselves. But we are in real danger when our diagnosis—or our self-given diagnosis, as is often the case—becomes a part of our identity and an excuse for why we can't help ourselves. *Oof, did the word "excuse" feel bad? Stick with me, I promise I'm driving somewhere.* You don't call someone with breast cancer cancerous. They are more than the disease within them and therefore they can fight against it or live a life that is not entirely made of cancer. Labeling the whole of a person any one diagnosis not only misses the complexities of being a human, not only reduces the entirety of you to one phrase, but it also robs us of our agency to change or help ourselves.

If I'm not anxious but simply frustrated and disgusted by the political landscape, I can volunteer and *do something* instead of endlessly fretting, my anxiety taking up as much time as action would. If I'm not anxious but angry with my father, but I no longer depend on him as I did as a child, I can tell him why I am angry so *we can have a chance to heal, so we can have the opportunity to change our relationship*. If I'm not anxious but furious with my boyfriend who keeps lying to me, breaking into my phone, pressuring me to have kids, and borrowing money from me, then instead of making *myself* feel bad and panicked, I can tell the motherfucker off. I can tell him exactly how I feel in a two-page takedown email the likes of which I had never written before. But if I'm simply "anxious," I end up spinning, unsure of what to do, because really, what can you do with anxiety?

While I know there are very real medical reasons for anxiety, and there are some people who suffer from pure anxiety with nothing underneath it, I think it's often the case that we use it as a blanket term. "Anxious" is a lot more socially acceptable than "furious," especially for women. It's almost like it's the new "hysteria," a broad label stamped onto women to explain, and often dismiss, why they are acting "irrationally" or "excessively." Isn't that the hallmark of anxiety? That it is outsize and unwarranted? But maybe we aren't as irrational as we've come to believe. Maybe the whole world is fucked-up and all we want to do is scream, to make a scene, to stomp our feet and demand change, but our healthy and deserved rage has been pushed down for so long that we have lost the ability to let it burst from our skin like lava too long festering below the earth's crust. And like lava, which has the potential to either destroy everything in its path or create fresh new earth, if we push our anger so far down within us that we don't know it's even there, then maybe we lose the ability to build something new and life-giving out of our fury.

Your emotions aren't curses to be avoided. They aren't bombs you can drop. They won't kill anyone. A feeling expressed calmly and without attack is SIMPLY A FEELING. It's got no power to hurt *anyone* unless you bottle it up, press it way down into the well that is your soul, and let it alchemize into something that wakes you up every morning, ten-out-of-ten anxious. *That* is dangerous. To you, to your family, to everyone you know.

* * *

> The stigma gone, Hester heaved a long, deep sigh, in which the burden of shame and anguish departed from her spirit. O exquisite relief! She had not known the weight, until she felt the freedom!
> —Nathaniel Hawthorne, *The Scarlet Letter*

Once again—I feel you, Hester, I really do.

If you want to know how I deal with anxiety, the answer is, I don't. I deal with rage, disappointment, and hurt. By dealing with what my anxiety is trying to tell me, not only has my morning worry disappeared, but I've ripped off the "A" society branded me with and thrown it to the ground. And like Hester, I can now sigh deeply, I can catch my breath, because I'm no longer ashamed or hiding from myself. I didn't even realize how much the "A" of Anxiety was dictating my life until I demanded the freedom to feel how I actually feel.

If any of this resonates, why don't you do like me and Hester and rip that "A" off of your chest? If only for one moment, so you can see if there's anything under it? You can pick it back up and put it on, but you might just learn that you are feeling more than a single "A," because you are complex and brilliant, and there's no way one word or phrase could define you. Except, of course, "made of star-dust," which is a label we all deserve to embrace.

Are you anxious or . . .
When you think you're anxious, it's not always because you are anxious. Use this list to investigate what your nervous energy might be about.*

- Is your bra too tight, corset-style, causing your heart to race?
- Are your tighty-whities too tight, causing your . . . you know . . . to something?
- Are you sleep-deprived? I know I would be if I was taking care of a newborn while working a full-time job and somehow managing to cook for my family. I'd be sleep-deprived and full of rage and lashing out at everyone. So . . . yeah . . . I guess no kids for me?
- Furious at your boyfriend for breaking into your phone, pressuring you about children, and constantly lying to you? Anyone? Just me?
- Frustrated that you didn't complete everything on your to-do list? Even though no person alive could complete your to-do list?
- Excited about an upcoming celebration or work project but it's hard to find the line between excited and anxious for you?
- On coke?
- Hyped up on a venti iced latte with four pumps of vanilla, your every nerve frayed and jumpy from the caffeine and sugar?
- Justifiably angry that Brian at work simply repeats YOUR ideas but somehow gets credit for them?

---

* This list, and much of my conception of anxiety, is inspired by Dr. Ellen Vora's book *The Anatomy of Anxiety* (Harper Wave, 2022). It challenges the notion that all anxiety is born of emotional turmoil. Sometimes it's just something weird you ate! I love Ellen, and her book challenged a lot of my thinking.

- Is the world actually a scary place right now? And you are feeling justifiable fear that's alerting you to the fact that *something* must be done?
- Are you thirsty? Please go drink some water.

Core State Journaling Practice

This written meditation has helped me to uncover how I really feel and relax my sometimes overwhelming emotions. I have shamelessly stolen it from Rabbi James Jacobson-Maisels (meditation chapter!) and Schustey'd it up. (I hate that Liam used "Schustey," because it's my most beloved nickname. Except, of course, for "The Artist Formerly Known As T$," which is a mouthful of words but I'm into it.)

1. Get out your journal. If you don't have a journal at this point in our relationship, this is never going to work. I love you, it was nice while it lasted, but maybe now is the time to go our separate ways? We'll always have the memories. Of course I'm kidding. I'M KIDDING! I love you! But for real, please get a journal. For your sake, and for mine.

2. Write the emotion you are feeling. If you're not sure, consult your feeling wheel.

3. Now ask yourself, "What does the feeling I wrote above want and need?" We are going to dig and dig until we find a core emotion. So, if I chose "anxiety," I would ask, "Anxiety, what do you want? What do you need?" I would pause and write down the first thing I hear: "My anxiety wants safety."

4. You'll repeat the above for "safety." "Safety, what do you want? What do you need?" I write down the first thing I hear: My "safety" wants peace.

5. What does "peace" want? Maybe my "peace" wants love.

6. Keep doing the above until you come to some kind of "core" feeling. Don't overthink it, just keep working until you feel an emotion that's "right enough." For me, it's usually around four layers of digging. Then pause.

7. Now sit in that core feeling for a few moments. Here are some examples of how you can do that:
    a. If you wrote "love," bask in those feelings by recalling all the people you love and who have loved you, or in any memory of love.
    b. If you wrote "relaxation," think of calming images, or times you have felt the most ease.
    c. If you wrote "tweaking out," I'm telling you—that's not a feeling, that's the coke kicking in. It's okay, we've all been there.*

8. Once you've taken a moment to give yourself the feelings of your core state, move back up the ladder, giving "love," the core emotion, to each emotion you previously identified.
    a. Do this by asking, "What if my 'peace' had love?" Then I would feel calm and connected.
    b. "What if my 'safety' had love?" Then I wouldn't be worried at all because I would know I was safe.
    c. "What if my 'anxiety' had love?" Then I'd know I was all right.

This is my go-to written meditation to figure out what's under my emotions and how I can help soothe them. You could also use

---

* Me, I've been there.

the emotion wheel. Who knew there were real tools for these things? Not me for thirty years!

A Little Thing That Helps

This is creepy, but it works to relieve nervous feelings. Look ahead of you. Now move ONLY your eyes to the left and hold your gaze there for thirty seconds. Now move ONLY your eyes to the right and hold your gaze there for thirty seconds. Now return your gaze to the center. HOW GOOD DID THAT FEEL? There's a scientific reason for why this works, but this isn't that kind of book.

Loneliness Is My Superpower

Your "Faults" Are Out to Help You

I RECENTLY ASKED MY COMMUNITY on Instagram, "What part of yourself do you most want to get rid of?" I thought I'd get a handful of answers, because it's a fairly intense question. Instead, in mere moments, I had *hundreds* of replies. I guess everyone had their answers locked and loaded. These are the top five things folks wanted to destroy in themselves:*

"My anxiety and my intrusive thoughts, they drive me crazy."

"People pleasing! How about being pleased with myself first!"

"Fear of judgment. It has held me back from really living my life."

"The part that hates how my body looks."

---

* Thank you to everyone who answered. You helped me see some of my own insecurities, and I think you are making a lot of new folks feel less alone right now. What a gift you gave.

"The feeling that I'm not good enough despite how awesome I am. Self-doubt is a bitch."

Oh, my friend, self-doubt is indeed a bitch. How do we quell our raging self-doubt, body-hate, and people pleasing? How do we eliminate the part of us that believes we will eventually be abandoned by our friends and family, by anyone who pretends to love me—er, I mean, *us*?

I have felt that I will be discarded and left behind my entire life. This fear is not irrational—for so much of my childhood, I was neglected, and not just by my parents. In one of my most vivid memories, I am five years old, wandering down a black asphalt road, terrified and alone, desperately trying to find adults. I walk, shouting, "Hello? I need help!" but because I live in an isolated canyon with few neighbors, no one hears me. While I can't find people, I know what else is out here: coyotes and rattlesnakes and deer that die in your pool (see *Buy Yourself the F*cking Lilies* for your dead-deer curiosity), and I'm petrified.

Before I found myself outside, I was in my bedroom with my babysitter Jaz, playing with my Lego-style circus set. On this particular day, I had decided that Jumbo the Elephant had been overworked and deserved to sleep in the Painted Lady's red bed. I picked up Jumbo to put him in the play bed when Jaz stopped me. "Elephants can't sleep in people's beds, stupid girl," she scolded. Jaz was often harsh with me. "If you put that elephant in that bed, I'll leave you." I paused for a few seconds, holding the plastic elephant in the air, then stared her dead in the eyes and put Jumbo in the bed. Jaz didn't say a word as she got off the gray carpeted floor and walked out of my room. I ran to my window and watched her get into her white Ford Tempo* and peel out of our long and steep driveway. She kept her promise.

---

* How could I possibly remember that she drove a white Ford Tempo? I guess I've been label conscious my whole life.

So that's why I'm here on this road, sob-walking toward imagined safety. I know that Mrs. Williams lives up a giant hill above our house and I think that maybe if I can make that climb, I will be safe. When I finally get to her front door, I bang on it and ring the bell, growing increasingly upset, bawling harder and harder, because now that I have found safety, I can really lose my shit.

"Tara, what are you doing here?" Mrs. Williams asks, frowning, as she opens the door, at first just a crack, then halfway. "My babysitter Jaz left me and I'm alone and don't know what to dooooooo!" I wail. Mrs. Williams looks down on my little face, snotty and glossed over with tears, and her eyes tighten. She takes a step back and sighs—in a way that I read as frustration and annoyance. She does not hug or comfort me. "Come here," she sternly instructs as she takes me by the hand and marches me into her in-home jewelry studio.

There are magical Lucite boxes full of gems and rhinestones all around me, and on a better day this room is one of my favorite places to be in the world. I love to look at—and even sometimes, when I am allowed, play with—all the sparkling, brightly colored crystals in their perfectly organized trays. "Stay here while I call your parents," she seems to scold me. Then she walks out of the room and shuts the door.

I have many early memories of being left alone, but this one has always felt particularly triggering. I felt so blindingly ashamed of playing how I wanted, of being abandoned for it, and then of needing help. A real shame trifecta, if you will. It's entirely possible that Mrs. Williams was not as unkind as I remember her, but it also makes sense to me that she might have been. My family was the "problem family" in the neighborhood. The house where you would often see cop cars, or animal control, or social services. The house with the remnants from my mother's failed medical practice—exam chairs and filing cabinets—sitting in the front yard for years.

We were the undisputed eyesore of a neighborhood that to this day self-describes as "an architecturally controlled community," its website boasting of the design awards it has won and the magazines in which it's been featured. It's not the kind of place that appreciated it when my mom spray-painted a scene of Hawaii over the garage door, nor is it the kind of place that welcomed a disheveled little girl showing up at their front door in a frenzy. I am sure Mrs. Williams was justified in how frustrated she must have been with our family. But this memory, perhaps more than anything, solidified a belief that had been forming in the back of my mind: I would always be alone, and for some reason, I didn't deserve being taken care of.

Now, maybe you could have shrugged this off and moved on, maybe you could have even found it funny with time, but for me, the belief in the inevitability of my abandonment has shadowed me my entire life. It lives as a second, slightly smaller and softer beating heart, just below my main heart. And because it's such a steady part of me, it often directs me to behave in ways that can be, well, really fucking annoying. To myself and to anyone who knows me. Try not to roll your eyes too hard: I regularly ask my friends if I am being "good enough" to them and frequently invite them to give me "feedback," because I don't want them to have a reason to leave me. When I share something intimate that's troubling me, I always end with the phrase, "I'm sorry to be a burden," in the hope that my friends won't begin to think I am solely a problem they don't need.

At work, my fear of abandonment manifested in profound panic *every single time* I was asked into my boss's office. At a place where I had worked for eleven years, where I had a *contract* and could not be fired without enormous cause, my first thought was always, *This is it, they're letting me go.* As I crossed the threshold into my boss's office, the first thing I usually said was, "What did I do wrong?" I disguised it as a joke, but for me, it wasn't. If I could first admit that I was wrong or bad in some way, I could beat you to the punch line, and get ahead of any rejection or humiliation.

As I've journaled and built my safe house, as I've meditated to calm my moods, as I've become a fucking doctor of disentangling my emotions with scalpel-like precision, I've noticed that this fear of abandonment rages the most in—*what else*—my relationships with men. Since my first boyfriend at the age of eighteen, I have been ricocheting from one guy to the next. If you wonder why I have so many outrageous dating stories it is because that is the subject in which I have earned my PhD (which I like to think stands for Perpetually Harrowing Dating). The reason I am always in a relationship—even if I know from the *first date* that it won't work—is because my goal is not to find love, it's to not be abandoned.

As I've grown older, my friends have unsurprisingly found their partners, and as I write this to you, I am the only single person in my friend circle. I'm usually okay with this; after all, I'm actually usually in a relationship hoping "this will be the one!" But last year, in the span of two months, three of my closest friends got engaged, one marked her two-year anniversary with her boyfriend, and another got pregnant. At first, this didn't bother me. *Good for them!* I cheerily thought. After all, if they were succeeding in love, why wouldn't I? I usually, and probably somewhat narcissistically, take other people's wins to be proof that I, too, can succeed, but this all came crashing down like a muddy hillside in an earthquake when the group of us went on a girls' trip shortly after.

Six of us decided to get away to Ojai. Guy readers, a girls' trip is like your golf or hiking dudes' trip but with a lot more tears and *days* of texting beforehand about who will bring the hair straightener. Since I am the ~~self-described~~ undisputed Ojai expert, I made all of the arrangements. I hired the "energy healer" to do whatever it is that energy healers do (in this case it was to reduce us all to tears by leading us to ruminate on all our past friendship mistakes—not quite what I had in mind). I picked the restaurants and made the reservations, I chose the hikes, I recommended what kind of clothing to bring, carefully considering each detail of our experience. I wanted this trip to be *awesome* and memorable, a celebration of friendship in a town that is sacred to me.

The first night in our rental house, while I was doing God-knows-what (probably sweating some last-minute details of our evening plans) a few of the girls decorated the living room with symbols to celebrate all of our wins over the last year. Such a sweet idea, right?! As I walked into the dining room I saw there were giant metallic balloons in the shape of wedding rings to celebrate the three engagements, there was an IT'S A BOY! banner to celebrate the pregnancy, and there was a birthday cake for another. I smiled, happy, of course, for my friends. But there was nothing for me.

Please know that I hesitate to tell you this story because I know how petty I sound, and you're probably thinking, *Aren't there much more horrible things that can happen than being excluded from balloons? And really, wasn't this THEIR time to shine and how could I be so selfish— wouldn't I have wanted them to do the same for me?* And yes, that is my internal monologue right now. But just imagine walking into a room where everyone but you was being celebrated in a very obvious and in-your-face way. In a best-case scenario, that doesn't feel *great,* and if you're a single woman then you know how painful it might be if the majority of the things being celebrated were wedding and family related. I'm not saying my reaction was fair or mature, but let's be honest, how many of us think our worth is dependent on finding and keeping love? How many of us think that if we don't find a partner for life, we have failed a central tenet of being a woman? My guess is it's probably a hell of a lot.

I walked out of the house and onto the hillside, to the exact spot where a bear had been spotted earlier in the day. I would rather take my chances with the predator than let anyone see me get upset. I started walking, to clear my mind, to cry (as I suspected it was coming), and to then let my face calm down before I walked back in, emphatically not wanting to be seen as bratty and petulant. The moon was shining so brightly that it lit the path for me in the twilight. *Maybe I was overreacting,* I thought. This must have just been an oversight on the part of my friends, there was no way it had been malicious, they were good people who had both celebrated and cared for me an infinite number of times in the past and whom I loved very much. Still, it brought up *all* the times I felt unseen, all the times I had not been considered, all the times I had been isolated and left alone and felt that I would always be alone. And then I flashed back to that early memory. Here I was again, walking down a path in the dark, desperate for someone to *see* me, desperate to not feel so alone. *Same old shit.* I wiped a tear from my cheek and inhaled a ragged breath.

At first, I threw myself a REAL pity party, getting lost in a common thought loop: *You're single because there's something wrong with you; there's something wrong with you for feeling bad about being single.* But as I calmed down, I quickly realized that I was not a child anymore. I was thirty-five years old, and I was not experiencing anything close to what I had endured when I was five. I had not been abandoned. I was a well-resourced adult on vacation and I had *chosen,* when I felt hurt, to leave the house, to have a moment to myself to help me decide my own reaction. I inhaled another, smoother, breath.

Standing there, I took stock of my actual, mid-thirties life, not the five-year-old trauma tantrum I was currently living in. I was mentally more stable than I had ever been. Every week I tasted more peace and freedom to just be my fucking self. I luxuriated in my actual dream job of being a full-time writer. My writing took me from Indianapolis to New York to Paris to Luxembourg to meet readers. And the more I met and corresponded with them, the more I experienced the most surprising sensation of all—*I felt less alone.* I had written my first book with the sole purpose of making *one* other person less isolated. What I had not anticipated was that YOU, in turn, would finally convince me that I belonged. I don't really know how to thank you for that but I'll try: *Merci beaucoup.* You've done your good deed for the day. Please let your boss know that I said you can take the rest of the day off.

And! And! If I really thought about it, had I not felt so solitary for so long I probably would never have become a writer. I probably wouldn't have the need to feel seen, to be heard, to want people who had endured similar experiences to feel supported by me. I wouldn't have the indefatigable desire to connect to others, not only through writing, but through my synagogue, my meditation community, the friendships I maintain like they are precious gems. My loneliness was not inherently bad; it had given me some of the most sacred things in my life. My loneliness, I could see now, was my superpower.

Loneliness is my Harry Potter lightning bolt branded into my forehead. It's my Bruce Wayne becoming Batman. And since the genre of action movies is really not my deal, that's where my examples end. Loneliness is something I would never have chosen myself, but it has served me well. It brought me writing, community, spirituality, meditation; it brought me compassion for other people who felt flawed in some way or ashamed, because I knew *exactly* what that felt like. It was my loneliness that probably led me to re-parent myself and give myself this beautiful life in the first place, because I so desperately wanted to feel whole and tranquil in my own company, and *not* like a miserable mess thinking of ending my life.

Now, when I look at my loneliness as a helpful tool, it allows me to understand the night my babysitter bailed in an entirely new light. I can see it as a painful memory of being left alone *and* I can see it as a testament to how smart and mentally healthy and strong I must have been at five years old. Left alone, I could have walked into the backyard and fallen into the ungated pool; I could have picked up a set of matches and started playing with fire; I could have turned on the stove to "cook," but instead, my profound loneliness led me out of my room, through the front door, and up to my neighbor's house where, even if I didn't find comfort and compassion, I found safety. It was not my fault that Jaz had left me, and it was not my fault that Mrs. Williams was unkind. Their actions said absolutely nothing about me. They were the ones who should have felt shame.

I don't know if you have abandonment issues or often feel lonely but I do know that *many* of us struggle with aspects of ourselves that we think are "bad," and that we feel powerless to change. We think we will never find a romantic partner or unconditional love because our parents' ugly divorce made us doubt that real love exists and we hate that about ourselves. We think we will never overcome our perfectionism because that was the only way we showed our worth and maintained control in a chaotic household that didn't value us as we were. As we grow older, we think we will never *ever* be able to get over the shame of a mistake in our careers or in our relationships and that we deserve to be punished—by *ourselves*—over and over again. We think the only way to deal with the unacceptable is to banish these parts or punish them, insisting on endless self-fixing. Thank God that we are wrong. The way to heal the unacceptable parts of us is to accept them, to hold them close, to love on and appreciate them for all the service they have done on our behalf.

Since realizing that my loneliness has aided me, I have learned about an entire school of therapy called Internal Family Systems that posits that *no* part of us is bad, *no* aspect of our personality needs to be rejected. Instead, *everything* within us—even the stickiest and most exasperating feelings—have a positive intent for us. In an IFS (as it is known) framework of looking at ourselves, we see all the different parts of us that make up our self. *Stick with me here, I know it sounds a little wonky but so did Pilates and now I love that shit!* If you've ever felt vindicated about someone else's failure while also wanting to help them, or melancholy when something good is happening to you, or torn about a decision, then you already know this to be true—at any moment we feel a range of emotions and thoughts, and often, they are seemingly at odds with one another. Most of us lose our minds trying to figure out what the real story is—what we actually feel—because, we think, surely it can only be one thing or the other. But we are not one thing or the other—we are all of these voices and emotions. We can hold them all at once. Our problems arise, however, when these darker parts try to "protect" us, because very often these parts are simply using coping mechanisms from WAY BACK WHEN.

As you know, I hold inside me a scared little girl who is always seeking touch, so in an attempt to shield me from deprivation, she leads me to date *anyone who breathes** and very often men who are hurtful. I have a distractor who, when I have a tough decision to make, tries to divert my attention to endless, meaningless Internet consumption so that I can delay facing the difficulty of a hard choice. I have a doomsayer who is convinced I am inherently condemned and thus shouldn't have ambitious dreams because I'll only end up embarrassing myself when I can't achieve what I set out to do. As I've gotten to know these parts of me, as I've gotten curious about them, about how they feel, about what they are afraid will happen to me if they stop fighting on my behalf, I've finally, for the first time ever, experienced self-compassion.

I've read about self-compassion on the walls of yoga studios, on the sleeves of cups of coffee from the snooty place around the corner, and in self-help books, but until Internal Family Systems, I had no idea what in the hell it meant nor how I could POSSIBLY achieve it. Now, when I sit with the lonely little girl at my core,

---

* Well, not *anyone,* but the same kind of person over and over again. We'll get to that later.

when I get curious about her, when I really *see* her, and hear how bad *she* feels, when I ask her how long she's been alone inside of me feeling abandoned, scrambling for touch, and she tells me she's been unattended for thirty years . . . Oof . . . I can *empathize* with that suffering. I am moved to heal her and since her pain is actually my pain, I'm moved to heal myself. That is the very definition of self-compassion.

And it gets better! As the founder of IFS, Dr. Richard Schwartz, so eloquently points out in his excellent, appropriately titled guide to IFS, *No Bad Parts,* as we feel self-compassion we learn how to feel for and help others. He writes, "If we can appreciate and have compassion for our parts, even for the ones we've considered to be enemies, we can do the same for people who resemble them. On the other hand, if we hate or disdain our parts, we'll do the same with anyone who reminds us of them."* *WOOOW. That makes so much sense!* Did that one *get* you like it got me? If what you are hoping to do is heal and show up as the most loving version of yourself in the world so that you can love and be loved, self-rejection is not going to get you there. *Ever.* I'm so sorry because I know that self-hate comes so naturally to so many of us.

As I've worked with the lonely part of me, as I've felt the abandonment and fear *it* has felt for thirty-five years, it is gradually easing up and becoming less afraid. I've even stopped dating for the moment so that I can give my parts the attention they need, and it has been a revelatory and completely *awesome* experience. So, if you see me at a wedding riding solo, dancing in a fucking *fantastic* little gold number, sipping a spicy marg (my drink of choice), know that I am not sad or embarrassed to be single.† I do not be-

---

* Richard C. Schwartz, *No Bad Parts: Healing Trauma & Restoring Wholeness with the Internal Family Systems Model* (Sounds True, 2021), p. 17.

† A word I shudder to use because you can be single and alone in a relationship, know what I mean? Yet "single" often has a tinge of a diss when referring to someone who is uncoupled. Can we come up with a new word, please and thank you? DM me if you have an idea!

lieve that being without a partner says anything about my past or my future. I'm too busy having the most excellent time with my internal family. We are no longer fighting, we are confidently vibing and most likely going *nuts* to Earth, Wind & Fire's "September" as you and all your parts shimmy over to dance with us. We let our arms fly in the air, we feel our skin get drenched in sweat, we notice our hair clumping to our faces, but we don't give a fuck how it looks because we are free! Free from self-hatred and rejection, free to finally embrace ourselves in all our imperfect, conflicting glory.

My Self-Compassion Party Trick

Self-compassion is one of those things that seems impossible to attain, like the utter perfection of style, intelligence, and beauty that is Zendaya. But I bet I can get you to feel self-compassion even if you think it's out of the question . ... because it's already in you. We just need to coax it out of hiding. To do so, I am borrowing HEAVILY from Dr. Richard Schwartz's No Bad Parts, from Jay Earley's Self-Therapy, from the hundreds of hours of meditation I myself have done, and from my experiences helping others to tap into this mind-state in workshops. I like to do it as a guided visualization, but since you can't hear my voice,* I'd like you to take out a journal, your pen, and get curious with me. Please write down all of your responses to the following questions. If at any point this gets too intense, back off. You can try again later. Remember: We're not trying to bully our way through healing, as tempting as that is. Ready?

1. What part would you like to work with? What just feels *bad* and you think you need to get rid of it, ten minutes ago? Try not to pick a part of you that has suffered intense

---

* Unless you are listening to the audio version of this book, or you visit my website, where you can hear me guide you through this.

trauma and that might overwhelm you. Pick a part that you reject, but that you can handle working with.

2. Where does this part of you live in your body? I want you to conjure it, feel it. Does it tighten your jaw, bring tears to your eyes? Do you feel it in your throat? In your chest? Get specific about where you feel the part and write that down. If you are not really feeling it now, think back to the last time this part of you was triggered. How did it feel in your body?

3. Pause. Let's not rush through this. Really *feel* this part of you.

4. Now can you visualize (on paper or simply in your mind) what this part/feeling looks like? A scared child, a raging tornado, the Wicked Witch of the West? Just a bunch of up and down lines like an EKG reading? It can be anything.

5. Really *see* this part. Try to discern all the details, slowly. See that it's not the whole of you, it's a *part* of you.

6. Ask this part, "Do you have a name?"

7. Now ask how *it* feels, not how *you* feel, not how you feel about *it*. Don't think too hard, just listen to its response.

8. Sense how much your part suffers through fear, exhaustion, loneliness, etc.

9. Once you have truly felt your part's pain, ask your part, "What are you trying to accomplish? How are you trying to help me?"

10. Now ask this part what it is afraid would happen if it stopped protecting you.

11. Now ask, "How long have you felt this way?"

12. Take the answer in. Realize how long it's been.

13. What does that make YOU, the whole self, feel? Are you sad for the part? Do you feel empathy? Do you want to help the part?

14. Identify that feeling you have right now. Do you want to relieve your part's suffering? If so, then, *wow, you just felt self-compassion*! That's my party trick!

15. Thank this part for sharing with you today. Thank it for all the work it has done on your behalf and let it know that it is no longer alone, you are right here with it.

Don't be afraid to come back to your part again and again. Lord knows it has been alone for too long. The more you allow it to exist, the more relaxed it will become, relieving both of you.

A Little Thing That Helps

Have a go-to phrase to soothe whatever part you are working with. When I feel lonely, I repeat to myself the truth: "I am connected to everyone and everything."

LadyGod
The Power of ~~Believing~~ Feeling

SO, NOW YOU KNOW "the Thing"—the frayed ropes of trauma reactions that had bound my heart so tightly it felt like it could never beat freely. I was reacting to the present like I was living in the past: I didn't feel safe, I couldn't regulate my emotions, I woke up with searing anxiety, and I believed in the most tender part of me that ultimately, I would be abandoned.

But there's one more piece to it. I want to share with you a memory that feels to me like the white-hot burning center of "the Thing." I am five years old and in a LIMO. *Do you hear me? A LIMO,* because I am the shit and life is not awesome but LIMOS *ARE* and I'm going on my first trip to Manhattan, which is where my hero, Eloise, from the children's books, lives. I am sitting on every inch of that limo. First on the back bench with my mom, then scooting and dragging myself along the side seating, then lying on the expansive floor. I pick up crystal glasses meant to hold liquor and marvel that there is a TELEVISION IN THE LIMO! WHAT?! The experience is nothing short of extraordinary and to top it all off, I'm wearing the black faux-fur coat my mom has just gifted me to keep me warm in Manhattan. This is easily one of the best days of my life.

"Tara, I need you to come sit next to me," my mom instructs. I get up off the floor, where I have been rolling and luxuriating in

LIMO carpeting, to do as I am told. "I want you to see some-thing." She pulls out white business cards. "You see these cards? These are the names of whores your dad is fucking. He's perverted. He doesn't love me and he doesn't love you." Time feels a little suspended and my body begins to burn. "No! Daddy loves me, I know he does," I protest. My mom says, "That's what you think but when you were inside of me, he wanted to abort you, he wanted you to die." I don't know what "abort" means but I know "die" is awful. "That's not true, Mom!" I start to scream, sweating and feeling hot fury flush my cheeks.

My coat is now unbearably oppressive; I rip it off myself and throw it to the floor. "I'm getting back at him, though," she con-tinues, "for us. I slept with one of his friends, Ernest,* to humiliate your dad. Now he'll have to see Ernest around and feel embar-rassed." "STOP, I DON'T WANT TO KNOW THIS," I howl. "Ernest was kind," she says, "and he asked me how I was feeling the whole time he touched me, your father never does that. I have needs too." I hate this limo, I hate my life, there is nowhere to es-cape to *ever* and there's never a way to help myself and by five years old I am desperate for a way out of my family.

Looking back, I now understand that my mom exposed me to things that no child should ever have to see or know about. I couldn't process the information. I was incapable of telling my dad about any of this because he, after all, was the object of my mom's savagery and potentially he didn't even want me. If I told him what I knew I worried he would feel embarrassed by all the dis-gusting things she was telling me and I wanted to protect his feel-ings. I couldn't tell my teachers because I was mortified by my family altogether and was not going to give them more reason to look down on me. And I couldn't tell Child Protective Services, who visited me at home and my school after receiving tips that

---

* Ernest is very much not this guy's name.

something was wrong, because I never knew if what I was going through was "bad enough" to mention.

Experiences like this led me to detach from reality. For my emotional survival, I had to pretend they were not happening, which eventually caused me to doubt myself in all aspects of my life. What I needed, I always felt, was a third parent, someone to love me and hold me and take care of me or at least not make my life unbearable. I think I've always been looking for a great protector.

In Jewish kindergarten class, I learned about a powerful man in the sky who watched and safeguarded us all. It was the most reassuring and magical concept I had ever heard. *Finally!* There was someone who could come to my rescue. Thank . . . GOD! I wanted to know more about the big man but unfortunately, back at home, my parents, who were strict atheists, told me that God wasn't real—"He's only for weak and stupid people who don't understand science. You're better than that." I learned to keep my curiosity to myself and decided that if my parents wouldn't introduce me to him, maybe I could forge a connection on my own.

After school I would wander out onto the redbrick patio in front of the kitchen in our house and scan the sky, looking for God, determined to get him to see me. To command his attention, I would pick up a metal pipe that for some reason lived in a bed of begonias and strike it as hard as I could against the trunk of a jacaranda tree, screaming, "HELLOOOOOO! I am Tara! Are you here, God? Come here! See me!" When no sign arrived, because it never did, I would continue my bashing the tree, desperate to get him to acknowledge me but also, I now recognize, full of a rage I did not understand and could not articulate. These moments felt crushingly solitary except for one saving grace—if I stood in the right position, my voice would resound in the canyon. The echo made me feel less desolate, like maybe there was something bigger, something more resonant, that was paired with my own little voice.

This yearning for God, or just some bigger energy that unites us all, has never left me. I have always wanted to find a benevolent protector to hold my hand, make me feel safe, and love me unconditionally. I have a recurring fantasy that two giant arms in long, cream-colored gloves reach down from a cloudless blue sky and scoop me up gently in their interlocking hands. I've always thought that life would be better if I believed in God. I mean, how much easier would it all be if there was some force in the universe watching out for you, if everything that happened was a part of a *plan* and not some haphazard shit show, and if God potentially could SAVE US from things! *How cool would that be?!* But as I grew into adulthood, I wasn't convinced. By the age of twenty-five, I believed in God as much as I believed in the "miracle" face creams I bought to "defy" aging. I knew it was nothing more than delusion.

Around this time, one of my best friends, Evan,* called me with an intriguing proposition: "T, have you heard of Birthright? I think we should go!" I had heard of Birthright. It's a program aimed at strengthening Jewish identity and community among young American Jews by bringing them to Israel for free! That's right. *For free*. The organization would *pay* for your ticket to Israel, for your food, for your hotels, and take you on a tour of everything the homeland had to offer. I'd known a lot of people who had gone, but I was still skeptical. "It has to be some kind of scheme, right? Don't you think they're going to try to convert us to Judaism?" I asked Evan. "We *are* Jews," he reminded me. *Oh, right.* So with the promise of a "free vacation," as Evan sold it, and

---

* OG *Lilies* readers: This is the same Evan who challenged me to hike and who has those V-shaped handles etched into his hips. He still has them, in case you were wondering.

the minuscule hope that maybe this was my chance to finally connect with God, I set off for Israel.

The moment Evan and I got on the bus at Ben Gurion Airport
and met our fellow travelers, I felt like I had made a huge mistake.
We were the elder millennials on the trip—everyone else was at
least two years younger, which at that age was basically a lifetime.
Within minutes, they were building a social hierarchy and pairing
off into hookups at the back of the bus—the place reserved for
bullies and popular kids—as they shouted and squealed with joy.
What did they even have to shout about?? THEY HAD JUST
MET!

Ilan, the leader of our tour, a short, sinewy, tanned, and hyper-
focused man in his forties, whom I would later see cinematically
catch a thief in the Jaffa Flea Market and pin him to the concrete
ground, held up a microphone and announced, "Welcome home!
I am passing envelopes for all of you with a little chocolate and
your pita and hummus money, our gift to you for coming home!"
Oh Jesus, I thought, *cue the homeland indoctrination.* They couldn't
even wait until we were out of the airport parking lot to start with
the propaganda?

A tall boy with a goatee and despicable parachute pants whom
"the youths" (as I was now calling them to Evan) had clearly
anointed their leader shouted at Ilan, "Hey, man, can we get drinks
with our pita money?" Ilan, not totally understanding the question, had the bus driver pull over so that the youths could get some
"soda pop." When they returned with Orangina and hidden handles of vodka, I felt myself fill up with unexpected animosity. Our
itinerary included visits to places like the Wailing Wall and the
grave site of Yitzhak Rabin—ya know, places where it would be a
tad disrespectful to be blackout drunk? At a natural hot spring later
that night, they guzzled their concoctions out of water bottles as
steam and booze and general horniness turned their faces bright
red. Look, I had been a disgusting drunk mess ~~hoping~~ scheming to

make out with any available person (regardless of gender, sexual preference, political affiliation, etc.) many times over in my life, but for some reason, I couldn't stand these kids. They were just so loud and obnoxious in a place that was supposed to be holy, a place where I was hoping to find God, and I couldn't stop making judgy comments to Evan. "That's the one who's never left home before and is doing her best impression of what a *Jewish Girls Gone Wild* would look like." I laughed. "And that's the guy who anywhere else is a three but on this bus is an eleven," he joked back.

Still, when I could get over my intense and irrational hatred of the back of the bus, I was able to take in some truly astonishing sights. One morning, before sunrise, our group marched up the steep pathway to Masada, an ancient fortress atop a sheer cliff, reaching the apex just as day began to break. The blue sky opened up with vibrant swaths of deep pinks and purples as the bright, gemlike sun emerged from obscurity, lighting up a view of the azure Dead Sea below. Evan looked at me. I looked at him. *Was this for real?* It was more than just a gorgeous vista. This shit was *ancient*. We had huffed and puffed our way up the mountain and now we looked onto the same spectacular view as so many who had come thousands of years before us.

There were more breathtaking experiences on our tour, the kind that arrest your attention and make you grateful to be alive. One night, we glamped in the Negev Desert, a remote and rocky moonscape where the stars shone so brightly at night that it felt like tiny flashlights were illuminating our campsite. And then there was the incredible shakshouka (baked eggs and tomatoes) that we inhaled at the Jaffa Flea Market, an open-air ancient trading post (and also the place where Ilan pinned that dude to the ground like a CIA agent in a TV show). When you bit into the hot egg, the yolk flooded your senses with the warming flavors of cumin and just the right amount of cayenne to alert you to enjoy it.

Evan was right, this was an awesome free vacation. Still, toward the end of the trip I didn't feel any closer to God. If anything, thanks to how much our traveling companions were getting under my skin, I felt like the most cantankerous, least compassionate version of myself.

Our last stop on the trip was a morning visit to Yad Vashem, the world Holocaust memorial museum, which I gotta tell you, I was not pumped to see. Kind of a brutal way to start your day, dontcha think? As we entered the museum, we walked on a downward slope, which, our guide informed us, was meant to signify that we were about to witness the lowest man could get. Again, *rough*. In one of the first rooms, I was struck by films of Jewish people living their best lives in their villages and cities right before World War II. There were fancy Euro Jews wearing fur coats, there were children singing, there were country Jews tending to their farms, there were Jews dancing in the damn streets, unapologetically bursting with joy and vigor. There were all kinds of Jews to be had! No one was afraid, no one was hiding. I actually hadn't known what Jewish society looked like before the terrifying images of stacked-up bodies I'd seen in textbooks. These weren't unnamed corpses, these were people—families and children (who, as far as I could tell, were not gulping down vodka and Orangina).

As I investigated the photos of people who, frankly, looked a hell of a lot like me and my friends, I worked up the nerve to ask our tour guide a question I had always wondered: "Why didn't the Jews just *leave*? If they could see that laws were being passed to strip them of their rights and that the culture was becoming so anti-Semitic and ominous, why not just go?" Our guide looked at me and in the most matter-of-fact tone possible asked, "Why would they leave?" She continued, "They were at home, leading their lives, they owned businesses, they were getting degrees, they were tending to their farms, they were busy living. Something like the Holocaust had never happened before so how could they even imagine what was to come? Why would they abandon every aspect of their lives to evade a catastrophe that had never occurred before in the history of the world?" Wow. I had never thought of it like that. *Why would they know to leave?* It would be like being submerged in a pot of water slowly being brought to a boil. At first you don't really notice—this is just the temperature of the water, you don't love it, but it's fine, then it gets uncomfortably hot and you start to get a little afraid but have no real reason to be alarmed, until finally it's painful and you know you need to leap out of the pot, but at the moment you recognize that you are in danger, it's too late—someone clamps the lid on and you have no way to escape. You knew the water was maybe too hot and the situation less than ideal, but you couldn't imagine how bad your circumstances could become.

As we went lower into the museum, our group came upon a living room plopped down in the middle of our path. The bookshelves were fully stacked with leather-bound books (Which, BTW, shouldn't all books be leather bound? The *height* of elegance!), the walls lined with family photos, and in the middle of it all was my favorite object on earth—a desk. This one was decadent, with brown wood, the kind of desk where you knew novels, or plays, or utterly romantic love letters had been written. Epic stuff. This living room could have been any living room from any of my friends' parents' houses. It kind of even looked like the fancy version of *my* living room.

At that very moment, I felt a surge run through my body, my skin breaking out into goosebumps, my vision blurring. I finally understood something—on a visceral level—that I never had before: *This could have been me.* The only thing that separated me from the Holocaust was seventy-five years and monumentally good luck.

And it wasn't just me. It was everyone on this trip. Everyone in Israel. It was *everyone on the planet,* because if something this horrific could happen to one group of people, why not any other? As

I stood there, I felt like I had instantly been plugged in to every person who ever lived. Even if I didn't believe in God, in this moment I couldn't deny that we are all utterly connected and all utterly vulnerable. None of us had any control, all of us were merely separated by history. And if we were all fundamentally the same, then we all must be made by the same . . . *something*.

A calm bolt of energy seemed to stream from high above me, through my chest, then through my body and then down deep into the floor, rooting me to the earth in a great current. This was God to me—I instantly felt it and knew it: My connection to other people and the truth that whatever essential flame animated me came from the same source of whatever essential flame animated everyone else. We each might look different, but the flame was the same. This whole time I had been searching for something external—some adult, or some being in the sky—to save me, to love me, but as I stood there in Yad Vashem, closing my eyes to take in this moment, I realized that the God I had been looking for had always been both present within me and shining from everyone else.

God was the unflinching, constant love I felt for my sister, the soul connection I felt to my best friend, it was the laughter, the waving hello in the street to neighbors, the smile someone gave me when I was having a visibly rough day. And this deep connection, this ability to see that I was tethered to everyone else, made it a fuckton more difficult to be annoyed with the youths. I opened my eyes and watched them walking through the exhibit. I imagined them as sacred flames, I imagined myself as a sacred flame. If I hated on them, was I not hating on myself? Who did that serve? Did I want to be that kind of person? It's really hard to despise, or even be annoyed with, someone when you imagine both yourself and them as *sacred flames*.

Maybe it's strange that I found God in the place that commemorates a chapter in human history that often makes people ask,

"What kind of God would allow this to happen?" Or maybe it makes the most sense? And by the way, you could call it God, source, the divine universe (as I most often do), nothingness, randomness, the history of us all, or LadyGod, as my dear friend Sarah says and of which I'm sure Saint Ariana Grande would approve (because if God is anything, for sure she is a woman). LadyGod would not intervene on my behalf, nor give me everything I wanted. No, she was simply present with me always, holding my hand with compassion while also gleaming from the souls of everyone else—lighting us all up in a transcendent glow.

To this day, I still don't believe in God nor do I try. I *know* in God. I *feel* in God. It's that special warmth and softness and soul power that runs through me when I hold an undeniably perfect baby on my chest. It's when I see something otherworldly like Mount Masada that is so beautiful that it just doesn't make sense. It's when I go on a hike and start talking aloud to parse through some problem I have and I hear an answer emerge from within me, a wisdom I didn't know I had. (Or at least I hope that's what's going on with these hikes because otherwise who the fuck have I been talking to on Sundays?)

Many of us are desperate to feel connected to something larger than ourselves but we get hung up on the terms—religion, God, Christ, etc. Fuck that. Every terrible experience you've had in your own house of worship (which I know can be devastating), every logic trap you've become mired in when thinking about God, it all gets in the way of *feeling* in God. Try this with me now: Let go of all of your hang-ups about a divine source (if you have them), pretend they don't exist for just a moment (I promise you can have them back), and put your right hand over your heart.* Do you know that within you there is a force keeping you alive,

---

* BTW, I basically walk through life with a hand over my heart. It feels soothing and when I whisper to myself, "It's okay, sweetheart," OH BOY am I on some next-level self-nurture. And it looks cool. Like I'm on another spiritual plane.

pumping blood through your body with NO conscious instruction from you? How can that be? Can you sense that even if *nothing*
made you, that nothing was still . . . *something* because you are
whole and real? Can you recognize that of all the possible permu-
tations of "human," you—utterly unique you—were born? Can
you recognize the majesty of the science within you that we all
share? If you do, you don't need to believe in God, you simply *feel*
in God, you know in something beyond our understanding, you
acknowledge that something breathed stardust into you and turned
on your shine even if it doesn't make any sense. And maybe that's
the way the universe wants it—for our lives to be a mystery that
we keep unfolding, our curiosity creating the paths of our lives.

Do I feel that spiritual all the time? Very much no. There are
days and months when I think I'm back to square one, whacking
that metal pipe against the jacaranda tree, desperate for something
to see me and hold me, but I feel absolutely nothing in return. But
I have felt the presence of a love beyond myself enough times that
I have given LadyGod the benefit of the doubt and the keys to my
internal citadel. (She built the place after all, at the very least she
deserves a spare set of keys.) She's in there, sitting at her desk trying to tend to all of humanity while sipping an old-fashioned,
when I bust in to complain to her about yet another dude situation
gone awry and how hurt I feel. "Baby girl," she tells me, "I happen
to know Liam, ya know, cuz I made Liam—and every other Liam
for all of time but that's an entirely different subject. Your Liam, *oh
boy* . . . he is going through *a lot*. That doesn't excuse how he treated
you, but it also means this ain't on you. Ya can't take it personally."

Or when I'm laid off and am terrified of the instability, fearful
that I'll never have a job again, she takes me on a stroll in my neighborhood and reminds me that even though losing a job hurts, "it
doesn't define you, darling. It's not a statement about who you are.
You're safe right now, honey, and it's impossible you won't find
some kind of job cuz you love to work." Or when I'm worried

about how the entire world seems to be unraveling, how conditions couldn't be any worse, and how this really might be the end times, she'll bring me a cup of freshly grated ginger tea (thanks, LadyGod, for going out of your way!), hold my hand, and softly ask, "Well, this kind of has nothing on the whole Noah's Ark thing if you'll remember, but what if these *are* the end times? How will you live them? By lying down, waving a white flag, and giving in to endless worry? *Or*. Are you going to enjoy the beauty that is present to you now, your friendships, everything that is so *right* in this moment? I'm not saying you don't need to work on helping the world; in fact, I expect you to! I'm just saying that it would be a real shame if you were so distracted by your fears that you let this perfect California day with its piercing blue sky and sun wrapping your skin in warmth pass you by. Now, can we get two glasses of rosé stat? It's five P.M. *somewhere*." LadyGod is just chill like that.

I have come to know LadyGod, the divine universe, and the miracle of straight-up science. And I know that just as she put a little stardust in me, so, too, did she put stardust in you. I imagine that LadyGod has a burlap sack (she's super frugal) full of gleaming stardust and a silver measuring cup that she scoops into the bag and then pours into each of us, into our own vessels, our own expressions of life. The dust builds layer by layer making us who we are; it can shift, it can change, it can grow into whatever magnificent sandcastle we want it to become, nothing is predetermined. LadyGod very purposely created us all from the same matter and the fact that she did it with *stardust* tells you everything you need to know—she is super baller and definitely as into jewelry and glitter as I am. And, perhaps most important, she is always with us and in us because she, too, is made of stardust.

We all have our "things" that we think we won't ever get over, things that make us feel like we are nothing but shame, things we pretend we don't know because knowing seems too painful to bear. Now I have someone to carry some of the burden of those things with me, I have LadyGod to see and acknowledge me, to take a little portion of my hurt and put it on her very capable, super-ripped shoulders. Sometimes just knowing there is a witness to my life is all I need to feel a measure of calm in an otherwise tortured situation.

LadyGod did not light us up so we could endlessly suffer, or get so lost and hateful that we become unwilling to hear anyone else out, so stuck in how "right" we are and how "evil" everyone else is that we forget our essential connection to one another. How different would the world be if we respected our individuality but honored and embraced our interconnectedness and sameness? What kind of place would it be if we were all just stars, flickering together, all of us recognizing how tied together our lives and fates are and that together we are so much more beautiful than alone? I think we would be living in a different world and it might be called "heaven."

I think LadyGod made me for a simple reason—so I could meet you. So I could have the chance to encounter all the other little sparks and flames and stars that get to dance on earth at the same time and bask in one another's light. What we choose to do with the spark we have been gifted is entirely our own decision. I know you are very busy and stressed-out, but at a minimum, don't you think it's pretty cool that LadyGod woke you up again this morning? How do you thank LadyGod for doing that? She didn't have to, but LadyGod is a real mensch.

I believe each of us is utterly important, one of a kind, bursting with glitter, and that each of our lives matters, a lot. At the same time, we're kinda nothing, just another soul in a body, no more special than anyone else. BUT WE ARE SOULS AND BODIES AND THAT IS FUCKING FANTASTIC! That push and pull of the personal and the universal, if we can recognize it, if we can see that both you and I are made up of the same stuff and the only difference is our exteriors, if we can see that, it becomes a lot harder to hurt other people because you realize that you are only hurting yourself. If you follow that logic, you instantly see that YOUR healing is so important because it is also my healing, and your sister's healing, and your child's healing, the healing of everyone who has come before us and the healing of someone you will never meet.

Do me a favor. Put a hand on your heart. Think of the person you love the most in the world, really see their face and look into their eyes. If you can't heal for your sake, can you heal for theirs?

What I am about to say to you I mean with every ounce of my soul: At your core, you are totally pure and totally good. Stop thinking about yourself as some individual person with faults who's made so many mistakes, and recognize that your most essential stardust self has no faults, no problems, and is *enough*. Stardust is enough and that enough is fucking fantastic. Now you have the chance to grow, and the opportunity to decide how you want to glow. Are you ready?

Fuck yes, you're ready, you've gotten this far already. If after all that work and healing, you decided to dim yourself, to recede back into darkness, that would hurt all of us, that would get all of us lost, and that's not how you roll, right? You roll brightly, with clarity, with shine that the rest of us can see. You've nurtured your glow, now let's help it grow.

A List of Weird-Ass Places I've Hung Out with LadyGod

You don't need to be in a house of worship to feel LadyGod. You don't even need to be religious to know LadyGod. You can show up in sweats, no bra, and a face mask cuz LadyGod don't give a fuck. Here are a few of the unexpected places I've found her, by simply paying attention to the present details of my life.

1. **Disneyland.** If you don't like Disneyland, I'm not sure how we'll continue this relationship because Disneyland is THE BEST. Every architectural detail—the rides, the cos-

tumes, the manhole covers with custom designs for whatever land you're in—it's ALL thought through, perfected,
and immaculately maintained. How many other places can
you say that of?! Walking among the crowds, looking at
the other people pass me by, I was struck by a thought:
*How incredible is it that we all have these different faces? We all are
made up of almost the same genetics, but our faces are endlessly different. We are all so beautiful, in our own way.* And then BOOM!
I felt LadyGod. She winked at me and said, "Yeah, it's my
best party trick."

2. **The Mushroom Stand at the farmers market.** I know
nothing of mushrooms. Don't know if I like them, don't
know where they come from, and I *definitely* don't know
how to cook them, but one day at the farmers market, I was
moved to ask a few questions. The Mushroom Man (which
I'm sure is his official title) handed me a pint of blue oyster
mushrooms to investigate. I looked at the whimsical, delicate caps that indeed looked like little oysters, examining
how all the mushrooms clustered together like a bouquet,
and THEN! UNDER THE MUSHROOMS! There were
hundreds of white, delicate gills, as if the mushroom were
alive and breathing like a fish. *OMLG, HOW IS THIS A
THING?* My body felt warm and light and tingly and high
AF. LadyGod held my hand and said, "Calm down, nobody likes a person who proclaims they are 'high on life,'
it's so annoying. But yeah, I felt pretty inspired when I
made all these mushrooms, so I get it, girl. I get it."

3. **Budget Car Rental, Albuquerque, New Mexico.** I was
picking up my car rental for a solo expedition when I realized, *DAMN, I forgot my USB cord at home. Now how will I
blast Paul Simon with my windows down as I pretend I am Georgia*

O'Keeffe surveying the land for places to paint? The car rental guy asked me if everything was okay with the Jeep I was splurging on. "Oh, it's great, I just realized I forgot my USB cord, which is a total bummer!" "That *is* a bummer!" he replied. "I think I saw one in the lost and found you could use, hold on a minute." He walked into a little booth and emerged out of it with the cord, handing it over to me. *With a smile.* Now, in Los Angeles, people can be just plain rude sometimes (tho they have nothing on New York), so this simple act of kindness brought me to the verge of tears. "Wow, thank you, you made my day," I said as my eyes turned glossy. "Hold it together," LadyGod whispered to me. "There are good, considerate people who will go out of their way to help a stranger, but let's not freak them out with waterworks over a USB cord, okay?" As I pulled out of the car rental agency, listening to Paul Simon at a respectable volume before I let loose on the highway, LadyGod sat in the passenger seat beside me.

4. **Listening to Beyoncé's "Love on Top" on the treadmill.** I was sweating and moving and maybe even grooving to Bey when I sang out the chorus with her,

> *You're the one that gives your all*
> *You're the one I can always call*
> *When I need to make everything stop*
> *Finally you put my love on top*

OH WOW, that's the way I feel about LadyGod—that if it's just her and me, it's enough, I thought. *Did Bey mean to make this a spiritual anthem?* "Anything Bey does is spiritual, she's my high priestess," LadyGod replied. When we got to the lyric, "And, boy, your lips taste like a night of champagne,"

I had to ask, "How does that make any sense in this con-text?" LadyGod took one second to reply, "Dude, we still need to sell some records." Touché, LadyGod, touché.

5. **On every single hike I've ever taken.** Hiking, even local hikes that are under twenty minutes, LIGHT ME UP! The warmth of the sun on my skin, the miracle feeling of sweat breaking out all over (how do we do that?!), the sky, the trees, *the moss!* Have you ever really looked at moss? First off: WHAT IS IT? Second: How and why did LadyGod make texturized tie-dye to clothe trees and rocks and streams? And when you touch it—fuck! Again, WHAT IS MOSS? Everything about being on a hike elevates me to LadyGod's level and I have been known to get off the path and literally hug a tree because, well, trees are amazing. As I stand to the side of the trail, my arms wrapped around a sprawling oak, my eyes closed as my face presses against the bark of the trunk, LadyGod calls out, "Get a room, will you?"

6. **When I'm with my sister, laughing so hard we cry.** It's never even that funny, nor can I *ever* remember why we are convulsing with laughter, but in those moments of hyster-ics, when I am with the person I care more about than any-one in the world, lost in the pure joy of her company, I feel LadyGod right next to us saying, "This is how it should be, this is what it's all for."

Where have you felt LadyGod, my friend? Where have you known something that is beyond yourself and just gives you a little spark of *YES, this is right*? If we can get a little better at recognizing the miraculous in the mundane, we open our perspective, and help ourselves to heal, little by little. It's not all pain, misfortune, and problems. Our days are STUFFED with beauty if we are willing to see it.

A Little Thing That Helps

Pretend this is voicemail you don't dread opening: Hi, I just wanted to say that I think you're doing a great job and that I'd like to hold you in my arms right about now. Which probably means I want *you* to hold me in yours.

II.

GROW

Oh, the Places You'll Grow!
Abandon Learned Helplessness

I HOPE THAT BY NOW I've shown you that if you want to inhabit your most authentic self, then there is no such thing as "moving on" from your emotional injuries. Time does not heal all wounds, it just gives them wrinkles. If you're responding to your present life like you're still in the past, you have no brain space to do much of anything except react. And that's exactly what I didn't want my life to be—a reaction. I wanted my life to be a joyous, deliberate declaration. But how do you do that? How do you grow into that kind of person?

I realize that the word "grow" might seem like a contradiction to the idea I've been obnoxiously belaboring—that you are *already* made of stardust, that you do not need to change, that you were born whole and glowing. But what I'm actually proposing is that you don't need to grow up or *out*—you don't need to change into someone else—you need to grow *in* to yourself. You must inwardly wipe away all the muck and debris of your past emotional injuries, of our culture's pressures, of everything that is *not* you, so that you can find what *is* you, and actively bring that clarified and brilliant self to every facet of your life.

Growing up is like going outside on a brisk night in the middle of a desert, let's say Joshua Tree, for an evening in the hot tub. You were wise enough to take this trip and time for yourself (go, you!).

You walk out of your Airbnb—with no homes around you, no light pollution, no noise—and feel a rush of chilly air wake up your senses. Looking up, you see the limitless sky, littered with stars so radiantly bright they appear to be turning, burning diamonds. *Mmmm, how dreamy does this sound?* You get in the Jacuzzi, naked, cuz why not, who else is here? Just LadyGod and she has seen it *all* before. After testing the water with your toes, you submerge yourself in the bubbling bliss and it feels so damn good. But! (Isn't there always a "but"?) The steam from the water immediately fogs up your glasses and you can no longer see. You *know* there's something beautiful out there, you've done enough work to get here and you *just* saw it, but now that lustrous light is obscured. That's exactly what it's like for us, or—I'll stop generalizing—that's what it was and sometimes is like for me. I had healed enough to glimpse the life I wanted and to know it was already somewhere within me, but I needed to clear everything away that was *not* me so I could reliably see my own shine and the shine of the world around me.

The first step in wiping away a lifetime of fog to return to the person we were before all the bullshit, before we were mistreated and learned to mistreat ourselves, is to reclaim our agency and power. Because you and I, just like the stars burning for billions of years above us, have *infinite power* to get rid of the distractions that bog us down in all areas of our lives. And we can find this power in small, consistent practices that lead to monumental shifts in our lives. There is no one on planet Earth who can stop you from being yourself except yourself.

My need to reclaim my strength was one of the main reasons I moved to Flagstaff in 2020. Aside from needing to escape a looming out-of-body-panic-attack-doom-spiral, I moved because I felt powerless in the face of the upcoming elections, and I wanted to do something about it. Those were some of the most important political races of my life, and possibly yours. The previous four years had been traumatic—and I'm comfortable using that word in this context because each morning American citizens didn't know what fresh hell awaited them. Threats of war? Hundreds of thousands dead from a virus for which there was no cure? A near civil war breaking out among the people themselves? A climate emergency with more and more devastating effects but less political will to confront it? It seemed like we were living in a nightmare's nightmare.

I felt FULL-CAPS ANXIOUS about how the race would shake out. But thankfully, I had the newfound wisdom to sit my ass down with my emotion wheel and dig until I could discern what was underneath my anxiety. And ultimately, I saw that it was anger mixed with an equal measure of helplessness. I felt rage over how the past four years had gone, but that rage had nowhere to go because I didn't think I was capable of changing any of it. This feeling of impotence was debilitating. I don't know if you know me, but I can be—*hmm, what's the right way to phrase this?*—a fucking weirdo about needing to be in control. The person who not only chooses the restaurant but then scours Internet reviews to find which dishes are deemed best, then proceeds to ~~aid~~ manipulate the entire table into ordering said dishes, and then shames anyone who doesn't want to share, all in an effort to curate the "best" possible experience for everyone, according to me. Also the kind of person who tracks her *soul progress* in a color-coded Google Document. Feeling helpless was anathema to my soul.

So, not knowing what else to do with my feelings of powerlessness, I turned to Google (like we do) and as you know, it brought me directly to Flagstaff. Part of my job was to become a "ballot healer." I immediately fell in love with the title, because what the fuck is that? Was it some kind of voting shaman? It seemed inscrutable, like when someone tells you they work in private equity, or that they are the chief engagement officer of their company, or how Lil Nas X is Taco Bell's chief impact officer. I'm not mad about it, in fact I assume that whatever Lil Nas X does is next level, I just have no idea what it means.

On my first day on the job, a volunteer with seen-it-all eyes that reflected gritty determination (and possibly exhaustion) told me that my job was to "cure rejected ballots." I raised my Zoom hand and asked, "I hate to be annoying, and maybe you've already gone over this, but, what does 'cure ballots' mean?" She looked at me like I was wasting her time (which I'm sure I was) and explained, "Look, a lot of legitimate mail-in ballots are being rejected because they're missing a signature, or someone lost the official envelope and put it in their own from home. Or—and this is probably the worst—the voter used the right envelope and signed it, but the signature doesn't match whatever form of ID they registered with."

WAIT! WHAT?! I didn't realize a ballot could be rejected for some clerical error and OMLG, at that point, I didn't have a "real" signature that was consistent in *any* way. I had what I would call a "marking," a lazy scribble that contained a line and one to two triangles but which more closely resembled a hieroglyphic from an alien civilization than a signature. I had never bothered to create a permanent one because (full disclosure) I kinda forgot cursive (if I ever knew it) and because in all my years, it had never mattered *once*. Even at the bank, you know the place that handles the most important thing in our society—cash money—no one had ever questioned my squiggle when I endorsed a check. I wondered how many of my ballots and how many ballots of my friends had been rejected because we had been playing fast and loose with the definition of "signature."

"Our job is to inform each citizen with a rejected ballot that their vote won't count as is, and then give them the available resources to fix it. That's how we 'cure' them," the coordinator explained. *Okay, seems simple enough,* I thought. My first assumption was that this job would be pretty easy, because it was the voters themselves who actually corrected their ballots, but *boy oh boy* was I wrong. I received a shoddy list of names, some with no information about how I might find the voter—no address, no email, no phone number. When the names *did* come with any information, it usually proved to be woefully incorrect. This was infuriating. But it left me to do what I do best when I feel backed into a corner: research the shit out of something and take notes in a Google Doc. I scoured the Internet using LinkedIn, Facebook, Twitter, every site I could find associated with the voter, keeping meticulous notes of my discoveries. For one woman, I only had her first and last name to go by. So, I started on LinkedIn and finally found her at a physical therapy clinic. She had no idea her vote had been rejected. I told her my intention was not to Internet stalk her but that I was a lowly unpaid volunteer just trying to help. She thanked me for my creepiness and fixed her ballot that day. Victory!

I was pumped up. Years of stalking ex-boyfriends online had given me an emotionally debilitating but *useful* set of skills. I was like one of those noir detectives, a little cynical about the whole "system," preternaturally talented, but tragically unable to get herself out of the game. The only thing that separated me from the plot of a Raymond Chandler novel were venetian blinds. And a gun. And drinking too much whiskey. And basically, every other trope of a hard-boiled PI in a noir detective caper.

One of my most perplexing leads was Bernard, a seventy-nine-year-old man whose ballot had been rejected for having an "incorrect" signature. All I had was his name and age. Bernard was a ghost on the Internet; he had no social media that I could find, but still, I sensed his spirit on the Web and kept digging. I saw that a local art gallery where I had *just* bought very dope green opal earrings—because *never* sleep on an opportunity to buy jewels from towns you visit—employed an artist named Bernard whose picture looked like he was an older gentleman. But, maddeningly, his last name was different. Still, I had a hunch, so I called the gallery and found out that THIS WAS *THE* BERNARD—he had a pseudonym for his professional work! I left word for ol' Bernie Boy asking him to call me so that I could walk him through the possible remedies for his ballot. When a few days went by and I didn't hear from him, I began to lose faith. Then, one night in a Target parking lot (Because for some reason I cannot help stopping at Target *everywhere* I go. Maybe it is because Target is the best store?) my cell rang. "Is this Tara Schuster?" a gravelly voice asked. "Who wants to know?" I quipped back. "I'm Bernard and you're my hero for saving my ballot! Will you marry me? I'm yours!" I laughed and told him I was not the marrying type. "At the very least, can I make you a stained-glass wind chime?" he asked. It was a sweet offer, but I had to decline when he started telling me he was "a local celebrity with a *notorious* reputation," and "quite the ladies' man." I wasn't here for a romance with a notorious local celebrity twice my age. I was here for Internet stalking and magical ballot healing, damn it.

In my pursuit of fixing ballots, most of the people I met were incredibly grateful that someone had noticed their votes had been rejected, and when their ballots were finally accepted, the voter and I would often celebrate together over phone or text, yelling, "Wahoo!! We did it!" and "YAAAY YOUR VOICE COUNTS!" Each vote that went from rejected to accepted felt like a personal victory. Many, many times I made the motion of clenching my fist and yanking my elbow down to my hips—the international symbol of "YESSSSSS!"

In an election cycle that was *the most chaotic thing I've ever fucking seen,* in a pandemic that made so much in life feel out of control, I felt like, at the very least, I was *doing* something instead of endlessly wringing my hands. The more I did to actually help, the more I asserted my efficacy, the less scared I became. As Election Day neared, I would get text messages from friends who were freaking out under a deluge of anxiety of *WHAT IS GOING TO*

HAPPEN?! But honestly, and not to be annoying, I didn't feel that way at all. The fact that I was doing something neutralized my feelings of powerlessness that had been masquerading as anxiety. I was calm, mostly because I was too busy to worry about what would happen—I had ballots to heal!

I had cured at least eighteen of them (that's eighteen "YESSSSSS!" motions), but there was one voter I just could not pin down— Mariella. Her melodic name became like a Beyoncé lyric I couldn't get out of my head.* From her records, I knew she was eighteen and that this was her first election. I also knew that her ballot was rejected for a missing signature. It was grade A bullshit. I became fixated on finding her because I didn't want her first vote to be denied due to a clerical error I probably would have made myself. After all, I regularly send mail having forgotten to write the person's address on the envelope. If Mariella was losing her voting virginity, I wanted to make sure it was a special, non-painful, and meaningful experience. I was going to make it count.

After much sleuthing, I arrived at her house at seven P.M. on a Wednesday, when I thought she might be done with work. It didn't occur to me then that it might freak someone out to encounter a stranger (wearing a face mask) showing up at their home in the VERY dark night (remember: International Dark Sky Community). I see now that I'm lucky I was never mistaken for an intruder. I knocked on the front door until a small woman with silky, thick black hair answered. "Hi, are you Mariella?" I asked. "Yeah, how can I help you?" *YES, YES, YES, YES, ALL OF THE YES MOTIONS!* I stood far back, *smizing* as hard as I could in my mask ("smizing" is smiling with the eyes—I'm pretty sure this term was invented by Tyra Banks on the seminal program *America's Next Top Model*) to show that I was a friendly, safe person.

---

* P.S. I think I'll be hearing "You won't break my soul," playing on repeat in my brain forevermore. I'm not mad about it.

Looking behind her, I could see moving boxes everywhere. "Where are you moving from?" I asked. "From living at home, this is my first apartment," she proudly explained. As I eyed her studio, I saw that although every single box was still closed, she had managed to hang one giant, framed black-and-white Led Zeppelin poster smack-dab in the middle of the living room. I remembered what it was like for me after graduating college and moving into my first place. Before I unpacked anything practical, I put a KEEP CALM AND CARRY ON red poster in a frame on my living room/ kitchen wall both because I was out of control and needed someone, ANYONE to tell me to calm down (even if it was Britain's World War II propaganda department) and also because it felt so . . . *adult* to hang something *framed* (not just stuck on there with double-sided tape). I had arrived!

I explained my job as a lowly, unpaid, slightly obsessed volunteer to Mariella, how her vote had been rejected, but—*have no fear!*—there was still plenty of time to supply her signature to the county registrar's office. I gave her the address and pointed out that it was under a ten-minute drive. Then I asked, "When do you think you'll be able to fix your ballot and do you need a free ride to get there?" She looked off to the side and mumbled, "I probably won't do it." I was so taken aback that I could barely make sense of her words. Remember, in 2020, this election was all *anyone* was talking about AND she had already taken the time to vote! She had enough interest to send in a ballot, but not enough to make sure it counted? Perplexing and upsetting, no?

"Can I help you in *any* way?" I begged. "I can also give you the phone number for the county registrar and, I don't know, you might be able to fix the problem over the phone!" She looked at me with her big brown eyes and said one of the most depressing things I have ever heard: "I appreciate what you're trying to do here, but either way, my vote doesn't count. I'm not fixing my ballot because it doesn't matter. Things always stay the same. I don't have any power." Mariella was only eighteen, but she was already so convinced that her voice couldn't make a difference that she had given up. "I have to go," she said, trying to end our conversation. We traded cell numbers, but I assumed I would never hear from her again. Here she was at the starting line of life, full of potential, with a *very cool,* FRAMED Led Zeppelin poster, surrendering her voice before she had even used it.

Correct me if I'm wrong, but I think many of us feel we have no *real* power. "Sure, sure, sure, 'Every vote counts' is a cute motto, but we all know it isn't *really* true, right?" So, we give up our influence in small ways. We don't vote in that local election because in addition to having NO idea what the issues are, we don't know the difference between the state assembly and the state senate (and I would really appreciate it if someone would explain it to me). When we hear a crude remark at someone else's expense, we let it slide because we tell ourselves it's not our business and who are we to speak on behalf of someone else anyway? We slack on recycling at home because after a hectic day at the office, then with the kids, who has the wherewithal *not* to push the take-out container down with the other trash instead of rinsing it and putting it in the already full blue recycling bin? These tiny individual actions, we believe, simply don't matter in the face of overwhelming world calamities—the political system, the climate crisis, the economy, the systematic oppression of so many people, *THERE ARE JUST SO MANY PROBLEMS AND WHAT CAN ONE PERSON REALLY EVEN DO?!*

Sadly, it's a self-fulfilling prophecy: The more we believe we are weak, the weaker we become. Psychologists call this kind of thinking "learned helplessness." It occurs when a person "continuously faces a negative, uncontrollable situation and stops trying to change their circumstances, even when they have the ability to do so."* When we throw our hands up in the air, convinced we can't make a difference, without really even trying, we cement our fates.

Let's look at a personal example of learned helplessness: Growing up, I struggled with math and just because it didn't come naturally to me, I labeled myself as bad and irredeemable, and felt helpless to change my situation. Eventually, I gave up on math altogether. I intentionally went to a college where it wasn't even a requirement! To this day, I still do not know arithmetic or multiplication and when the bill arrives at a restaurant, my mind goes blank and my friends know they will just have to tell me how much to tip. I'm so convinced of what I can't do, that I no longer try.†

We so often let our experiences in the past tell us what we can and can't do in the future. This is obviously nonsense. We *all* have the infinite potential we were born with—the potential to learn and experiment and approach the world without the shackles of the lies we've been told about who we are and what we can do. I know I said earlier that I don't care about late-stage capitalism, but, surprise! I guess I actually do now that I decided to look up the definition instead of condescendingly rolling my eyes and tuning out. While the term means many things, one of the definitions I find most compelling is that in this stage of history, there is a plethora of people and corporations who make money off our perceived defenselessness. If you think you can't change the world, you stop trying, and ultimately, you become a doormat to what companies, politicians, and social systems want. It's even like this with your family and friends. If you have no boundaries with your mom or dad, if you *let* them walk all over you, why would you expect that they'd ever treat you differently? They have no reason to, because they suffer no consequences. If you're with someone

* Psychology Today (psychologytoday.com/us/basics/learned-helplessness).

† Note to self: Stop being lazy and look at a multiplication table ONE time and I bet some math will come back to you!

you desperately want to leave but you focus on all the reasons you "can't" leave them instead of all the reasons you can, you create a self-fulfilling prophecy. But when you decide to claim your power and move in the direction YOU want? You fling open the door to all of life's possibilities. There is only one person who can turn the handle and walk through the threshold, my dearest. You. Only you.

Mariella's story does not have a happy ending. She waited until the evening of the election, felt a sudden pang of regret, texted me to ask what polling location she could go to, but missed the cutoff time to vote by *seven minutes*. Her defeated statement that nothing was going to change turned out to be dead wrong. Arizona was one of the deciding states in the election, every single vote was incredibly important, but she didn't get to be a part of the change.

The reason I am telling you this story is because *you* can be the happy ending. You can vote, you can look up how your local government works. You can smile and look people in the eye when you walk about your neighborhood. That may seem insignificant, but if you're sick of the rancor and partisanship in this country and feel like there is nothing you can do to help with the big picture— here's an idea: Start with yourself. Act with civility and respect toward *everyone* you encounter—the neighbor you've never met, the super of your building, even the telemarketer.*

No one person is responsible for fixing all of our problems. You are not Atlas with the entire world resting on your very toned shoulders nor are you Luisa from *Encanto* needing to be strong for everyone. In Judaism, one of the core principles that I am pretty obsessed with is called "tikkun olam." It teaches that human beings are here to *repair the world*. We arrive on an Earth that is fucked-up and always changing. And it's our job, part of our meaning, to patch up the cracks we inevitably find, to create bonds with one

* Yes, telemarketers are people too. But how did they get my number?

another, to heal what we can, and enjoy the everyday miracles that are available to us, like the opportunity to get into a Jacuzzi on a cold desert night, or track down an artist named Bernard and help his vote count. We are not obligated to do *everything, right now*—that would be overwhelming and impossible. But we *are* charged to do *something* and if that something makes you feel proud and you witness your own effectiveness, your doubt will quickly transform into confidence because—as hokey as it is to say—you know that you are a part of the solution.

In this section, I'm going to share with you the small, free rituals I rely on to help me get back to myself and reclaim my power time and time again. Because it is through practice and repetition that we strengthen our sense of self.

We are going to look at how we can deal with some of the main stressors in our lives so that they don't overrun us: finding motivation for change in the first place, our relationship with money, beating imposter syndrome, our hateful feelings toward our bodies, how to navigate our workplaces, honing our communication skills so that we express our true natures and can hear the truth of others, and, finally, how to cope with the seemingly uncope-able.

Rip off your glasses with me and wipe away the fog. We are going to clear the distractions that impede us from truly seeing ourselves and living our best lives. We are going to give ourselves tools to navigate back to who we are, again and again. And as the shine that is our birthright becomes clearer and brighter, we can help those in our communities to do the same. We all have the ability to become the beacons of light that lead one another back home when we are lost in the desert on a cold night.

So step into my Airbnb. Come get close to me, where it's warm. We have work to do. And let's start with the one person we *know* we can change—ourselves.

A Little Thing That Helps

Instead of doomscrolling, find ONE thing you can do to help our world this week. Make a phone call, send a letter, reach out to a friend who's having a hard time . . . just like muscles, your sense of power grows with repetition.

Bribery
The Best Way to Build a Habit

RIGHT ABOUT NOW, YOU MIGHT be thinking, *Okay, cool, rah rah, power, et cetera, here for it, but how do we actually DO this? How do we grow IN? And how do we stay motivated to keep it up?* That is in fact the first question I am typically asked in the workshops I teach on bringing self-care into our lives, and I always have the same response: I wouldn't know because I'm not motivated. I'm scheduled and prepared. I plan and set myself up for my success before I've begun. I don't start out inspired to do jack; rather, I let the *doing*—the pleasure, the pride I feel in accomplishing a ritual—help me to continue. If you wait to get inspired to achieve everything you want, you might be waiting a very long time. Just *start,* there's magic in motion. Let the momentum of what you're creating propel you forward.

So, do you have a ritual in mind that you think might make your life more enjoyable or fulfilling? Wanna work on turning it into a habit? Not *someday. This* day, and the next and the next, again and again, until it becomes a part of your daily routine. There are SO many books about building good habits, but what I want to talk about here is how I create rituals that are comforting and beautiful and that help me feel more contented and in touch with myself, no matter what's happening in the world. These are completely self-centered, and because of that I am typically centered. And as my happiness and sense of safety increase, so, too, does my ability to grow in all facets of my life, because I have the headspace and perspective to be imaginative, nonreactive (at least 70 percent of the time), and open to possibility.

After years of establishing maintainable rituals, may I present to you:

The Artist Formerly Known As T$'s Eight-Step Plan to Stop Thinking About the Good Rituals You Want in Your Life and ACTUALLY DO THEM and Keep Doing Them, So That You No Longer Feel Guilty That You Aren't Doing Them

Catchy title, right? I might trademark it.

1. **Pick *one* thing.**

   I always take ONE THING AT A TIME! Do not try to start journaling, meditating, and making your bed all at once! That usually, if not always, leads to failure and even shame. Pick one thing and make it as simple as you possibly can so you feel PROUD when you accomplish it.

2. **Know your *why*.**

   Why is this important to you? Keep asking yourself that question until you get to a powerful truth. I usually ask *why* at least four times when trying to get to the heart of something. For example: The reason I started journaling was because other people told me it would be beneficial for me. Why? Because they were worried about me. Why? Because I was out of control. Why? Because I hated myself, was contemplating ending my life, and was desperate for a better existence. Now, it's hard to hit snooze when I know the reason I am getting up early to journal is to save my life. *Oh man, things just got serious!*

3. **Schedule that shit.**

   I have never *once* been able to stick to a ritual if I don't make actual time in my actual calendar to do it. Putting it on my schedule forces me to think it through. If I am supposed to meditate at six-thirty A.M. tomorrow, then I must go to bed NOW instead of staying up to binge-watch *Bridgerton*—which, WOW, how does Shonda Rhimes do it?

4. **Make it nice.** *

   I also make my rituals as beautiful and pleasurable as possible *to me* so that they feel like an extravagance. When I work out, it's in the sexiest spandex I can find because it makes me feel fierce and stealthy and like I am walking off the screen of a James Bond movie and right into a set of squats. That might not be your speed, but it most certainly is mine. Have the tools you need for your ritual before you begin, and make sure they SING to you. Also, make sure they are somewhere you can see so that they taunt you into action. *You win, hot pink journal with bronze pen sitting on my coffee table, staring up at me. You win.*

5. **Pick a measure of success.**

   I usually have a numerical measure of success so I always know when I've "achieved" something. When I write, I set a timer for one hour, when I run I have a certain number of miles in mind, when I journal, it's always three pages. I know you think you can't measure something like "build contentment in life," but you for sure can! I know this for a fact because in an effort to have more days in which I feel content, I printed a calendar and each night, I measure how content I was on a scale of one to ten. I then look for

---

* Did you catch the *Real Housewives of New York* reference? All hail, Dorinda!

clues to why I might have felt more content or less content. If I see that I felt "seven-out-of-ten content" today, what did I do differently to lead to success? If I'm only "two-out-of-ten content," what went wrong? For each day I'm at or above a five (my measurement of content), I put a green star on the day and for every day I'm below five, I put an orange star. I KNOW THIS SOUNDS TERRIBLE AND KIND OF PROVES HOW CONTROLLING I AM but it's *really* helpful, because then nothing is abstract. You know the ritual is working if you are actually measuring what the fuck is going on.

6. **Shamelessly reward yourself.**
When I'm trying to establish a new habit I always, always reward myself for *any* effort. I may not have a dog, but I have expertly treat-trained myself. When I first started exercising, if I achieved my weekly goals, I bought myself a candle, or a fun pen, or something that was pure delight. I'm pretty sure that in the beginning I only moved my body because there was a reward at the end of an interminable workout. With time, however, the prizes fell away and now, the feeling of exerting myself is the most invigorating treasure of all (I know, annoying, forgive me). We don't want to admit this, but most of us do things because we think we will get something in exchange. That's just a fact. Can we be real that bribing ourselves works? We don't have to be saints, especially when we are trying to do something hellish like establish a running practice. OH! ALSO! I *never* beat myself up for missing a day or even a week of a ritual. The point of having these practices is not to make myself miserable, it's to bring me to a plane of contentment and joy and ease. That's your goal, too, right? Take a shortcut to building your ritual: Reward yourself lavishly.

7. **Soak in the feelings your rituals give you.**
   I pay close attention to how good a ritual feels. I let myself
   linger in the way my body tingles with aliveness after I've
   gone on a run. I acknowledge that I feel emotionally lighter
   after I soul-vomit into my journal. This is also true in the
   opposite direction. If I don't journal, I try to really *feel* how
   much worse my day goes. If I don't work out, I recognize
   that I have less energy. That way, I know, in my body—
   which, as we all know, "keeps the score"—that these rituals
   make me feel better. It's not a philosophical exercise; I have
   physical proof.

8. **Rinse and repeat.**
   My life is boring and predictable and because of that it's
   easier to be creative and content. BEING BORING IS
   AMAZING! I spend almost no time thinking about how I
   will structure the "free" blocks in my day because the rituals I have created have taken the heavy lifting out of the
   mundane. I wake up, meditate, journal, work, eat lunch,
   eat dinner, and go to bed basically at the same time every
   day. On vacation, on a workday, it really doesn't matter. All
   of that structure, safety, and reliability makes it a lot easier
   for me to experiment with a new project or a business ven-
   ture because, almost daily, I feel pretty good and secure! I
   am way less risk averse than I once was because the details
   of my life are soothing.

Ritual Building Worksheet

Pick *one* thing you would like to incorporate into your life.

_____

Why are you doing it? *Keep digging until you get to the larger truth of what you are trying to accomplish. (I usually use four "whys.")*

_____

When will you do your ritual? How long does it take to complete? Can you pick a consistent and realistic time to do it? Why not write it in your actual calendar?

_____

How will you make your ritual fun and delightful?

_____

Do you need anything special for your ritual? A notebook? Running shoes? A meditation pillow and the best-smelling candle? FIND THOSE THINGS NOW, not at the moment you are scheduled to start your ritual.

_____

How will you measure your success? PICK SOMETHING REAL! Not "because I will feel better." WHAT DOES THAT MEAN? That's too vague!

_____

How will you reward yourself for meeting your measure of success?

_____

How will you build this into your life so that you can rinse and repeat?

_____

Remind yourself frequently of *why* you are working to make this ritual a part of your life. Maybe even write it down somewhere you'll see every day. You wouldn't go through all this trouble if it wasn't important to you. And ultimately, that's what this is all about, right? Actively choosing how you want to live and then DOING something about it instead of wishing on it? As you build your rituals, you also build your confidence because you embody what it looks and feels like to lead a life in which you take yourself seriously.

Your rituals are reflections of your values and priorities. Do you really care about your mental health? Do you put kindness to yourself and others above everything? Are you actually acquiring the skills for your dream job or are you just thinking about it? One of my favorite quotes in the whole wide world comes from the author Annie Dillard—she wrote, "How we spend our days is, of course, how we spend our lives."* Spend your days living what you care about and feel yourself light up with life. *Your* life.

---

* Annie Dillard, *The Writing Life* (Harper & Row, 1989), p. 32.

A Little Thing That Helps

Find a supportability[*] buddy who is building the same habit as you are so you can troubleshoot, celebrate, and hold each other accountable.

---

[*] A participant in one of my workshops came up with this term! She elevated "accountability group" to a much higher level.

Moneysick

You Own Your Money, Your Money Doesn't Own You

HAVE YOU EVER HEARD THE term "dopesick"? Aside from being the title of a book and then a TV series on Hulu staring Peter Sarsgaard (who I did not realize was a famous person married to fellow famous person Maggie Gyllenhaal, but instead thought was an under-the-radar actor and therefore someone I could possibly date), "dopesick" is the excruciating withdrawal people who are addicted to opiates—heroin, fentanyl, oxycodone, to name a few—undergo when they do the superhuman thing of trying to get off of the drug that has ravaged their lives. The reason the narcotics are so devastating is that they actually rewire your brain so that you can no longer feel pleasure without their aid.* That's just one of the explanations for why it's so hard for so many to quit: The drug alters your personality and the way you think, making you believe that it's impossible to feel good without it. Not to be dramatic, but you know what this all sounds a lot like to me? My relationship with money. I am moneysick.

Through my decade of re-parenting myself, I have healed a

* That's not *exactly* how the article from the National Library of Medicine put it, but that's how my dramatic mind interpreted it. As always, for your *real* science needs, please consult a credited source!

LOT of my own moneysickness—I've managed to see that I don't need massive funds in order to feel joy or contentment and that my value does not hinge on how much I have in the bank. That is nothing short of a revelation and one of the achievements I am most proud of in my life given where I started. See, I grew up in a house with finances that were seemingly tethered to a leaded yo-yo swinging wildly and with force in every direction. One week I'd be on a luxury Hawaiian vacation with my parents, stuffing my face with Oreo smoothies (so good), and the next I would be under the covers in my bed, hoping to muffle the sounds of my parents howling about how our home was going to be foreclosed upon. "THIS IS YOUR FAULT, CAROL! *YOU,* you put us in this debt," my dad would bark before my mom fired back, "You're *obsessed* with money, it's all you care about and it's disgusting!" There was never any stability. In high school, my dad would burden me with *all* his financial woes, despite my repeated protests that he not. "I'm in so much credit card debt and the interest rate is twenty-nine percent! TWENTY-NINE PERCENT! I don't know what I'm going to do!" I think what killed my dad about his rocky finances was that he believed the only thing that made him a father or, really, a person was having money. So, no money? No person. By my mid-twenties, I had come to believe that I was cursed by my parents' tumultuous finances, that I could never find economic security, and that because I wasn't extremely wealthy, I wasn't valuable, and, therefore, I wasn't worth the very basics of self-care.

I would stretch the life span of my socks until they were more holes than cloth; I'm not proud to admit this but I would (sometimes) steal toilet paper from restaurants because I thought I couldn't otherwise afford it, or that I needed to cut any corner I could. Even though I had a job with a future, by twenty-five I *sweated* every single dollar, feeling ten-out-of-ten panic when a friend at dinner ordered more drinks than everyone else and then asked to split the bill evenly. *Today,* that's a mere annoyance to me, but a few years ago I would break out into a cold sweat at the table, flashing back to my dad's strident screaming about how we were headed toward economic calamity and there was nothing to be done about it.*

As I re-parented myself and nurtured my mind, body, and relationships, I saw that taking care of the basics was actually a luxury I could afford and one that made me stronger. I could manage pants without holes, the co-pay to see a doctor, I could even afford the elegant, bursting-with-delight seven-dollar lilies from Trader Joe's, as long as I planned for these things and understood my budget. For *years,* I operated in this place where I felt good, or at least not miserable, about money. But then, of course, I was laid off and experienced an instant relapse into being utterly and hopelessly moneysick.

Throughout my career, I had been an aggressive saver. This is not because I am a virtuous or completely unfrivolous person (I am currently considering buying a pair of Valentino rubber flip-flops just because the word VALENTINO is plastered across the front of them in this way that is just in-your-face cool), but because I am terrified of financial ruin. Some kids dream of becoming firefighters, others of becoming veterinarians, but I only dreamed of monetary security. I decided that I wanted to create my own "trust fund," something that could help me if the bottom fell out, or something that could simply give me a cushion if I wanted to switch careers. In order to grow this fund, I skipped many fun trips with friends, lived FAR below my means (a habit I keep to this day)—and I never EVER tried to keep up with anyone else. I saved

---

* PSA on behalf of the world's people: If at dinner you are the one ordering more drinks than everyone else, you are probably also the one ordering the raw fish side dish that is for some reason double the price of all the other appetizers and you should pay more. Your friends might say, "We don't care!" but they do care and so do I.

as much as I could as often as I could, which was not that difficult given that I wasn't supporting anyone but myself.

By the time I was vice president of talent and development at Comedy Central, I had accumulated a comfortable cushion—maybe even a fainting sofa—of savings for myself which I could fall onto if something went south in my career. That security allowed me to not only pay off my student loans, but also to stop worrying about going to jail for stealing toilet paper (Sorry, Joseph Leonard on Waverly Place! I can pay you back! *Maybe*.) and it gave me some of the ease that comes with knowing you have a small, but real, net to catch you.

But the instant my boss called me on May 1, 2020, to tell me that I had been laid off, I felt my heart beat faster than it had in years. Pins and needles broke out across my skin, and the money-sick tremors started. *Even though I had savings!* I want to be really clear: I had my fainting sofa of cash, which I had built for this very situation, and was wildly privileged to have *no* obligations—no kids or mortgage, no partner to support—but even with all that, I woke up every single morning stressed about money and went to bed feeling even more alarmed. *I need more,* I thought without rest. *I don't have enough to keep me safe*. I needed to get a steady job, any job, *right this second* to get me off this path of ruin. And the more financially frazzled I became, the more I found myself spending a good portion of my time doing the catastrophe math.

Are you familiar with the catastrophe math? It's when you plot out all of your assets against all of your projected expenses and figure out how long you can survive on what you have (with no more funds coming in). It's the math of the worst-case scenario. Now, this might be a healthy, prudent thing to do *once, when you need it,* but I became obsessed with running these numbers and finding little places I could save in my budget. Maybe I could live in a less nice place? Maybe I could trade in my car for something cheaper? And every time I did the math, I instantly forgot what I had learned, almost as if a cloud of amnesia had descended on me for only this one particular piece of information, necessitating that I do the exact same exercise the very next day and the next, and the next. The only thing was—nothing was wrong *yet*. I hadn't even had time to put together my resume, much less put in the effort it takes to get a new job. (SO MUCH WORK JUST TO MAKE THE RESUME, NEVER MIND GET AN INTERVIEW!) And instead of focusing on what I could gain in this time *because* I had been a responsible saver (e.g., learn something new to make me more valuable in any career), or recognize that I had done a GOOD JOB OF BEING AN ADULT by even having savings, I was laser-focused on how much I had lost and how much I would lose in the future.

I am going to share with you one of my—hands down—most unflattering moments, one that makes me feel gross about myself: I became so debilitated by my fear of losing money that one night, when I wanted Thai takeout for dinner but saw on Uber Eats that it would cost eighteen dollars, I began to . . . *oh my God, this is agonizing to tell you* . . . I began to cry. I know this is pathetic and offensive. It was an entirely irrational reaction, but it was real. I felt helpless, like if I spent that twenty-three dollars (because every delivery for me includes a *minimum* five-dollar tip, no matter my financial situation) it might kill me. I felt like my life was in danger. As I looked in my living room mirror at the tears streaming down my face, I felt pathetic and humiliated.

Remember the phrase, "If it's hysterical, it's historical"? As I looked at my phone, going back and forth trying to decide if I could afford the Thai food, I realized that I wasn't crying about this decision in particular. I was distraught about a lifetime of financial insecurity from which I hadn't fully healed. I hadn't recovered from all those times my dad told me our family was financially cursed, or forgotten the rusting exam chairs and other office detritus that filled our front yard after my mom lost her medical license and her livelihood. The years of my parents bemoaning how broke we were and how our lack of savings was destroying what little family we had—all of that money stress had left a deeper impression on me than I had realized, until now. The lesson I had learned in childhood was that money was scarce and something to be lost, never gained, and that you had no control whatsoever over your finances. So even though I was a grown-ass, successful woman—*with savings!*—there was a part of me who was still fucking terrified that I would lose the cornerstones of my life—my hard-won stability and my safety.

It was at that point that I realized I needed money therapy or something or someone to HELP me, *for the love of God help me once and for all,* to recover from my belief that impending loss was always looming and that I couldn't rely on myself. (See how bad learned helplessness is? SO bad!) I asked friends who they talked to about money and learned that many actually shared my same fears. I also learned that a few of my friends with family wealth had financial advisors whose job it was to explain foreign concepts like the "stock market" to them and help them come up with a plan for their fiscal futures.

One friend suggested I talk to her wealth advisor, Barbara, a no-nonsense, wise woman with a thick Boston accent. My homework before we met was to look at my entire financial picture and report back to her on what my assets were, what debts I had, and what I expected to make in the next year. That one really got me. I HAD JUST BEEN LAID OFF—and for now, I was going to pursue writing, so . . . negative money? Zero future? I almost felt ashamed that I didn't know what my salary would be, or even if there would be one at all.

In our first meeting, Barbara opened by saying, "Tell me everything. I need to know about your entire history if I'm going to help you." "What do you mean 'everything'? Like, the complete financial picture and my 401(k)—" "No, not that," she interrupted. "You emailed me that. I want to know how money functioned in your family, what you thought about it growing up, and what you think of it now." *Where to even begin, Barbara . . .* "Well, I grew up thinking money was the most important thing in life because my dad basically told me as much pretty constantly, and made not having money seem like a death sentence, and since my family didn't really have it (or we were losing it all the time) we would always be 'doomed' (that was the word my dad used most often) and we would never ever be safe and there was no way we could help ourselves and this was all a disaster because the only thing that made you a valuable human being was how much money you had in the bank." "I see," Barbara responded after a short silence. "So, yeah, I had to do a lot of work on myself, and eventually, I learned how to be okay with spending money to take care of myself . . . but . . . really my main thought today around money is that I'm going to lose it." Barbara looked over the Zoom screen with a tight stare and asked, "Do you know what clients I have that talk about money the way you talk about it?" I had no idea. "The only people who talk about money the way you talk about it are people who survived the Great Depression."

There's nothing like being told you are living as if you are in the Great Depression to shock you into reality. I burst into tears— like, cartoon-character burst, where water droplets explode from the eyes out of nowhere. I was young, healthy, able-bodied, and LUCKY, SO LUCKY to have savings and no mouths to feed, but I was acting like someone who was barely surviving. I felt ashamed. The kind of shame that reminds you that you are not behaving like the person you want to be. I didn't want to be an ingrate who didn't see her many and various blessings. Money had hypnotized me and put me under a painful hex from which I wanted to be free once and for all.

Considering all the other rituals I had developed to take care of myself, I came to the conclusion that I had to give myself some kind of structure to cure my moneysickness. I decided on four steps to take in order to (try to) heal:

1. **I admitted I had a problem.** I faced up to the fact that I was obsessed with money. Sure, I had done a great deal of work to heal, but if I was honest, I still thought about money *all* the time. It had gotten out of my control and it was time to stop saying "I shouldn't feel this way" and just admit that money was playing an outsized and deeply negative role in my life.

2. **I acknowledged how afraid I was.** Once I took a step back, I saw that my number one emotion around money was not anxiety but terror. It is no exaggeration to say that I was *terrified* of losing my savings. But! I realized that my fears were pretty vague and I didn't actually know shit about money, something I could remedy by finding actual information.

3. **I decided that it was now my *job* to know how money works.** Financial literacy would become another self-care tool right up there with journaling and meditating.

4. **I would put my newfound knowledge into action.** I didn't know exactly how yet, but I recognized that part of my issue was that I just felt so debilitated with fear that it was extremely difficult to do anything to help myself. And as you know, when you feel helpless, you lose the power to be an active participant in your own life.

I started small, reading books on finance just like I would *any* subject I didn't understand, and the more I read about the stock market and how wealth is built in America, the more I saw that it wasn't all that complicated, financial jargon just made it sound that way. I went to friends and had honest conversations, asking them the unthinkable—"How much money do you make?" "Is family money supporting you?" "Are you as crazed about money as I am?" and "What exactly do you feel about money?" I was surprised to learn that everyone had complicated relationships with money and most (no matter if they were living paycheck to paycheck or had a giant trust fund) knew little to nothing about personal finances. I sought out professionals in my network and respectfully begged them to teach me what they knew.

One friend in particular, Khe, a former Wall Street banker bro, had given up his career making seven figures a year because working a hundred hours a week in that business meant he was saving incredible amounts of money for a life he didn't have the time to lead.* He had not been born wealthy; his parents were Cambodian immigrants who arrived in America with barely any savings and a rudimentary understanding of English. Khe grew up thinking the thing he lacked, money, would bring him acceptance and respectability and maybe even love—something I could very much relate to.

I wanted to talk to Khe, but I was . . . well, *humiliated* by my moneysickness. I thought I was probably a bad person for being as haunted by money as I was but I decided that with Khe, I could be totally vulnerable because though the details of our stories were different, the truth behind them was the same: We thought money would be the cure-all for our insecurities and fears. I called him one night and was just straight-up honest. "Khe, I'm tormented by money, I can't stop thinking about how I'm going to lose it and how I'll never be safe without it, and how I need more." I had

* Khe runs radreads.co, which I love and learn from. Its mission is to help people be more productive, examine their lives, and ultimately find a little joy. My mission is to soak up as much as I can from Khe.

never been this frank with someone about how desperate and preoccupied I was regarding money, and as I waited for his response, I felt totally exposed, like I had peeled off all of the layers of respectability I had so painfully painted on myself. "I get it, when you lose a job, a guaranteed salary, and that's been the thing you thought would make you safe and lovable—it's terrifying," Khe offered. "But you have enough savings to help you figure out what you want to do next, right?" he asked. "I do, but I think I need more or else . . . I don't know . . . or else I'm *doomed*," I confessed. "I get that, we all want more! It's like a drug, we need the next fix," he said with a laugh. "But have you ever asked yourself, 'How much money would be *enough*?'" A small bomb denotated in my brain—*no,* I had never for a second considered what would be "enough."

Khe was not talking about the baseline income we all need to take care of ourselves, which in 2022 is increasingly difficult to obtain. He was talking about the above-and-beyond money, what is referred to as "disposable income." I had no end goal in sight, no number I was aiming for aside from *infinity,* so anything below infinity felt paltry.

With Khe's question ringing in my head, I asked myself, "Okay, beyond taking care of my fundamental needs, what would be enough? What's the actual number?" Did I want to have a second home (never mind a first!), wear all designer clothes, and compete with my friends for luxury vacations like I was some celebrity's kid even if that meant I had to work until the moment I died, constantly bailing myself out of credit card debt along the way? If so, how much money and how much of my soul was that going to cost? The immediate answer I found was, "No thanks. That sounds awful."

I answered my own question by creating a budget of what a "comfortable" life for me would look like (what my rent would be, how much I would spend on groceries, restaurants, clothes, travel, etc.) and then added 20 percent of that to either save or buffer me from things outside of my control. And also, I had to admit that there was a certain point beyond which I couldn't protect myself and believing that I could was only leaving me permanently disappointed. I couldn't prevent unexpected doctors' bills, being laid off, or global factors like inflation. I could prepare for them, but there wasn't going to be a point at which I was immune to them. I also had to give up thinking that if I just had "more" money I would be safe. With a new framework in mind, I saw that I didn't need to endlessly pursue more for more's sake. As my meditation teacher Rabbi James likes to say, "Even if you win the rat race, you're still a rat," and I was no longer about that rodent life.

The point is, instead of being scared of my financial situation—looking at it with one eye shut, one eye barely open—I owned it, all of it. I embraced the fact that I had been financially insecure for much of my life and it had left me money-obsessed. I decided that learning about personal finance and the economy was a critical component to taking care of my physical, emotional, and spiritual life. I gave up being proud and pretending I was "cool about money, y'all" and had real, vulnerable, sometimes painful conversations with people I trusted to compare notes and learn from them, and then I decided on a number that was "enough" for me—a number that gave me a solid life but didn't mean I'd be constantly scrambling and hustling, trading in almost all of my time for more money. Because *time,* I've come to realize, is the most valuable thing, the thing we can never get back. I can never get back time with my friends, with my family, and with *you.* There's usually a way to make more money but there is never a way to make more time.

I do want to be clear: To come to this conclusion is SUPER privileged. Just to be able to *decide* what is enough is an incredible miracle that much of the world does not share and I am knocking on every piece of wood in my home office to ward off the evil eye.

And. Still. There are more of us who could take our financial destinies in our hands. Have you *ever* asked yourself what would be sufficient, and what *exactly* you are trying to get to? Or what about, "I like my life now, do I really need any more? Would more make a big difference?" Maybe you have and if so, YOU ROCK, but when I've posed the question to friends, not a single person has been able to answer what level of income would satisfy them.

In my experience, money rarely makes anyone happy, and in fact, oftentimes, I've seen that the more people make, the more they are dissatisfied and stressed as they trade their hours and their health for money. Research from the Center for Health and Well-being at Princeton University shows that an income higher than $75,000 a year does not *significantly* raise one's overall level of happiness.* Can you believe that? Cognitive scientist and Yale psychology professor Lori Santos explained to *The New York Times Magazine* that for a higher salary to increase your happiness, you'd have to "change your income from $100,000 to $600,000." But even then, "your happiness goes up from, like, a 64 out of 100 to a 65."† Let me ask you this: Is that *one* point worth all the stress you know it would take to sextuple your income? You might not be able to control how much money you make, but you can control how you feel about money and what you're striving for.

I don't think it's just me who's moneysick, I think it's our whole culture. We're relentlessly sold the idea that *more*—of everything—will make us happier and prettier and better. If you want to feel bad about yourself, just go on Kim Kardashian's Instagram and ask what I ask myself: "Am I supposed to look casual and off-the-cuff in a private jet? Should I be working toward owning nine refrigerators, one just for beverages, one that is an actual walk-in room,

---

* Daniel Kahneman and Angus Deaton, "High Income Improves Evaluation of Life but Not Emotional Well-Being," *PNAS Early Edition*, August 2010.

† David Marchese, "Yale Happiness Professor Says Anxiety Is Destroying Her Students," *The New York Times Magazine*, February 18, 2022.

and a pantry that houses my own personal frozen-yogurt machine?" Or go on Kylie's page and look at the photo of her closet full of Tom Ford, Chanel, and Hermès all in FALL colors, as if this is just a fraction of her treasures, as if she has this finery for all seasons. NO SHADE toward women and people who have more than me—GOOD FOR THEM! WAY TO GO, KIM AND KYLIE! GET THOSE EMPIRES!—but when I compare myself to that level of wealth, I feel self-hate, my heart wrings with jealousy and anger at how much I must be fucking up if I'm not *anywhere near* that nine-refrigerator life. And maybe that's a moral failing on my part and maybe I'm just as bad a person as I thought I was, but it's the truth. I've had to unfollow celebrities who boast of excess because I can easily get swept up by the central tenet of capitalism they convey—you need more money and more stuff to lead the good life. I've even unfollowed friends who flaunt their wealth because, again, I don't want to let my moneysickness taint my feelings toward them or myself. The more I've stuck to *my* measure of financial success and blocked out everything else, the less I find myself praying at the altar of money, which in America today, thanks to social media, is directly in front of my face at all times.

Many of us, regardless of our financial situation, labor our entire lives in a moneysick culture that holds up two great false prophets. The first is the God of Infinite Funds: We sacrifice endlessly at this god's altar, working and hustling and saving—but we always feel like we need more and that more would be attainable if only we worked harder. Isn't that your understanding of America? Cuz it sure is mine. The sense of possibility we've cultivated in this country has a potentially problematic side: There is no end goal in sight and so many of us never feel satisfied with what we have. That, in fact, is the premise of the stock market, the economy, and all of our major financial institutions: Money is infinitely expanding and more is always better. The second is the I Can Do That, Too, God: We mistakenly believe that because someone else is extremely wealthy, we can be too. I hate to burst all of our bubbles, but many of our money celebrities, people like Mark Zuckerberg and Bill Gates, are not entirely self-made billionaires we've been taught to admire. Mark Zuckerberg went to a high school that cost $47,000 a year and where he had a private tutor in computer science *before* he even got to Harvard. Bill Gates's mother, Mary Gates, an influential Seattle businesswoman, helped get her son and his start-up, Microsoft, their first contract with IBM. The system is stacked in favor of the already affluent. I'm not saying that's good, it's fucking awful, but if you can accept that fact, you won't feel quite as bad looking at the part of Kim Kardashian's pantry exclusively reserved for ice-cream sprinkles on Insta. You'll see it for what it is—a hardworking, smart, and savvy businesswoman, born into privilege, who used her position to raise her status even more. THERE IS NOTHING WRONG WITH THAT! But we have to recognize that reality if any of us are going to keep our sanity and maybe even help others. We have to clearly see how money is operating in all of our lives if we are ever to be cured.

This is not to say that I would not take your money; if for some reason you want to cut me a check right now, I'll gladly take it. Please make it out to "Tara E. Schuster," though I won't ever tell you what the "E" stands for even if you offered me all the money in the world. I'm lusting after owning my own home right now (which given the current economy seems like a flirtation that will never be consummated), I'm an investor in the stock market, and I would have bought those Valentino pool slides except they were super uncomfortable, which, for what is typically referred to as a "shower shoe," is just offensive. BUT! The difference now is my eyes are wide open, I understand how money is operating both in my life and in the broader economic context, and I have no delusions about what money can and can't offer me. Money is not happiness, it's not safety, it's not salvation. Money is an unevenly distributed tool that can provide for the basics and, beyond that, can give you the lifestyle you want, but it can never give you a life. Simply put: I own my money, my money doesn't own me.

No matter what your relationship to money is, or how much you have in the bank, I think we could all do ourselves a great favor by getting more informed about what the fuck is even going on with money in the world. We needn't feel haunted by the specter of finance without any idea of how to break the curse. Consider these questions: What's your relationship to money? How often do you think about it? Are you moneysick like I was (and can still be) and do you think it would be helpful to find some antidotes? Do you have a number that is "enough"? Do you need a money mentor like I had in Khe? If so, do you have any friends who can help you? Have you considered reading a book on personal finance, just as you would research any other topic? What can you actively do to help yourself?

No matter your finances, you can and must understand that in a totally unequal, unfair, largely random system that favors and prioritizes the already wealthy, it's cruel and even a form of violence toward yourself to feel like a failure if you don't have as much money as someone else. It's also just not true. You don't have to be born rich to be rich in time, relationships, experiences, happiness, or *any* of the things you and I both know really matter.

Every one of us deserves a life of financial freedom, a life in which we do not live in fear of bills, or how we will help ourselves in an emergency, or one in which we make health decisions based on financial constraints. But unless you were born wealthy, financial freedom eludes most of us, especially if we say things like, "I don't know anything about money," and then proceed to learn nothing about it. That's like saying "there's a fire raging through my house, but I'm not going to put it out because I'm not a firefighter and don't know how." And the more you give up your power and agency, the more companies, friends, con artists, you name it, are going to take it from you. So, let's demystify our understanding of money by educating ourselves and then *acting* on that new information. Say it with me again: "I own my money, my money doesn't own me."

Moneysick Q and A with Tara

Hello and welcome to a generic theater in your hometown! My name is Tara and I have no professional finance qualifications whatsoever and none of this is investment advice because I don't have any! I hope you enjoy the free popcorn and fresh mint tea I've provided, but if you don't, don't tell me! *It wasn't free to me!* Let's get to your questions.

Woman in Magenta Blazer: Hi, Tara, how do you get wealthy in America?

Me: You have three options: (1) Be born into wealth. (2) Marry into wealth. (3) Work in finance. End of list.

Woman in Magenta Blazer: Um . . . isn't that depressing?

Me (*enthusiastically*)**:** Yes!

Woman in Magenta Blazer: Okay . . . so there's no hope?

Me: I didn't quite say *that*. It's almost impossible to become wealthy in America unless you start off with money or you have a high-income job and you *aggressively* save. And even then, if we are talking about real, lasting generational wealth here, you can't just sit on that money, you need to know how to properly invest it. The wealthy in this country didn't necessarily get rich because they worked harder than everyone else, it's because their money *makes money* in the stock market.

Someone throws an empty popcorn box at my head.

Me: Hey, I didn't make this system! I would burn it to the ground if I could and then stomp on the smoldering remains of this unequal bullshit while singing a Viking hymn of victory. I'm just trying to be realistic with you.

Man in Blue Checked Shirt: So there's no chance I'm going to be rich?

Me: You need to define "rich" for yourself because the word is so arbitrary it barely has meaning.

Man in Blue Checked Shirt: But isn't that kind of a cop-out? By my own definition, I could be rich *today*.

Me: YES! As my friend Khe would say, I am "infinitely wealthy by my own definition" because within my own context, I'm living the exact lifestyle I want and my time is my own.

Young Woman in All Electric Green Who Looks Like Billie Eilish: What should I invest in?

Me: Great question! But first, can I quickly point out that you are a walking example of why color blocking works? Wait, are you Billie Eilish?

Young Woman in All Electric Green Who Looks Like Billie Eilish (*apathetically*): Yeah.

Me: Love. Your. Work. Well, before you invest, you need a cushion of three to six months in case something goes wrong. . . .

Billie Eilish: Um, I'm Billie Eilish. . . .

Me: DUH, sorry, okay. So after that, you should max out your 401(k) ESPECIALLY if your employer matches what you put in because you won't be taxed on that money (for a while at least). If you have ANY 401(k) questions, google "John Oliver retirement plans episode." In twenty-one minutes you will learn everything you need to know. And you will laugh. And cry. Any other questions about the fundamentals of investing? Read Burton G. Malkiel's *A Random Walk Down Wall Street*. It helped demystify the stock market for me and taught me how to make responsible, non-schemey decisions.

Woman in the Back: How do you budget?

Me: The short, superficial answer is the rule of 50/30/20. Fifty percent of your monthly income goes to the essentials you NEED to pay for, like rent, transportation, groceries, etc. Thirty percent goes to your wants, the things that it's just nice to have. Twenty percent goes to savings and debt repayment. And on debt—there is no designer bag *ever* worth going into debt for. Credit card debt is truly the stuff of my nightmares.

Dude in the Back: How can I make a lot of money quickly?

Me: IDK. If I knew that, I wouldn't be here. Okay, folks, time to wrap it up because I need to take advantage of this moment to fangirl-out on Billie Eilish HARD. Please don't leave yet, Billie! Any more Qs, please direct them to my Instagram or google them. Don't you think Google should pay me some kind of commission at this point?

A Little Thing That Helps

Use an online, free budgeting tool like Mint to get real about what you're spending. Choose a date each month and set a reminder in your calendar for when you will review your finances so that you can make any needed adjustments. The key to financial well-being is awareness of what the fuck is even happening.

In My Next Life, May I Be the Dude Who Has Never Heard of Imposter Syndrome

I Promise You Are Not a Fraud

RECENTLY, I SPOKE AT A women's empowerment conference on the topic of self-love—tho when I give a talk, lord knows what I end up discussing. Usually, the session quickly devolves into a spiritual communion in which the attendees and I become witches and sorcerers, casting spells and dancing around a (metaphorical) fire pit where we burn our self-hate, find everlasting freedom from our limiting beliefs, and enjoy the warmth of the flames and community radiating through our bodies. *Or at least, that's how it feels to me.* BUT ANYWAY. In the "ballroom" at the conference, I really regretted not bringing my sweater because the space was cavernous and meat-locker cold. As I shivered from the tundra-like conditions, I watched as a local newscaster asked the activist, actress, and all-around excellent, funny, and unfairly beautiful human being Jameela Jamil the following unbelievable question: "Can you tell me what imposter syndrome is?"

"What do you mean?" Jameela asked. "Well, I hear that term a lot, but I have no idea what it means," he said and laughed. In a room of one thousand freezing women, there was DEAD silence.

You could have heard someone cut through a continental break-fast muffin with a butter knife. Women sighed and shook their heads in clear astonishment and disapproval, and some muttered, "Whaaat?" and "Oof," which reminded me of heckling at a comedy show. *Of course* this dude had never heard of imposter syndrome, something every woman in the room probably felt at least once a day, BECAUSE HE WAS A GUY AND DID NOT UNDERSTAND SUCH THINGS.*

Before we go any further, let's get on the same page about what "imposter syndrome" means. I define it as doubting one's abilities and feeling like a fraud despite one's talent and accomplishments. It's when someone congratulates you on a promotion and you tell them you were just "lucky," because heaven forbid you take credit for working your ASS OFF and earning every ounce of that recognition. It's when you're asked to give a presentation and you feel a full-body panic that now you are one step closer to being "found out" for your incompetence. Imposter syndrome is not just reserved for those in the workforce (lucky us). I have friends who are stay-at-home moms (a job I FOR SURE don't have the patience or strength or courage to attempt) and feel judged and like they are less than for choosing to have arguably the hardest job in the world. I know people who never graduated college and feel like they don't belong in social conversations because they don't have a degree. Imposter syndrome can pop up anywhere, but my worst experience with it has been at work.

I'm not sure why women are particularly susceptible to imposter syndrome in the office. *Oh wait—yes, I am*—it's because they are censured, questioned, spoken over, reprimanded, and second-guessed. Meanwhile, their male counterparts are praised for aggressively sucking up all of the oxygen in the room as everyone

---

* DUDE NATION: You might actually feel imposter syndrome, but because you are not allowed to emote or express uncomfortable feelings, I would not know this about you. Maybe slide into my DMs to discuss limiting and poisonous gender roles?

else gasps for air, like fish stranded on the shore after a high tide of corporate bullshit spat them out and left them to suffocate. In that environment, why *wouldn't* you feel like a grifter? It can be especially horrible for people of color and all folks in the LGBTQIA+ community, who already may feel out of place in work spaces that are mostly white, cis, and straight. If you think I'm angry right now, please know that I'm not. I'm fucking furious.

Of all the impressive and lauded writers, directors, actresses, artists, C-suite executives, and other UTTERLY ACCOM- PLISHED women I have met, I have *never* heard anyone say that they didn't feel at least a *little* like a charlatan in an elaborate, multi-decade, identify-theft operation. I certainly feel it from time to time, especially in a room where I think everyone else has a sheen of prestige from wealth that I lack (there's that old moneysick again!). I go to a conference every year where I am, by far, the least influential person in the room and the least well-to-do. I'm not being faux-humble. This room is full of CEOs and billionaires, the people (mostly men) who hold the levers of power in our society. *My* former job was mainly focused on answering the age-old question, "How many dick jokes is too many dick jokes in a half-hour comedy show?" (Final answer: No limit.) But how many of my fellow conference attendees can spot creative artists and help build critically lauded and commercially successful TV shows around them? HMMMM?? HOW MANY?? Still, when I mingle with these ultra-rich corporate board members, I tend to feel like I made a wrong turn somewhere. Like these people are better than me; they figured out how to make fortunes and hold real power and I should just shut the fuck up lest I say something uninformed and reveal that I do not fit in here.

But with time and intentional work, I have been able to bring down my overall level of imposter syndrome discomfort and *sometimes,* even for months on end, manage not to feel like a con artist in work-appropriate attire. So, without further ado, I'd like to present you with my five-pronged approach to vanquishing imposter syndrome!

1. **First, I ask myself, "Am I experiencing imposter syndrome or is this place a nuclear war zone for self-esteem?"** Is the issue that *I'm feeling* like a fraud? Or is the ground here so toxic that not even cockroaches can survive, and I have legitimate reasons to be full-body sick with self-doubt? A noxious work environment can cause real harm to your self-esteem—and that is NOT in your head. So, when I feel the imposter syndrome pangs, I ask: "Is this coming from my own insecure brain? Or are the women in this job marginalized, excluded, and at the mercy of unconscious bias *especially* at the intersection of race and gender? Do they lose promotions to men who have nowhere near as much expertise? Are they picked apart for their leadership styles? The point is, a lot of the time NOTHING is in our heads AT ALL! We aren't making shit up and it's just *mean* to blame ourselves for a bad environment. So, first I figure out: *Is it me, or does this place just suck?*

2. **I decide what makes *me* proud of myself.** I can easily get carried away by my fears of how others perceive me, so it's important that I get clear on how I perceive myself. On an index card next to my computer, I write down the unshakable, un-take-away-able sources of my confidence. For me, as long as I write, am a reasonably kind person, and use my body at least once a day in a way that feels good, I am confident and proud of myself. It doesn't matter how my writing *performs,* it matters that I show up and scrawl what I think is true. It doesn't matter if others see me as kind, it just matters that I (mostly, but not always) consciously choose to act with goodwill. And I don't need to have

shredded arms to be proud of the effort I put into my body (tho my arms are rather nice!), all I need is to sweat a little every day to feel good about myself. When I can easily identify what makes *me* respect myself, as opposed to what I think others might value about me ("She's rich! Successful! With great arms!"), I am way less concerned with what other people think. I'm doing my own thing, *thank you very much*. If your self-esteem is anchored by your position at work, your salary, feedback from colleagues, or how much your boss values you, or even how much appreciation you are getting from your kids, then *luck be with you, my friend*. You have just handed over your self-worth to somebody else.

3.   **I have convinced myself that I have a good soul.** Maybe you always thought your soul was good, but I didn't until I heard a Jewish prayer thanking the universe for giving us pure souls. The prayer prompted me to ask myself, "Do I even believe that I am basically good?" The answer was, "No." Over the next two years, I woke up every morning and sang the prayer, hopefully declaring to—and eventually convincing—myself that despite my mistakes or ugly thoughts, I was born inherently good. Sure, I might get lost from time to time and act in ways I'm not proud of, but the most essential part of me—the stardust part—is virtuous. When I pray, I'm not asking to be made good, I'm reminding myself that I *am* good. And when I say "prayer" here, this does not have to be religious (and it isn't for me). Just find a phrase to remind yourself that you are already whole and good. If you are edgy about this and want to scream at me, "BUT YOU DON'T UNDERSTAND, I *am* bad and it's only a matter of time before everyone leaves me," let me ask you this: Are babies inherently bad, or not enough, or

selfish? No? Were you a baby once? That baby stardust is still in you and *is* you. Therefore, sorry! You can't be bad!

4. **I actively heal my negative thoughts, daily.** Positive affirmations can heal critical self-chatter. Our natural tendency is to register pessimistic things more than positive ones and then dwell on them (as you know from that one piece of critical feedback your boss gave you a year ago that outweighs your employee of the month status in your mind). As we evolved as humans (OMG, I'm into some scientific stuff!) we needed to constantly scan our world for threats. For example, we had to discern the difference between toxic mushrooms and special, good-time mushrooms; we had to learn how to navigate an unmapped world so we wouldn't get lost (I can't even navigate Los Angeles!); and most difficult for me, we had to track and kill animals in order to eat (before they ate us) cuz sadly, there was no Instacart yet. Because our survival was on the line, it makes sense that we were hardwired to find faults. The problem, though, that arises from this negativity bias is that the more you think something negative about yourself, *the more you think something negative about yourself.* When I tell myself I'm not worth taking care of, I don't take care of myself. This is why I have spent a decade reminding myself, daily, that *I am a worthy person who is allowed to nurture herself.* The more I think that, the more my brain is able to create new neural pathways and change its factory settings. Neurologists have a saying for this: "Thoughts that fire together, wire together." Your thoughts actually create your brain's landscape! So if you have a tractor in your head, driving in circles all day long with the thought *I'm not good enough to take care of,* like I did, then you're digging those detrimental trenches into your brain more deeply. Fortu-

nately, you can disrupt those thought patterns with positive affirmations. So, I would suggest you pause, exit the tractor,* find the nutrient-rich affirmation you need to be reminded of, such as "I am ALLOWED to take care of myself," and let it fill in the ragged ditches of your mind like life-giving soil. Soon, you'll have level ground on which you can forge your own path—one *not* based on limiting beliefs—and let yourself bloom. Our minds are malleable and impressionable, just like the ground beneath our feet. So, pay attention to how you till the land of your brain, you tractor-driving sorceress, you!

5. **I decipher fact from fiction.** When imposter syndrome comes up, I draw a line down a piece of paper and on one side I write "fact" and on the other "fiction." Whatever negative belief I am hung up about, I write it down in the fiction column. For example, about that fancy conference, I write, "You are the least important person in this room." I then ask, "Is that true?" Usually it's not! In the "fact" column I write that "I've done TONS of very important things in my career. I've contributed to the show *Key & Peele,* which changed our *culture.* Who else in this room can say that?" This exercise brings me back to reality. Another awesome formula I use with *any* negative belief is to write down the "fiction" I am telling myself in one column, and then zoom out and ask, "What *else* might be true?" in the other. So for example, if I wrote down, "Everyone here thinks I am less important than they are," I then write down a larger truth I KNOW: "I was invited here because I earned my place. And no one person is more important than another. I'm just as important as Billie Eilish (and

---

* Do tractors have doors? Or is it a jump-out situation?

maybe even know more about personal finance than she does!).

By understanding the circumstances I'm working within, defining the sources of my self-confidence, realizing my own inherent goodness, healing the negative thoughts I am pre-programmed to believe, and deciphering the difference between fact and fiction, I largely no longer feel imposter syndrome. I kind of don't care what anyone thinks of me anymore because it just doesn't matter. Once you define your unshakable sources of self-respect and remind yourself that most of the negative stories spinning in your head are works of (not very good) fiction, then other people's opinions of you just become . . . boring? Beside the point? And when someone genuinely does know more than I do (which is often), I don't get weird, I ask questions. How cool to be in a room with someone who can teach me!

I'll even go as far as to say imposter syndrome can be a good thing, as long as I don't get swept away by it. It can be a warning sign that something isn't aligning within myself—that there is a gulf between the person I know myself to be and the person I am presenting to the world—or, it can alert me to the fact that I might be in a dangerous environment and just like our ancient ancestors who had the wisdom to protect themselves in their caves when a grizzly came around, I either need to get the fuck out or grab the metaphorical bear spray.

The point is, I take setting my own standards, and living up to my own personal integrity, extremely seriously so that I can see that the opinions, or perceived opinions, of others are actually kinda meaningless. Let me ask you this: If I know and inhabit myself fully, whom exactly would I be impersonating?

There are many people in this world who are so worried about what others will think of them that they've abandoned who they fundamentally are for a cheap version of themselves they think other people will like better. But that serves none of us. At this exact moment in history, the world is desperate for you to be you. *My God,* we have enough fakery, please and thank you. When you shine your individual light—purely and truly—you give me permission to do the same. And I just can't thank you enough for that.

A Little Thing That Helps

No one knows anything and everyone is lying and trying their best. The end.

Body Gratitude
It's Time. For the Love of God, It's Time.

I RECENTLY HAD MY HAND x-rayed in order to figure out why the flesh between my thumb and index finger on my right hand was swollen and painful and made it impossible for me to pick anything up, or write or type or eat or lift weights or brush my teeth or screw the lid on a jar of vegan mayonnaise.* Before the doctor came in to discuss the images, I sat waiting in her office, looking at the scans lit up on a wall display. *WOW*, I thought. *Wow, wow, wow.* I had never seen my fingers x-rayed before and therefore did not know how elegant, how stunningly perfect they were. Each sculpted phalange connecting to the next. The carpal bones in my wrists looking like perfectly stacked, prehistoric, rough-cut gems that magically fit together, like embellishments on a fabulous Marni handbag, understated but still blingy. As I sat, my hand throbbing with pain, I couldn't help but marvel at how lucky I was to have this glorious human body.

I didn't always feel this way, in fact, for much of my life I felt ashamed and uneasy about my body because . . . *woman*. I don't need to tell you this, but my guess is that all women have hated

---

* I'm not vegan but I am vegan-curious.

their bodies at some point in their lives and probably all dudes have, too, but just like with imposter syndrome, dudes are not allowed to voice their body image issues or display any vulnerability, which I'm sure is good and healthy and easy for them to deal with and has no unintended damaging consequences for society as a whole. Right, my gentlemen friends?

In middle school, I was embarrassed by my little potbelly that stuck out from the bottom of my novelty baby tee and the double chin that every photo of me at that time seemed to document in rigorous detail. In high school and college I would stand in front of the mirror scowling at my boobs, which I considered matronly and unattractive, so far from the ideal, Kate Moss–waif body of the era. By the age of twenty-five, I had spent so much energy picking my body apart that it became hard to be naked by myself, much less with anyone I was dating. Fed up with the effort it took to tear myself down, as a last resort, I went against every one of my instincts and chose to honor my body, even if I didn't quite believe it was worth honoring. To get over my boob hatred in particular, I bought fancy bras to give my breasts the highest-end support. In time and with practice, faking self-love, I was able to unabashedly wear bikinis, which I hadn't done since I was eight. One of my favorite childhood pictures is, in fact, of me at that age on the edge of a pool, wearing a black, rhinestone bikini with my arms straight above my head, the fiercest look of determination on my face, ready to dive into the water like my goddamn life depends on it. I am trying, and probably will always be trying, to get back to *that* level of body acceptance. The kind where you don't even think about it—you inhabit it, and make it work for *you*.

Paying tribute to my body helped so many of my low-grade (but real) dysmorphic thoughts, but I still found myself carping at things, especially my weight. Having never had a flat stomach, I lusted after "perfect" abs and thought, *For just once in my life, I want to have something resembling a six-pack. It doesn't have to be permanent* *but like, for five minutes, can I have abs?* To help me, I hired a personal trainer, Vlad, who I found on Instagram. If I'm being honest, part of the reason I hired him was that we were living in lockdown and this dude was HOT—very hot—and I figured it wouldn't be such a terrible thing to spend two hours a week with a beautiful person on Zoom, right?* Maybe that would make the arduous task of lunges slightly more bearable?

During our first session, Vlad asked me about my health history. "So, any sports-related injuries? ACL tears, breaks, anything like that?" "Nope," I replied. "I was more of an 'indoor kid' most of my life, so I haven't ever had an athletic injury. I got two concussions during theater productions . . . long story . . . I don't think that counts." Vlad broke out into a smile. "A theater kid! That's perfect!" At first I thought he was making fun of me (we theater kids are defensive because you have been making fun of us our whole lives—sorry—*see*, I'm super defensive!) but he went on to explain, "So many of the people I train played sports when they were younger and have all kinds of injuries I have to work around, but you have a clean slate! We can start fresh and make you into an athlete." I smiled back. I had never once thought that the fact that I hadn't played sports was anything other than embarrassing. But from Vlad's point of view it was *the very thing* that could make me an "ATHLETE," which would be the most unlikely label I had ever attached to myself.

At Vlad's instruction, I bought adjustable weights, those rubber bands that go around your legs, and a pull-up bar. The pull-up bar was a cute idea but I knew where it was headed—directly to the curb outside of my apartment. I mean, when I was a kid, and weighed my absolute lightest, I had never been able to do a single pull-up; now I was going to have a whole piece of bulky equip-

* Vlad, I am so sorry to objectify you like this ESPECIALLY after I noted that men often suffer in silence over their body image issues. But, like, you're so hot.

ment dedicated to them? I laughed as I said to Vlad, "I'm so glad you think I need a pull-up bar, but I guarantee you I'll be sending it right back." "We'll see about that," he teasingly replied.

Starting with basic moves, Vlad not only taught me exercises, he also showed me how to maintain proper form. When I did my dead lifts using a Swiffer mop to steady me, he'd point out, "You see how your left hip is pointing upward? We want it level with the ground." I moved my hip down and saw how that micro adjustment made *all* the difference—I could feel each separate muscle working in unison, my glutes pulling up my abdomen muscles. As we worked together, steadily building up my strength, I saw myself doing things I never imagined possible—push-ups! *Real* push-ups, not the kind you do on your knees! And chest-presses with twenty-five pounds in *each* hand. And every day I spent a little time with the dreaded pull-up bar, at first just hanging on it, then building up the amount of time I hung on it, then, little by little, pulling myself up until one day I DID A FUCKING PULL-UP!* It was incredible, I felt the pressure of my hands pulling down activate my core with life as I was able to bring my chin up to the bar. IT WAS A MIRACLE and one I truly never believed I would accomplish.

I was learning how friggin' marvelous and powerful my body was, but there was no flat stomach in sight. So, I got a little . . . I don't know . . . *out of my mind obsessed and totally intense and somewhat disordered* about reaching my ab holy grail. I started counting my "macros"—the measurements of how many carbohydrates, fats, and proteins you take in—and I started eating . . . a lot less. A lot, lot less. I did more intense weight-lifting workouts, and I upped my running game, training for a half marathon in my quest to burn calories. Within a few months, the combination of weight

---

* PLEASE do not ask me if I did a "pull-up" or a "chin-up." I neither know the difference nor care. Let me have this one.

lifting, consuming less food (read: barely eating), and running conditioned my body into the leanest and strongest it had ever been. In pictures, you could see the difference, and friends remarked, saying I looked the "best" and "skinniest" I ever had. I won't lie, comments like that went straight to my ego and made me feel proud. But every time someone said this to me, I felt a tinge of something I couldn't quite articulate—something that felt a little like embarrassment, or like I knew I was doing something not great to myself.

This amount of physical activity and watching my diet began to drive me nuts. If I had dinner with friends at a restaurant, beforehand I had to make sure there was something on the menu I could order, or if I was going to their houses, I had a list of totally obnoxious requests that there be no grains, no sugars, no fatty proteins, and *for sure* no carb-laden anything, which really complicates things if your host wants to make it a fun and easy pizza night. And I "couldn't" snack because I couldn't afford the calories. And . . . I was hungry. Pretty fucking hungry, to the point that I'd wake up in the middle of the night craving food. I'd find myself night after night standing in front of the refrigerator at two A.M. trying to figure out what to eat so I could go back to sleep. Sometimes I woke up thinking about bread. At this point, I had to ask myself: *How much further was I willing to go in order to get those early-aughts-Britney abs?*

Turns out, I wasn't willing to go any further. I had worked as hard as I could, the abs hadn't appeared, but a lot of the fun in my life had disappeared. Was a flat stomach even something achievable? How far could a person go? I brought this up with Vlad and he told me something I had never considered before. "You know, it's not really healthy or sometimes even achievable because, as I understand it, women store fat in their stomachs to protect their reproductive organs. It's an evolution thing." *WAIT, WHAT?! Why hadn't Vlad told me this when I first went on my "flat stomach" quest,* I thought, before I asked him that question in a much nicer way: "What the fuck, Vlad?!" "Well," he said with a chuckle, "who am I to tell you how your body should look? My job is to support you, not tell you what you can and can't do." *Ugh, fine, be the kind, professional guy you are, Vlad. Sorry I originally objectified you.*

I realized that I needed to stop focusing on a meaningless and—now I knew—impossible goal that was starting to dictate how I was living my life. What even *were* abs and why did I really care? I had a feeling it MIGHT have something to do with a lifetime of brainwashing by the two-hundred-and-ninety-five-billion-dollar diet industry who needed me to feel bad in order for them to make a profit. After one minute of research, I found that Vlad was completely right, a flat stomach was nearly impossible for most women because *we*—superhuman goddesses that we are—are built to protect our reproductive parts FOR THE BENEFIT OF HUMANITY. The thing I had coveted was impossible and just like my never-fulfilled dream of being a Beatle, it was time to give up instead of torturing myself.*

I now have my own standard about what I want my body to look like and it is . . . drumroll, please: my body. I did nothing to earn it, it was a gift given to me from whatever weird force is out there, and as you know, it's full of celestial glitter, which is WAY cooler than having a flat stomach, can we all agree? I now focus on all the genuinely inexplicable things it can do. For example, what is sleep and how does your body know to do it? Or, how can our joints last as long as they do? Or why does the warmth of my sister's body feel *so* good when we hug? And how have I been given such a privilege of having a body that works the way mine does?

---

* When I saw Peter Jackson's documentary about the Beatles I fell into a depressive state because I knew, definitively, that I would never be the fifth band member who, through mediation and compassion, kept the band afloat AND wrote iconic music. Also, I have never played an instrument, and could not go decades back into the past, so I guess that, too, was working against me.

There are so many who do not have that advantage, and how gross and small is it to criticize something so valuable? No, now I see my body for what it is—a living, breathing, moving sculpture, one of a kind and priceless, worthy of my absolute care and adoration.

There's so much talk of body positivity and body neutrality and whatever new term is being promoted by the time this book comes out. These labels drive me wild because they have weirdly become political (like everything else) and, frankly, how someone feels about *their* body is just none of my fucking business. You see *you* however *you* want and me having an opinion about *your* opinion is intrusive, divisive, and a GIANT waste of time. But what about a term I think we can all agree upon? What about body gratitude? What about the fact that if you have a body, even if it comes with complications and pain, you can ultimately be glad to be on earth? Can we have *some* amount of appreciation for that? What about stopping our relentless judgments and conversations and acknowledging that *any* body is already an incredible feat of creation that can't be explained. I mean, do you know how we are even made? It's mystical and ancient and gives me the lovely, cosmic chills when I consider that my body knew how to grow itself in a womb. Like, what the heavenly fuck?! Each one of us is a mystery at the nexus of art and science, and after spending so much miserable time disparaging our bodies, there is only one thing left to do: Thank them.

A Thank-You Note to My Body

Hey you,

Thank you for letting me be here. Without you, brain, I wouldn't know it, and without you, heart, I couldn't live it. I'm sorry I've been such a dick in the past and I'm going to try really hard not to be a dick in the future. I will not always live up to that standard, but I'm trying to focus on the truest thing I know about you—you are mine and I love you.

Thank you,
The Artist Formerly Known As T$

Maybe this is how you always thought about your body, but for those of us who have not, I know that initially, it might make you feel bad to recognize how mean you've been to your anatomy. I know this because I currently have tears in my eyes for how much self-inflicted mental brutality I've put myself through. That "bad" feeling is self-compassion. We are looking our suffering in the eye, extending our hand, and offering to help. This is the way toward growing back into that eight-year-old in the black, rhinestone bikini, unapologetic and ready to dive into life.

So if you'll do me the honor, can we do something together?

Let's Write a Thank-You Note to a Part of Ourselves We Know We've Been a Dick To

Let's pick a part of our physical selves toward which we have been cruel (because that's really the right word) and give it what we formerly thought was impossible—love.

1. Pick one part of your physique that you have not appreciated and maybe even loathed. I'm going with the weird skin flap that is beginning to develop under my chin.

2. Now let's give it a warm welcome with a salutation of honor.
   ★To Her Highness, the Royal Duchess of Tara, the Skin Flap That Is Beginning to Develop Under Her Chin

3. We'll admit where we've gone astray and be as honest as possible about it.

*I am deeply sorry for spending so much time wishing you away and staring at you like you were a mortal enemy every time I looked in the mirror. I have been hard on you. Just so you know, I don't feel good when I malign you, I feel much worse.

4. Now we are going to affirm all the work this part has done for us:
    *I'm not sure why you're here, but my guess it's because the rest of my body has allowed me to live to this day and you are the hard-won proof. I know you're a part of my neck, which allows me to drink coffee (one of my favorite things in the world) and water (when I remember) and to have a voice. A voice! You make it possible for me to communicate, which makes *everything* better. Tho maybe not everyone agrees.

5. Let's thank the part like we *mean* it:
    *"Thank you" is not enough to express my gratitude, so instead, I'm going to dedicate a new ritual to you, so that every day you feel a little bit of my love: Every day, I'm going to use face cream on my neck and give you a nice little massage. That shit is expensive and precious to me, and it's also the least I can do.

6. Now we sign it, but not with a squiggle and a triangle because we learned from ballot curing that we all need adult signatures.

Love,
Tara Schuster

A Little Thing That Helps

Even with my new perspective, I still find myself bad-mouthing my figure. When this happens, I pause, put a hand on whatever part of me I'm nit-picking, and let it know, "I love you and I'm learning," or I say, "This body is divine," cuz that's the truth.

Mission to Mars
Please Stop Calling Your Colleagues Your Family

HAVE YOU EVER LIKENED YOUR colleagues to your family? Or said that your best friend at the office is your "work wife" or "work husband"? Are you willing to go the extra mile so often that now it's just expected of you? Do you plug away late into the night, missing special occasions with friends and family, and ~~risking~~ destroying your mental health because everyone in your office shares a special familial bond and you are loyal AF to them? Do you find yourself jumping from Zoom to Zoom[*] with barely a moment to catch your breath, forgetting to digest what just happened or prepare for what's next, regularly describing yourself as overwhelmed? Have you ever hesitated to ask for a raise because you know your manager so well that it just feels awkward? Any of this sound familiar?

Many of us think of our workplaces like home and of our co-workers like family. We all have different reasons for how we arrive here but for me, I'm not too proud to admit, it was pure neediness coupled with desperation. When I entered the labor force, my family situation was small and strained. No one lived near me and the only person I spoke to with some regularity was

---

[*] Are we still doing Zoom, BTW?

my dad. I had always wanted a big family—a raucous group with whom I had inside jokes and shared memories from family reunions like that one time Uncle Mark got stuck on the Slip 'N Slide! *Do you remember that?! It was hilarious!* When I started at Comedy Central, I saw the opportunity to have the large, loving brood I'd always pined for. I imagined that a wise, funny senior leader was my "Loving Dad," and I did everything in my power to earn his approval. My actual boss, whose expressions were inscrutable, but who I knew had deep respect for me, I thought of as my "Harsh Dad," and I took his criticisms as statements about my character. Loving Dad regularly took time out of his schedule to catch up with me, and Harsh Dad once told me that he was more exacting on me than the rest of the team because he wanted to teach me how to handle pressure under any situation. Emotionally, I felt like a Ping-Pong ball being rallied between two opposite personalities.

My best friend at work was my "Work Mom," and I'd bolt to her office whenever the dynamic between Loving Dad and Harsh Dad became too strenuous. *MAN, this is all so embarrassing to admit to you.* Many times over, I accidentally referred to my office as "my room." As in, "I'll be in my room if you need me." And "my room," by the way, was cozier and better decorated than the one in my apartment, with scented candles so delicious smelling, people randomly dropped by just for a whiff, a brightly colored rug covering up the industrial carpet, and a gallery wall full of posters of shows I had worked on. I had spent more time decorating my office than my bedroom.

While my friends darted from job to job throughout their twenties, earning new experiences and higher salaries as they leapt from one thing to the next, I stayed put at one company for eleven years, partially because I was too afraid to leave the security of what had come to feel like "home," and partially because my job was mostly awesome and I could not imagine a better way to earn a living than being paid to know about comedy. . . . I mean . . . *how is that a real* *job?* But another reason I stayed was out of a sense of fidelity. When I was offered a promising position at a rival company that would have set me up for a bigger career in an area of television that actually had a future (streaming), I turned down the chance because I thought of myself as "the good daughter," loyal as fuck and afraid of breaking the rules. I reasoned that my work family *needed* me and that they couldn't handle the load without my efforts. The company could control my schedule, lay me off, fire me, tell me what to wear, keep the AC at freezing, speak over me, and determine my economic future, but I just couldn't *dream* of leaving them in the lurch with a project (a project that was technically *theirs,* not mine). I thought I was *the only one* who could handle my share of the business.*

I took my position as the good daughter seriously, persistently educating myself on the changing landscape of media and new managerial techniques I had learned from the countless professional development seminars I attended. I was the Lisa Simpson of the office—informed, well-meaning, but, I'm sure, *really annoying.* And by being a "good girl" (*groan, GOD, no*), I was given responsibilities far beyond my pay grade, which helped me climb the corporate ladder with speed. I relished this special familial treatment because it was a substitute for what I didn't get in my real-life family—a sense that I was valuable and talented. But, the flip side to my job being so personal was that when I received feedback, it felt like it was about *much* more than my work performance. It felt like it was a verdict on me as a human being and it often had devastating effects on my sense of self.

One day, Harsh Dad called me into his office and from his brown leather armchair (how dad-like!) informed me that I was "starting to get a reputation for being too aggressive. You're com-

---

* You're going to kill me and might throw away this book, but if you feel like I did, then I have to be the bearer of bad news: Your job will get along fine without you. I KNOW, *painful.* Yes, even *you.* So, let's step away from the martyrdom vibes, shall we? Says the girl who once, at a work party, proclaimed, "I AM INDISPENSABLE." I was not. I was drunk.

ing on too strong. You need to let the job come to you a little bit instead of always going after it." I don't know how *you* would react to these words, but they went straight into my guts like a spear, penetrating my being with a sharp razor of embarrassment. Set aside the fact that telling a woman she is "too aggressive" is a land mine in the battlefield of things you *really* just shouldn't say given the implied sexism (only men can be aggressive, women should be friendly)—for me, the reason his words were so incisive was that he wasn't just criticizing my work style, he was criticizing *me,* my personality and my status as the "good daughter." My mind filled with thoughts that others must be talking about me behind my back, that I wasn't liked, and that this meant something about me as an individual as my self-esteem circled the drain. Instead of stopping and asking myself, "Wait, is being aggressive really a bad thing?" or "What truth might I take away from this review that will make my *work* better?" I took his critique like a scolding from a strict parent. I felt ashamed and knew that in order to be loved, I had to fix this flaw in me.

I had to change. While I tend to be stubbornly determined and tenacious in all parts of my life (hi, every single person who knows me!), I can also be a mush-ball of optimism and love, going out of my way to affirm others (hi, *some* people who know me!). I resolved to bring the sweet side of me to the office more often, explicitly praising the contributions of others in meetings, and going out of my way to let my colleagues know how much I appreciated them. (I was constantly saying "I appreciate you," *way* before Ted Lasso. Jason Sudeikis, I see you copying my style!)* I brought my

---

* Sidebar: I once was on set with Jason Sudeikis and because I think he's super talented and seems like a nice guy, I wanted to look extra cool in front of him. I set up my "director" chair, a wooden, collapsible seat, directly in front of him, thinking that by being within his eyesight I would . . . impress him? Get him to notice me? For some reason? One moment after I sat in the chair, the entire thing crumpled under me and I fell to the asphalt like a lead weight. Now whaddaya think of me, Jason Sudeikis?

favorite chocolate chip cookies to meetings, I called out the achievements of others in front of upper management, I even tried not pursuing deals or talent as "aggressively" as I might have in the past. Emails came in from my teammates letting me know they were grateful for being acknowledged and that my meetings were some of their favorites (ya know—for the demonic, interminable nightmare that is a meeting). Clearly, I had found my Goldilocks "just right" personality at work and I was *proud*.

Then! One day, as I was sprinting on a treadmill at the gym, trying to exercise a stressful day at the old comedy mill out of my body, I received a call from Harsh Dad. Our biweekly check-in meeting had been moved around so many times that even though I knew this wasn't an ideal time to talk, in fact it was *my* time to decompress, I picked up the phone figuring it was better to just get this conversation over with than let it linger in rescheduling purgatory any longer. I hit "answer" but didn't stop the treadmill, instead straddling my legs on the solid frame of the machine so I could stand still, the belt below me still operating at race pace since this was going to be a quick conversation. Harsh Dad launched right in. "I've been hearing around the office that people think you're disingenuously nice. They think you don't mean your compliments and that you're faking it." It felt like a fully inflated, rock-hard dodge ball had been heaved directly into my stomach, my breath completely knocked out of me on impact.

Dumbfounded, I told my boss that I was having trouble hearing him because of the cellphone reception and hung up. *First, they thought I was too aggressive? Now too nice? How can I win?* I stepped back onto the treadmill, ready to REALLY go after this run, completely forgetting that the treadmill was *already on* and moving at eight miles an hour. I put one foot down and—WHAM, I was ejected off the back of the machine into another treadmill behind me like something from a lesser Jim Carrey slapstick comedy. As I lay crumpled on the ground in a true state of shock, a trainer who had seen the whole thing go down darted over to me, scooped me up in his buff arms, and deposited me on one of those tables that trainers use to "stretch" clients but that often make it look they are doing a lot more than stretching? As soon as he laid me down, I broke into tears.

I have to tell you that launching off the back of a treadmill in the middle of the gym due to receiving professional criticism has got to be one of the most humiliating moments of my life (which is saying SO MUCH), and because it was so extreme, so visible, it prodded me into considering that maybe, just maybe, my office would *never* be my home, and it was time to stop acting like it was, because, ultimately, thinking that way was becoming literally painful (the bruises were already forming on my knees).

After that mortifying fall (From grace? IDK what that expression means but I like the word "grace"), I decided it was time to bring a different version of myself to work. Instead of trying to please people with my winning personality, I focused more on the actual business at hand, talking less about my personal life, going to fewer after-work drinks and meals, trying to become a better listener to those around me, and directing personal conversations back to, well, work. Funnily enough, just as I was trying to cultivate a more professional identity, HR launched a campaign urging us to be our "whole selves" in the office.*

In one meeting, they showed a graphic of an iceberg meant to represent an employee. On the surface of the iceberg—which signified the parts of us that everyone can see—there was a person's race, the language they spoke, and their age (tho in LA I'm not sure how easy it is to gauge anyone's age; given the beauty standards and anti-aging regimens, someone could be thirty-six or sixty-six and I wouldn't know the difference). We were then told that there

---

* I think this happened because more traditional companies were trying to imitate Silicon Valley to stay hip, but just like open floor plans, it was a terrible idea from the start. Also: a Ping-Pong table in the office does not qualify as a "work benefit," k?

was no need to hide what lay below the surface: our social class, background, mental health issues, or religious beliefs. In order to be "authentic" workers, we were encouraged to bring our vulnerabilities, our emotional lives, ALL of ourselves into the office.*

As I sat in the overly air-conditioned conference room (again, they controlled the AC and for some reason were interested in petrifying us all in ice), I became increasingly sure that this HR training had it wrong. My own *parents* couldn't handle my whole authentic self; hell, sometimes *I* couldn't handle my whole self, how on earth could my colleagues? And what about those with more extreme mental and physical health issues? Were we really the best people to "see" them for who they were, to responsibly handle their most fragile parts? Having zero training, might some of us judge others—and maybe even treat people with less respect? It seemed deeply unwise to proclaim we were in a "safe workplace" without taking any of the steps necessary to earn that designation.

I stuck to my strategy of being a more professional version of myself without losing any of my enthusiasm for the job and over time, I gained more respect from my colleagues, which allowed me to take bigger swings, and eventually I felt more comfortable, safe, and oddly, *more myself* at work because my personality and my "whole self" were no longer on the line. Just my "work self." This also made me a better team player because I focused less on my individual need to prove myself as a worthy member of our work family and more on how I added to the group. I was more likely to think of the good of all in the long term, laying up assists for colleagues and engaging in less office politicking and gossip because, just, *enough*. Truly, if you have time to be a gossip in the office you have too much time and need a new hobby for the benefit of us all. While I used to be casual with my workmates, spending lots of

---

* Did you see this chart, BTW? Was it in every HR training in the year 2018 and onward? Did you also think it was weird to use an iceberg as the symbol for self since icebergs are famously harbingers of doom?

time socializing, I became more professional and again *felt more like myself* (!) because the lines between my job and my life were much clearer to me. And I didn't feel like a corporate robot AT ALL. I still joked with and genuinely adored (many of) my colleagues, I still offered compassion and all the help I could when someone was dealing with a personal issue, but I no longer saw the office as some weird substitute for family.

Here's the thing: No matter what anyone says, no matter how much time you spend at work, or how much HR rattles on about office culture, the actions of a company will always reflect *their* best interests, namely making money. Because it's a business, plain and simple. And unless your family is set up as a strictly hierarchal organization that maximizes profit over all other considerations, a company will never be like family. End of story. As Adam Grant, the thinker and organizational psychologist, and one of my personal heroes, notes in his newsletter, *Adam Grant Thinks Again,* there's another reason not to model your work life on your family life: "Families are dysfunctional!" In fact, research shows that when kin and commerce mix in family-owned firms, it often breeds environments of "nepotism and selfishness and irrational risk-taking."* *No thank you* to that!

Now, you might view this as a somewhat cynical and maybe even a tad bit resentful take on workplace culture but to me it's been monumentally liberating. Just as I don't want to bring my "whole self" to my job, I, frankly, don't really want to meet anyone else's whole selves, either, at least not in a professional context. I'm not a mental health professional, therapist, or life coach equipped to deal with all the problems and intricacies of the people I work with and neither are my boss and co-workers, and that's for SURE not why any of us signed up for our jobs unless we are actual therapists.

* Adam Grant, "No, a Company Is Not a Family," *Adam Grant Thinks Again,* January 31, 2022.

So how the hell do we expect Morty,* who dressed up as Santa Claus at the Christmas party and forced younger staffers (me) to sit on his lap, to really "see" us and "give space for our feelings"? You might want to take your chances with that one but I don't.

I'm not saying that we need to hide ourselves but it can actually backfire to be our most genuine selves at work. I have to quote Adam Grant one more time because he is just so smart; in his podcast, *WorkLife,* he points out that a meta study of more than twenty thousand people found that "on average, the more people focused on being themselves at work, the less successful they were. . . . [T]hey got lower performance reviews and fewer promotions."† It turns out that revealing too much about ourselves can lead to others questioning our competency. Do you really want to risk that? Just as you would show up to a date with a romantic partner differently than you would dinner with your sister, you have multiple authentic selves and choosing a work self that is more professional than personal exposes you to less risk, plain and simple.

AND OH GOD! We haven't even talked about the sosh med yet! The rise and ubiquity of social media has made it increasingly difficult to set boundaries between our work selves and our personal selves. A 2018 study, "Friends Without Benefits: Understanding the Dark Sides of Workplace Friendship,"‡ suggests that one of the pitfalls of "friending" or "following" a colleague on social media is that you don't have the same control you would have IRL to filter what others learn about you. Your exposed feed is an open invitation for your colleagues to judge you for your

---

* Not his real name but God do I wish I knew a Morty. Such a good name.

† Adam Grant, "Authenticity Is a Double-Edged Sword," *WorkLife with Adam Grant,* April 7, 2020.

‡ Is this not an incredible title BTW, so ominous! Julianna Pillemer and Nancy P. Rothbard, "Friends Without Benefits: Understanding the Dark Sides of Workplace Friendship," *Academy of Management Review* 43, no. 4 (2018).

lifestyle choices, perceived wealth, values, *anything,* and it can even incite jealousy if you are unwise enough to post a picture of yourself with another colleague—or worse, with your boss—where others weren't invited. Nobody wants to see you at an exclusive BBQ with the person who signs the checks. It's bad for morale on every conceivable level.

It's on us, the worker bees of all levels, to present business selves we feel good about, and it's up to our employers to provide the resources, time off, and benefits so that experts, people trained in these domains, can actually help us or so that we simply have the time, the sweet precious *time,* to help ourselves! Because sitting through a one-hour management class on how to deal with the emotional life of an employee when you were mostly on your cellphone scrolling Instagram is not exactly the three thousand hours of professional experience needed in California for someone to become a licensed therapist. And here's an idea: Instead of your boss rewarding the team with #ThirstyThursday drinks, how much more helpful would it be if you had those hours off to go to the doctor or dentist—to deal with your REAL life?! Wouldn't that be way more appreciated?

It should be the responsibility of our workplaces to give us the support and space to take care of ourselves, not to pat themselves on the back because they provided us with a birthday cake three years ago and know the term "unconscious bias." In order for us to be the best we can be at work, wouldn't it make sense for our companies to *invest* in us like they would any research, marketing, or new resource because employees are the ultimate resource? *That* certainly aligns with their bottom line.

Rather than thinking of the office as a home and my colleagues as family, I now have a much more powerful, professional, and, I think, ultimately healthy way that I view a workplace. I see a job, in a best-case scenario, like a mission to Mars. Hear me out on this analogy, please, because I think you are going to really agree.

Why Your Job Is Like a Mission to Mars

1. **There is nothing casual about a mission to Mars.** You better bet that everyone at NASA is aligned with the mission and performs their duties expertly because *it's a mission to Mars!* The stakes are high! There's no time to overshare about a romantic issue or to sit through endless Zoom happy hours (a contradiction in terms). The focus is the mission. And if a team member needs time to themselves or professional help, that is taken seriously and resources are deployed to them. But the electrical engineer never has to step in as a marriage counselor for an astronaut because that's simply not their area of expertise.

2. **Your CEO/president/boss person is the launch director.** The launch director sets a clear, attainable (if ambitious) strategic vision for the entire company and gives them the resources to accomplish it.

3. **The executives and managers are mission control.** Mission control takes the launch director's objective and decides exactly *how* they are going to get from Earth to Mars. All departments in mission control—marketing, IT, finance, operations, etc.—can't let cliques or territorialism or politics get in the way because, again, *mission to Mars*. Each domain is essential and needs its *own* vision that supports the overall mission, but no department can survive on its own. You can't have a marketing department if there is no product to sell, but it's also hard to sell a product without marketing. It's mission control's responsibility to carve out the time, space, and resources, not to burn out the employees.

4. **The employees are the astronauts (!!).** If the launch director gives the destination and mission control comes up

with the plan, then it is the astronauts who interpret and execute said plan. The astronauts know the real conditions on the ground (erm, in the air) and must be trusted to work with autonomy because micromanaging them would be dangerous to all (you can't have mission control loudly squawking in your ear during your space walk). If, however, mission control is checked out and barely cares, then the astronaut won't feel the motivation nor will they have the backup to complete the mission. If the astronaut has a problem they can't solve on their own (they are out of astronaut ice cream, say), then it's their duty to alert mission control and for mission control to secure whatever the astronauts need to get the assignment done. Astronauts do not bring their whole selves to the spacecraft, they bring their competent, incredible, innovative work selves to the job, so they are judged on their performance, not on how well liked they are. Also, an astronaut can't take work home with them and can't be expected to, which is a huge benefit of the job.

5. **The launch is the goal.** All of these departments join forces to catapult their spacecraft (or product) to stratospheric success. To an outsider, it might look easy, but the squad knows all the excruciating striving that went into the spacecraft fighting gravity (the endless meetings, the rounds of market testing, all of the hard realities of doing business) and making it into space (the marketplace).

Doesn't that framing make a whole lot more sense than a family? I'm not saying we can't have fun at work, I'm not saying we need to skip Brenda's birthday cake, but actually I do need to skip it (I'm more of a savory than sweet person—I would go if it was pizza or veggies and dips). Maybe instead we could recognize the incredible grind of those around us more? I think the fact that I was called "disingenuously nice" had nothing to do with me. I think that compliments were just so rare that mine stuck out as odd. We should tell Alexis that the way she managed communication with the difficult, indecisive client was stellar and ask her to share her strategy with all of us both so we can learn and so Alexis can get some well-deserved shine. We should tell Monika that her nonjudgmental leadership and ability to not be reactive in contentious situations makes it safe for everyone to take calculated risks. And given how hard launching anything is, why not throw a parade for the entire crew when these milestones go right or when we successfully navigate away from crisis?

If you think of the workplace as a space center where everyone has different jobs but the mission is unified, there is less friction overall, less chance for squabbles and miscommunication and letdowns and hurt feelings and taking things personally. Most of us already have a family of some sort, but how many of us have a *flight crew*? Suit up, my competent, responsible, innovative friend whose best work is yet to come. There's no limit to how far you can go.

A Little Thing That Helps

When my body tenses up and I feel like I NEED to send this email NOW, that is how I know not to click "send." I get up from my desk and go for a short walk to give myself time to cool down. Nothing good comes from my desperation emails. Also: If you're not comfortable with every single person you know reading the email you're about to send—don't send it. Cuz that possibility is just one "forward" away.

Ask a Question, Listen to the Fucking Answer

Communication Hot Tips

THE NIGHT BEFORE I MOVED to Arizona, I did something incredibly wise, healthy, and in my own best interest: I downloaded a dating app, created a bio, and started scrolling through my prospects in Los Angeles. Because why *wouldn't* it be a good idea to, in a doom-spiral-out-of-body-panic-experience, start dating someone in Los Angeles *twelve hours* before moving to Arizona for an indeterminate amount of time? WHAT COULD GO WRONG?! The real reason I wanted to scope out potential gentlemen callers was not because I wanted to be in a relationship, it was because I ached for those sweet, sweet likes. For years, if I was feeling soul-level bad, or even mildly annoyed, I used dating apps to self-soothe. Each person who right-swiped on me was a tiny victory (and a dopamine hit) that told me I was valuable and wanted. Like I said, HEALTHY.

I figured my last-minute dating binge was harmless because there was no way I'd match and chat with anyone *that* quickly. I would be in the dating world only long enough to be a cat burglar of likes, quietly and quickly robbing some men of their validation before exiting without a trace into the Arizona night. If you are right now thinking, *But what made you so sure you would get likes and* *not passes?* let me tell you! With a certain curation of photos—the tasteful but *tiny* bit risqué bathing suit pic, the well-edited and filtered portrait, and of course, the full-body shot in which you stick your leg out, lean back, put one hand on your hip to create a triangle, and lift your chin in a contortion worthy of a bronze medal in gymnastics—I can *guarantee* you likes.* Now, a healthy, real relationship where you can be your genuine self and fall in love? That is an entirely separate subject of which I have precious little knowledge.

I lay down on my too-small sofa, my phone held in my outstretched left hand above me as my right index finger scrolled through human beings as if they were menu items, and came across Oliver, a seemingly attractive man who listed his hometown as London. *Hmm . . . could this be one of those London boys Taylor Swift so appealingly sings about?* I swiped right.

Within moments, London Boy was messaging me. "Hi, Tara, did you know we matched before, on another dating app?" he asked. "I feel like a jerk but I don't recall! If it helps, I also don't remember what year it is today," I typed back. "LOL, no big deal but I'm glad we matched again," he replied with a few well-chosen happy-face emojis. I realized it was pretty ~~uncool~~ callous of me to be on this app if I knew I was leaving the next day, so, in a pang of human decency, I disclosed to London Boy the truth. "I know this is annoying, but I'm moving to Arizona tomorrow and I don't know when I'll be back. So, it was lovely to meet you and I hope we match yet again!" I explained. "Wait, wait!" he rapidly typed. "I work in music, I can make you a road-trip playlist! Let me call

---

* To my gentlemen friends reading this right now: Your dating app photos are trash. No one cares about your ski photo where you're leaning against a stake in the ground denoting the distance to Mount Everest. And it's impossible to tell what you look like with sunglasses on in a group shot. Plus, don't even get me started on why so many of your photos are puzzlingly taken either in the bathroom (a place not known for romance) or from the ultra-unflattering "under chin pointing upward angle." Delete *everything* and ask a woman in your life to help you help yourself.

you!" *Oh boy, what I have I gotten myself into?* I thought as my heart fluttered. Okay, he could call me, *but!* only for his music recommendations. I was NOT going to date anyone long-distance while I was in Arizona. That would be difficult, limiting of my options, and a distraction from my mission to help with the election.

You know what happened, right? The *second* I heard his soft upper-crust British accent all of my resolve melted and all I could hear was Tay crooning, "You know I love a London boy, boy, I fancy you."* I ended up phone-dating Oliver from Arizona, texting him during the days and talking to him almost every other night. It was fun, and sexy, and I loved hearing his aristocratic words roll off his tongue. But there was one pesky, non-ideal detail: He never used that delicate and delicious accent of his to ask me personal questions. Like, ever.

When I told him the reason I had moved to Arizona was to "ballot heal," he didn't have a single follow-up question. *Hmmm . . . maybe he knows what that term already means?* I gave him the benefit of the doubt. One night, I finally mentioned that I had written a book (something I really try to hide early in a relationship because you try telling a new dude that you wrote a book based on your childhood of neglect and psychological abuse before your drinks have arrived at the table—it doesn't really "set a mood") and while I thought he'd say something like, "Oh—what's it about?" he had no questions, no comments. Finally, I decided to test him, like anyone does in a healthy relationship. As we wrapped up a call one night, I said, "After I finish my volunteering tomorrow I'm going to explore a *volcano,* I'm so stoked." "Great, talk to you later," he flatly responded. *WAIT, WHAT?* I hung up the phone as my jaw dropped to the floor. Who wouldn't ask for the particulars of a

---

* BTW, London boys do NOT LIKE THIS SONG. And especially not *this* London boy. Apparently, there is some anger and questioning over the veracity of Tay's knowledge of London. Because songs have to be 100 percent factual and contain no creative license. If you didn't know before, now you know for sure—you have a full Swiftie on your hands. . . .

volcano? I mean, how many volcanoes were there even in the WORLD?! In what universe was a volcano odyssey just another mundane, ignorable detail of someone's day?

When I moved to Arizona, I had promised myself that I would be more honest and up front with people, because it wasn't something I was good at. I avoided (and still avoid) confrontation (though I'm really trying to do better now!) and often ended up trying to make other people feel better after *they* hurt *me,* insisting that I was "fine," even as my heart broke. So I decided to tell Oliver how I felt.* "Hey, I don't think you are doing this on purpose, but when you don't ask me questions about myself, it makes me think you aren't interested in me, which makes me feel unvalued and bad," I explained. "Oh my God, no, that's not what's happening at all!" Oliver quickly interrupted. "Let me explain. I was once backstage at a concert and Jay-Z walked into the room. Of course, everyone knew it was Jay-Z, but you don't want to act like you're totally intimidated, right? You don't want to seem like *you're* a nobody. So you just give him a nod without letting him know that you are in total awe of him," he explained. My silence conveyed how confused I was, so Oliver clarified: "I'm very, very interested in you but I'm afraid that if I ask questions about you, or seem to be too keen on you, you'll think I'm a nobody and lose interest in me."

For my whole life (and I bet a solid portion of yours too?) I had thought that if someone didn't voice their curiosity about you, or if they exclusively monologued about themselves, the only possible explanation was that they were self-centered and not eager to know you. But Oliver turned that assumption on its meticulously coiffed, London boy head. He wasn't asking questions precisely

---

* Although, I'd like to point out that I really bristle when someone (usually a romantic partner) declares, "That's just my truth," followed by a long, meaningful pause. I have never once heard it used in a way that was not to excuse some questionable and often sketchy behavior. Just say what you mean, we don't need the preamble.

because he *was* interested in me and he was scared of what I would think of him. Mind. Blown!

The more I thought about it, the more I was able to see that asking questions is the sex of communication. In order to "do it" you have to lay yourself down, totally exposed, and admit that you don't know something but that you want to. You also can't predict precisely how the other person will react to you—maybe they'll laugh, or feel offended, maybe they'll turn off the lights because they don't want to be seen?—but you need them to engage. All you know is that you have laid down your armor in a bid for intimacy.*

As I sat dumbstruck in my condo in Flagstaff, I had to ask myself: If I had been so wrong about the meaning of Oliver's lack of curiosity, what else was I getting wrong about communication in general? Had *I* been truly listening to Oliver as he told me about his life? Or was I so irritated by his lack of questions that I spent most of our conversations retreating into my mind, spinning stories about what this all meant and scheming about how to get him to ask me questions without actually absorbing anything *he* was saying? For real, what *had* Oliver said? He worked in music but what did he do? How long had he lived in America? What was *his* favorite road-trip music? It dawned on me that maybe I—infallible me—was a part of the problem in our communication. He wasn't a great question-asker, but maybe it was also true that I wasn't a great listener.

The reason I had the impression that I might be a poor listener, aside from the fact that I had retained zero information about Oliver, was that often (like, every-day often) I would forget the names of people I had just met *and* what we had discussed. Even when we had talked about extremely serious and important things! I could have a heartfelt conversation with you about your nasty divorce

---

* I hope you find this analogy helpful and right on and not gross.

and how you felt like you would never find love again but three days later have absolutely *no* recollection of your face, name, or the salient details of the exchange. I'm really not trying to be an asshole; I just act like one when dialogue amnesia hits. It's the amnesia's fault, not mine, I swear! There were also many, many times when, as someone spoke to me, I mentally checked out, crafting my response before they finished talking or letting my mind drift to the other things I needed to do that day. And Zoom culture didn't exactly help my cause.*

In an effort to get more of an understanding for what it took to truly, effectively listen to others, I turned to the small collection of books I'd brought to Arizona with me, with a hunch that the one written by a Zen priest might have some answers, cuz what are those dudes doing on their cushions all day *aside* from listening and cultivating mindfulness? Maybe they were getting annoyed at their Internet relationships like I was, but I suspected they probably had more wisdom than that. In his book *Taking Our Places: The Buddhist Path to Growing Up,* the author Norman Fischer's definition of listening is "to simply be present with what you hear without trying to figure it out or control it."† *Fuck.* That felt like a personal attack. What did one do in a conversation besides try to figure it out or control it?! Wasn't the whole point of talking to figure something, or someone, out? In dating especially, wasn't the goal to look as good as possible while simultaneously trying to manipulate the other party into liking you?

I resolved to train myself to be a better listener, and using Norman Fischer's book, the Buddhist psychologist Tara Brach's trainings on receptivity and presence, and my own meditation practices,

---

* If we are video conferencing, 70 percent of my attention is allocated to looking at my own image, 10 percent is set aside for (not so) clandestinely scrolling through my phone, and the remaining 20 percent is divided among my to-do list, some of what you are saying, and praying this Zoom will soon be over. You know it's true for you too.

† Norman Fischer, *Taking Our Places: The Buddhist Path to Growing Up* (HarperOne, 2003), p. 44.

and begging my therapist for tips on how to "stop being the jackass who doesn't really listen to other people," I came up with my own tools for how to actively listen.

1.   **Listen to *yourself*.** I noticed that often, if I thought something like, *Ugh, I'm so jealous of Chloe and her family's vacation to Bali, where everyone is staying in luxury tree houses,* I usually dismissed it as "bad" thinking and tried to ignore it. But I now realize that the feelings I wanted to dismiss were popping up because they wanted to be *heard* and if I rejected them, they didn't go away, they simply morphed into an anxiety din that hung around me constantly, distorting my hearing and giving me a headache. To become a better internal listener, I worked through my "parts"* more frequently, and if in a conversation I heard internal chatter that made me uncomfortable, I would pause, try to be as nonreactive as possible, and later I'd try to decipher what part of me had been speaking up. As attachment-theory pioneer John Bowlby wrote when explaining how important our earliest communication is in forming our identity, "What cannot be communicated to the [m]other cannot be communicated to the self," meaning that if a child is angry, let's say, but doesn't have the safety, space, or ability to communicate their feeling (to their mother in this case), they end up disowning and disavowing that emotion. It's hard to hear yourself when you've been drowning out your internal dialogue your whole life, and it becomes impossible to hear anyone *else* if you are distracted by your own internal conversation about how you should and shouldn't feel.

---

*   Remember? From way back when from the chapter about loneliness. *Keep up!* That's a note to myself because I got a little lost.

2. **Listen for clarity.** When I couldn't tell the difference between my many irrational fears and my true gut instincts, I just decided to go with whatever sounded and felt more true in that moment in an effort to amplify the voice of my intuition. If part of me said, "Don't bother with that guy, he was sketchy about plans and you met him while you were drunk, outside of a pizza place, how great can he possibly be?" instead of endlessly weighing the pros and cons of "how should I act?" I just went with what felt truer than not. I let go of needing to be "right," maybe I would be wrong but I just wanted to hear what within me was most clearly speaking. And by the way, I was right about drunk pizza guy. His Insta was full of Lamborghinis and videos of him "in da club," need I say more?

3. **Gauge whether you are READY to listen.** I am a completely different person at seven in the morning than I am at seven o'clock at night and I needed to respect that. If a romantic partner wants to have a serious conversation while I'm getting ready for work, it's on me to decide if I have the capacity to be present. If I'm stressed and rushing and bound to be a terrible listener, I can say, "I really want to be present and hear what you have to say but I am totally distracted right now. Can we talk about this tonight at six when I'm done with work?" I can also do this with friends who sometimes just need to vent. I want to listen to them but simply can't if I'm also in a mad dash to finish a document. Of course, the key is to return to the conversation, and it's on me to make sure that happens. But it's worth it because I know I'll be fully present for it and ready to truly listen.

4. **If you are the listener, ask the speaker what they want and need from you.** Do they want to vent to you or do

they want your advice and opinion? One of my own pet peeves is when someone tells me how I "should feel," or offers me unsolicited advice, so I always make sure to ask, "How can I be supportive?" at the onset of a conversation, and if they have no clue I offer two options, "Would you like me to lovingly and supportively listen to you vent or would you like advice or potential solutions?"

5. **Listen with your whole body.** So much of communication is nonverbal; it's in the way we smile, laugh, in the way we nod our heads. I use my whole body to take in information and often validate the other person's emotions. "That sounds so annoying," I affirm while nodding my head. "I am so excited for you!" I exclaim with a huge smile on my face. I try to make sure my entire body is in the conversation so that the speaker really knows I am taking in their words, ESPECIALLY on Zoom where emotion and interest are hard to read.

6. **Don't get it twisted.** I often repeat back in my head what the other person is discussing so that I am internalizing their words. It helps me pay attention and absorb their message. Sometimes, I even repeat back to them, aloud, what they just said to confirm I didn't confuse things. The benefits of this are manifold:

   a. It forces me to pay attention because in order to repeat anything, I have to hear it the first time!

   b. When I say something aloud it makes it more likely that I will retain the information.

   c. It helps clear up misunderstandings immediately. I can recap my takeaway and make sure I'm on the same page as the speaker. For example, if I'm understanding YOU correctly, you just said you want to turn this book into a movie and that you think I have great style. *Thank you so much.*

More than anything, I've realized that most people really want, and in some cases are desperate, to be seen and heard. Often when people feel misunderstood or hurt, at the bottom of it all is the feeling of not being acknowledged, so by tuning in and validating my nearest and dearest, I can give them a gift I know they'll love.

Sticky Communication Q and A with Tara

Q: I don't like my best friend's boyfriend, he's totally the kind of guy who cheats, should I say something?

A: Yes, if you no longer want to have a best friend. Otherwise, absolutely not! Unless your friend is in physical danger or there's something egregiously wrong, of course. But if we're just talking about a "bad feeling," or not liking him, it's not your place to insert an opinion because #Boundaries. On top of which, who are you to stop a friend from learning from their experience? On top of which! what if they get married? Hmm? I'll tell you what—you'll stick out to them as the disapproving friend and the whole thing will backfire because they won't come to you when Bryce *does* eventually cheat on them, just like you knew he would. *Fucking Bryce.* I know you mean well, but the way to help your friend is to simply be there, not tell her what to do.

Q: I know my friend didn't mean it, but she really hurt my feelings. Do I say something?

A: The "therapy wisdom" I've heard most often on this one is that if you're close with the person, you can ideally express anything you're feeling. But I can't imagine always abiding by that. For example, let's say you lose your job and a good friend of yours chimes in for the group consolation text at the beginning, but then doesn't check in on you months later? It hurts your feelings, but is it even worth it to tell him? I use a tool developed by the spiritual writer Eckhart Tolle. When someone's behavior really bothers you, you only have three options: Speak up for yourself, change the situation (as in expand your friend group or maybe give this person a little distance), or let it go—just nod your head and kind of laugh at it. This is what I now always do when I'm not sure if it's right to say something because who are we kidding, some things we just need to let slide and hope our friends let things slide with us too.

Q: I want to choose to speak up! But how do I do that?
A: I use this formula: "When you did X, it made me think/believe Y, which made me feel Z." So, "When I lost my job and you didn't check in on me, it made me think I wasn't important to you, which made me feel disposable." It's rare that someone is going to bite your head off when you are that level of vulnerable. Generally, those closest to us, if they learn they have inadvertently made you feel shitty, want to mend the situation. Your friends, if they are friends, I promise do not want to make you feel shitty.

Q: But I'm scared! What if they get defensive and angry?
A: Then you know a lot more information about this person. Confident, self-assured people don't get super sensitive when you tell them your feelings, because they recognize there is nothing to defend against—you're simply telling them how *you* feel.

Q: Okay, but let's say I get critical feedback, what if I'm the one who didn't check in? Now what do I do?

A: Breathe. Listen. Remember you are not bad, and remember that it's GOOD AND HEALTHY for other people to tell you how your actions made them feel so that you can examine yourself, clear up any miscommunication, and ultimately grow. When I'm on the receiving end, I listen as hard as I can and then repeat back what has just been said to me so I make sure I understand how the person feels and validate them. Even if I disagree with them, it's never useful to deny how someone else feels *no matter what* because that's not something you can control. Instead, use this as an opportunity to learn about the other person and yourself. You have just stumbled upon AFGO (Another Fucking Growth Opportunity).

Q: Okay, but what do I do in the moment? How can I say something smart instead of getting flustered?

A: Um. I don't know because I can't do this. If you are able to overcome your surprise, shock, pain, whatever feeling that comes up, *and* to respond kindly, thoughtfully, and coherently . . . then you are some kind of communication superhero. Don't beat yourself up if you struggle to say the "right" thing in the moment. The fact that I am not good at comebacks has saved my ass so many times from saying something I regret. So choose the "let go" option and cut yourself some slack. You can come back to this later. There's no benefit in being quick to the draw in these situations.

Q: When I tell someone "no" to a plan, I feel like I have to explain myself, but then I end up overexplaining or sometimes even lying. What can I do?

A: This one depends. If I'm saying "no" to a best friend, then they probably deserve an explanation, but it doesn't have to be a long-winded excuse involving a migraine, a work project, and my aunt's health. Keep it simple. If it's an acquaintance, you can just say, "No thank you," or "That sounds great but I can't," with a smile.

Q: Is it okay to ghost someone?
A: Only if you want your soul to suffer. I know that's extreme but it's kind of not. People aren't disposable, it's weird and unkind to just stop talking to them and it's bad for your sense of self to ignore a fellow human being. Unless, OF COURSE, they're harassing you or there's a real reason to abruptly cut off contact. That's not ghosting, that's protecting yourself and I applaud you, *brava*.

Q: But Tara, you completely ghosted me after our first date, how do you explain that?
A: *OH wow!* I totally didn't mean to! The thing is . . . I had a migraine that was so terrible that I couldn't see and I also had this huge work project and my aunt wasn't feeling well so it just got lost in the shuffle! I'm *so* sorry!

A Little Thing That Helps

I want to be the kind of person who knows the name of everyone who works in my favorite bookstore or coffee shop. But since my memory is shit, in the notes section of the contacts in my phone, I'll write something to remember each person by. "Chevalier's Books, Dan, smiles, suspenders." "Tara, amazing writer, chic as hell."

The Hot Rabbi
Deal with Depression Before It Deals with You

I TRIED TO MAKE MY rabbi my casual hookup. Well, not *my* rabbi because I'm not completely sadistic and I didn't want to alienate myself from my own synagogue should things go fakakta, Yiddish for "messed up," so I guess "a" rabbi would be more of an accurate description.* This rabbi was handsome—not handsome "for a rabbi," just flat-out "Wow, you're very good-looking, sir, would you mind if I ran my fingers through your purposefully tousled, gelled into a 'just woke up' sculpture of hair?" He was funny (*drool*), stylish, sporting sparkling new black-and-red Air Jordans (*get it, Rabbi!*), and above all else, he was SUPER into God, which was something that, as you know, I wanted for myself, so when a mutual friend offered to introduce us, all I could say was *"l'chaim"*!†

I LOVED the idea of dating a rabbi, mostly because, in a different life, I would want to *be* a rabbi. I have no interest in becoming a rabbi in *this* life because there is no way I could pick up Hebrew

---

* Shout-outs to my Rabbis Brous, Kasher, and Tsadok. It's not that I have anything against you, I just like to maintain a separation of church and state.

† A Hebrew expression of joy meaning "to life!" To get the vibe of it, just remember the Black Eyed Peas song "I Gotta Feeling," or listen to it for the first time. I might be the only one, but I think this song really holds up.

this late in the game. I took French for eight years in high school and college, lived in Paris—where I attended a French university for a semester and dated a man for seven months who ONLY spoke French—and the best I can now muster is the grammar and eloquence of a three-year-old: speaking slowly as I grasp for words and completely avoid most verbs. "Why is it because I am not able to make the work on my computer here?" and "If you please, sir, I would like this one here in chocolate, please," being my most-oft-used phrases. If I could barely order food in French, how would I ever be able to learn Hebrew *and also* talk about high-level concepts like the personal experience of God or the epically storied tradition of Judaism? The answer is: I wouldn't. *But if I dated a rabbi?!* That had to get me AT LEAST one step closer to the animating force of the universe and the gates of heaven! Though do Jews have heaven? I actually didn't know, and that was *exactly* why it would behoove me to date a rabbi.

~~My friends~~ I started referring to Simon, the rabbi in question, as "the Hot Rabbi" and was eager for our first date, trying on at least four thousand outfits in anticipation, determined that my look match the beauty, mystery, and power of the four-thousand-year-old history of Judaism. Could I wear a short dress, or would that be too much for a holy man? Were bare shoulders allowed? When I was a kid, I seemed to remember they weren't, but at my own shul,* the leader, Rabbi Brous, didn't give a fuck what you wore as long as you were using your life to relentlessly pursue justice and you were down to sing the Beach Boys' "God Only Knows" at the end of services.† Was Simon Orthodox? And what was that, aside

* A word I only recently learned means "synagogue."
† If you're looking for someone to inspire you, animate Judaism, and help you find your moral footing in a multi-faith and multi-generational setting that sometimes serves Scotch, look no further than Rabbi Brous at Ikar (a Los Angeles–based but global synagogue). Google "Rabbi Brous Kol Nidre Sermon 5780," one of my favorite sermons of all time. I dare you not to feel your own heart break and come back together again.

from something TV shows at the time (unfairly) made to look like extremist groups? You might be surprised to learn that I, a totally modern, rocketing-to-Mars woman, was so willing to alter how I dressed for a guy—but I had an agenda. The way I saw it, my first job was to ensnare the rabbi in a love trap. Then, when we got married, which was obviously going to happen *soon* (because you can't casually date a rabbi) I would drop the act and wear whatever I wanted.

I'm stalling a little bit here because I need to tell you that a quirky, sexy rom-com vibe is not where this story is headed AT ALL. This is not going to be my update on the amazing 2000 movie *Keeping the Faith,* starring Ben Stiller as a rabbi and Edward Norton as a Catholic priest who grew up together but who both question their faith when their childhood friend, the enchanting Jenna Elfman (where did you go, Jenna Elfman?!), comes back into the picture and hilarity ensues.

Instead, right here and now I am going to hit you with a trigger warning: This story is about depression and suicidal ideation (didn't see that one coming, did ya?) and so if that is something you do not want to read about, if it would ruin your day, or at least mess up your afternoon, please skip ahead to the next chapter. I'm not being glib or joking around. Please protect yourself if you need to. If, however, you feel comfortable reading about what it feels like to trek through that darkest night of the soul and make it into the morning light, or if you want to commiserate about how fucking awful that experience feels, or perhaps if you have the inclination to learn some skills to help others who find themselves in that rayless place, then this story is for you.

Okay! Where were we? First-date outfit! I settled on a short, body-hugging black dress with a black "all-business" blazer and white Converse sneakers because I'm classy like that. I met the Hot Rabbi at a low-key, hip Korean BBQ joint where he ordered us beer and soju and was very much interested in my suggestion that we end the night with some hardcore karaoke bar action.* "I'm so down to go *all out* tonight," he said with a laugh. "Work has been tough this week." I instantly wanted to know more. "It must be kind of intense for a synagogue to be your workplace. What's that like?" I asked. "I'll tell you, but you have to promise me I'm not your token rabbi, okay?" After seeing my puzzled expression, he turned serious as he explained, "Sometimes women get involved with me thinking I *am* my profession and that by dating me they're gonna learn more about Judaism or somehow get closer to God but my *job* is to be a rabbi, it's a job that's really important to me and that I love, but it isn't the whole of me. Ya know? I don't want to be someone's experiment or funny story they tell their friends about someday." *Um . . . yes . . . sure . . . I wasn't doing that AT ALL, Hot Rabbi.* "Oh, so weird, I never even thought of that!" I lied, feeling singed by embarrassment.

As the booze loosened us up, Simon revealed why his week had been so stressful. "All I want to do is my rabbinical work—teaching Torah, it's my calling and the thing I'm best at. But I end up being so tied up by useless committee meetings, weird political situations, and paperwork that I only spend a fraction of my time doing what I'm actually good at." As I listened to him rattle off his complaints, I realized that not even rabbis were exempt from the monotony and frustrations most of us experience at work. His description didn't match with the cliché I'd imagined his job to be: a harmonious and blissful refuge for the soul where all he did was burn incense and bless babies all day. "But it's a great place to work, ultimately, right?" I asked, fishing and praying that the Hot Rabbi would say something to show me that even with those flaws, the synagogue was still a place of holy commune. "I mean . . . it's a

---

* My go-to song is Alanis Morissette's "You Oughta Know." If we got enough women together in a witchy communion to scream-sing this anthem, I bet we could raise Ruth Bader Ginsburg from the dead. Do you have a go-to? DM me cuz I need more options, please!

place to work. Truthfully, I'm re-evaluating everything. The bureaucracy has been demoralizing."

I found myself getting sweaty and nervous (and not because he was hot, which he was, have I mentioned that to you already?). I realized that despite my initial curiosity, I didn't really want to know how the synagogue sausage was made because it threatened my perception of something dear to me. Temple was a sacred place for me. You see, aside from the fact that it's literally sacred, immersing myself in that community had become the most reliable way I could pull myself out of a depression sinkhole.

Since childhood, depression had been my shadowy playmate, lurking in a corner until she threw a fit and demanded all of my attention. When I was sixteen, I went through my first major episode after my mom was admitted to the hospital with an illness that doctors could not initially diagnose. My mom called me, sobbing, "I'm so scared, I'm on my deathbed, you have to come visit me." But I wasn't so sure that was a good idea. First, you already know the tortured relationship I had with her. Second, she had feigned or exaggerated medical issues and injuries since I was a small child. One time, as we walked to our car in the parking lot of Staples after buying me new school supplies (the best day of the year for me!), a car drove uncomfortably close to us. My mom dropped to the ground and wailed, "They've run over my foot! They've destroyed my leg! I COULD DIE!" as my Lisa Frank binder, mechanical pencils, and rubber cement bottles came tumbling out of the shopping bags she had been holding. I collapsed down next to her on the asphalt, frantically yelping over her body, "Maybe you're okay, Mom!? PLEASE don't die!" Soon enough, my mom got up, gathered the school supplies, and walked me back to our car, apparently just fine to drive. So, when she called me from the hospital "on the brink of death," I didn't know if I could believe her.

And at this point in my life, my parents were in the midst of a divorce so acrimonious that it would take ten years to settle and would cost them all of their money and energy as they waged vicious campaigns to ruin each other's lives, never realizing they were destroying *all* our lives in the process. Hands down, the most traumatizing part of this divorce was when they decided to separate me and my sister. My sister lived with my mom and I lived with my dad. It felt like they were divorcing *me* from the person I loved the most in the universe. My parents made no plans or formal arrangements for how my sister and I would *ever* spend time together. Instead, I had to barter with my mom for playdates with my little sister. My mom was especially cruel during these negotiations, yelling things like, "You torture your sister and all you value is status and wealth and it's disgusting. When the wave comes no one can predict what will be washed away." This was her magical combo: a cruel jab about something that was wrong with me paired with a bleak reference to some greater wicked force in the world that I did not understand. Her words trounced my self-esteem and made me feel like I was the most horrible person to ever exist.

And yet. For all that, somehow, I optimistically held out hope that one day my mom would change and see that I wasn't monstrous—that I was good, and decent, and deserved love. Maybe it was naïve, but I wished that my mom would find a reason to love me and treat me tenderly. So when she called me from the hospital, gasping with mania, I was deeply conflicted. I was afraid of her and angry about how she treated me, but at the same time, if she died, and I hadn't given her a final chance to mend our connection, then I would seal my fate of never having a loving mom.

Finally, I decided to go to the hospital, but I knew I needed my dad to come with me. My relationship with him wasn't perfect either. As you know, he made me feel unsafe and like I was in charge of his emotional health, but I had always had faith he was a dad in *some* way and that as flawed as he was, if I *really* needed him, he would drop his selfishness and be by my side. It was one of the few comforts I had—if things got really bad, I thought, I would always have my dad. But when I asked him to accompany me to the hospital so that maybe he could protect me from my mom's potential barbs, he was . . . not generous. "Go to the hospital? For *that woman*? She's trying to *destroy me*! There's no way I'm going anywhere near her. She's wrecked my life!" His words felt like a sucker punch to the gut. While I always knew I didn't have a mother, this was the first time I had asked him for emotional support and he rejected me. I felt the most alone I had ever been. My sister had been taken from me, my mom was apparently breathing her last breaths, and my dad wouldn't help me. There were no aunts or uncles to call, no godparents, no mentors or even friends, because I was so ashamed of every last detail of my home life that I never told anyone about it. I crawled into bed that night helpless, deserted, in despair.

When I woke up the next morning for school, it seemed to me that I had lost the ability to lift myself out of bed. I was surprised, I could move my arms but even as my brain screamed at my torso to get up, I just couldn't get vertical. I felt like I was being weighed down by wet cement, like a freshly laid sidewalk was built on top of my skin pushing me deeper and deeper into my mattress. My dad knocked on the door. "Tara, you're going to be late," he shouted. But I couldn't move; I could barely speak; and I couldn't imagine that I would ever not live in this bed. I wanted to be asleep forever.

I don't recall how that episode ended, but it was not the last I would endure. My worst was triggered just a few years ago, when I went on vacation in Brazil to celebrate my tenth anniversary of re-parenting myself. It was the most daring solo adventure of my life, an expedition to Iguazú, the world's largest waterfall. Located in a lush and still wild rain forest in Brazil, the rapids are among the Seven Wonders of nature. The explosive curtain of water is so grand that upon seeing it, Eleanor Roosevelt is rumored to have exclaimed, "My poor Niagara!"

I had splurged on a bright pink hotel located within the national forest so that I could see the falls before the park opened, though I quickly questioned my decision when, upon check-in, the front desk's receptionist handed me a brochure listing the dangers of jaguars in the area. When I smiled, thinking it was overkill to shield the hotel from liability or maybe a little overhyped to give all of us tourists a thrill, she put her hands on the desk and solemnly warned me, "They broke into my car last night. A big SUV. They tore it apart, who knows what they could do to you." *Okey dokey . . . So. I would be on the lookout for jaguars!*

Because I don't have the strongest concern for my physical safety, as you know, my first morning in Jaguarland, when the park was completely devoid of people, I took a run on a catwalk above "the Devil's Throat," a horseshoe-shaped part of the falls where rushing water drops down to the river below in a sheet as tall as the Statue of Liberty. As my Nikes bounced off the metal grating, my soul leapt up with joy. The falls were throwing off a mist that looked like liquid glitter in the morning sunshine as it landed on my skin and woke up my whole body with gratitude. I had triumphed. I had overcome a harsh start at life, I had stopped the neglect I had lived through by taking care of myself, I no longer saw the world as a pure threat, and now I was the kind of person who could write a book, go on countless adventures, and take a victory lap over a waterfall just cuz she wanted to. In other words—I was the shit.

Annoyingly high on life, with a dumbass smile plastered across my face, I returned to my hotel room and looked at my phone, where there was a text from my roommate and best friend, Lauren, who was back in Los Angeles. "Hey, roomie, I know you're on vacation but you need to know . . . we were burglarized. Everything is a mess. I don't know what they took but they smashed in your window and I think they got your jewelry."

In that instant, even though I knew I was safe and standing perfectly still in my hotel room, it felt like everything within me was rapidly cascading downward and plunging through the floorboards with a force that could match Iguazú. I felt like something was pushing me down, holding me under violently churning water, my head visible just below the surface as I drowned, unable to see or catch my breath or help myself. Though deeply disoriented, I had the presence of mind to text Lauren, "Are you okay???" before quickly calling her. "Can't pick up, I'm with the police," she replied. "But I'm fine, no one was injured."

I was relieved that Lauren was unharmed, but I felt totally flooded by this sudden loss. See, despite everything that had gone deeply wrong in my life, my jewelry was the proof that I had been loved, that I had mattered. As a kid, the only sign of affection I did receive with some consistency was trinkets. The turquoise heart necklace my mom had given me on Valentine's Day when I was ten, the silver charm bracelet with a Scottish terrier, a clown, and a snowman my dad gave me for my twelfth birthday, the gold-and-pearl bracelet my deceased grandmother had left me, all of these things stood in for what I always ached for—love and connection. And so, I imbued them with special meaning, treating them like relics that redeemed my miserable childhood. The jewelry was tangible proof that I wasn't totally worthless.

Because I counted these objects as my absolute most important possessions, I had always held them close and taken excruciatingly good care of them. Through the never-ending construction site that was my childhood home, through the initial back-and-forth of divorce before my parents separated me and my sister, through college, through every apartment move and life upheaval, I had kept track of my jewelry—and frankly, everything I owned—so well that I could count on one hand the number of times I had *ever* lost something. I was maniacal about knowing where my things were at all times. But after all that, someone had just waltzed into my closet and taken it all away. . . . I'm embarrassed to admit how bewildered I was, because I know these were just "things," and I was *so* lucky that Lauren and I were safe, but I was undone. I felt like the identity I had earned as someone who could take care of herself and avoid disaster had been snatched away from me.

I flew back home to the rainiest winter I'd ever seen in Los Angeles. I felt engulfed by the perpetual gray clouds and my own grief. *I let those precious items be stolen. How could I be so irresponsible?* I thought, blaming myself both for the burglary and being an ungrateful, vain piece of shit for caring so much about their loss. It was my Christmas vacation from work so I didn't have my job to distract me, and my closest friends were all out of town with their families. I was alone, just like I had been as a child, with no one to comfort me. I spent days in bed crying under the sheets, at times unable to move, just like when I was sixteen. I lost five pounds in just a few days as I stopped eating and doing much of anything. Brushing my teeth alone felt like an unfathomable exertion of energy. Still, I denied how depressed I was, because I felt I shouldn't care about losing things. I was consumed with hate for all parts of me—the part that was depressed, the part that knew *I* was actually the bad guy, not the robber, and the part that felt sorry for herself for being so shaken over something so trivial.

After at least a week of this, and without a therapist to help, one day I decided that *I* was the only person who could help myself and that I would have to if I ever wanted to leave my bedroom. I turned to the one place where I found consistent safety—my journal—and poured out everything my rational mind knew about depression as I brainstormed ideas for how to help myself.

Eventually, I drafted a plan for lifting myself out of the bowels of severe depression:

1. **Stop denying the truth.** I was depressed and couldn't wish it away. Instead, I let myself *sink in.* I'm talking Fiona Apple on full blast, *Eternal Sunshine of the Spotless Mind* playing in the background. I didn't drink any alcohol because I was afraid of how I might behave or think but other than that, I allowed myself to do any "bad" thing I wanted. Sleep for a day? Marathon the *Real Housewives* until three A.M.? There was no way I was "supposed" to act other than whatever felt natural.

2. **Strip your to-dos down to the bare minimum.** All of the rituals, all of the things I "had to" or "should" do, I let fall away in a bid to make my life as simple as possible. What was ONE thing I needed to do to be a human? Not a good human, not a productive human, but just an alive human? And after each task, I would celebrate myself. If I could brush my teeth I would tell myself I was a GOD. If I ate a peanut butter sandwich instead of saltines I would celebrate for being the fucking Julia Child of depressed cooking. I REFUSED to think about the future beyond the present moment. My only responsibility was to be depressed and keep my life simple.

3. **Reach out to your community—your closest friends, your church or synagogue or sponsor, to any community—to remember that your life is enmeshed with others'.** I forced myself to see friends even though I really, really did not want to. I went to temple to be around people who were singing songs and praying and not melting down, to remember—*I won't always feel the way I feel.*

4. **Don't freak out if you fall back down.** I realized that part of standing up from depression is toppling back down, it's inevitable. And when I did, rather than punish myself, I treated myself. I took a loving action like taking a bath, or drinking tea, any small, kind thing to boost me up.

5. **Repeat steps one through four until you feel like your-self again.**

And all of this was the reason I was nervous to date the rabbi. (Yes, that's where this story started and I appreciate you letting me take you on a meandering ride. I promise the destination will be worth it, at least for me.) Going to synagogue was my refuge from depression, and the Hot Rabbi knew everyone at my synagogue and visited frequently. I realized that if we were to break up, I would probably feel uncomfortable seeking refuge in my spiritual home. I knew I was playing with fire, and not in a good Moses-at-the-burning-bush-being-given-an-awesome-mission-to-rescue-his-people kind of way but in an uncontrollable-wildfire-that-has-decimated-everything-in-its-path kind of way.

As Simon and I continued to date, it quickly became apparent that he and I were incompatible in almost every single conceivable way. And not in a cute "opposites attract" way. I couldn't find anything even slightly entertaining about how out of sync we were with each other. When I suggested an afternoon of walking and gawking at the glorious houses in my neighborhood built in the 1920s (ancient for LA), he scoffed, "Who cares about a bunch of rich people's houses?" On a movie date at home, I asked him if we could watch something light and fluffy, and he suggested *Minari,* which turned out to be about the harrowing struggle of a family to make ends meet. The movie culminates in a devastating fire and was so depressing that I asked multiple times if we could stop watching it. "It's one of the best things I've ever seen," he protested, refusing to turn it off. When, one Sunday, I suggested we go to the farmers market in my neighborhood, he griped, "Ugh, no, I don't want to run into anyone from my congregation." I thought I understood. "Oh, because you don't want to explain me?" "No, not at all," he replied. "I just don't want to see anyone. I don't like people." It was odd. *For a rabbi.* Although I don't love being social all of the time, I did LOVE running into people at the farmers market because how cute is that in an otherwise not-cute culture?

It was obvious that Simon and I weren't going to work out but I decided to give us one last date, one last chance to get to know him and find some common ground. On a hike I asked him, "So, tell me about your parents?" "They're happily married, twenty years of bliss. It's almost intimidating how in love they are. I talk to them almost every day," he explained. I fake-laughed. "I'm so jealous, that's not my family at all. I actually no longer speak to my mom." Catching his quizzical look, I continued, "She was . . . abusive. Always lambasting me or feigning medical problems. Or other things that I don't really want to talk about. And at a certain point I decided I was worth more than allowing myself to be put in emotionally damaging situations over and over again." Simon was silent at first. "You know, the Ten Commandments *command* us to honor our mother and father. You're going against that. . . . Are you sure you want to make that choice?" His words were like a mallet beating on my heart and making every nerve in my body throb. Not speaking to my mom was not something I relished; it was an excruciating reality, close to the worst-case scenario! "It's not like I'm in love with this situation," I stammered. "I wish things were different, but they're not. I made a determination, for my health, to protect myself." Simon considered this and then explained, "You know, part of my job is to be the stopgap for family situations like this. To be the one who intercedes and says, 'You only get one mom, do you really want to do this?' "*

Aside from Simon's advice being generic, it cut me to the quick because he, the expert, someone trained and paid to be in the service of the divine, was saying that I was hostile to God's will. I hadn't ever considered before that in protecting myself I could inadvertently be going against the universe. Though I am not particularly religious (I'm spiritual but I don't follow all of the rules of the Torah—mostly because I don't know the rules!), in that moment I felt just as alone and misunderstood as I had felt when I was sixteen and couldn't get out of bed and later, in the aftermath of the burglary. As we finished the hike I fought back tears behind my oversized sunglasses, feeling like such a weirdo, with such a strange family, so solitary in my experience that a rabbi, the person whose whole job it was to comfort and relate to people, was telling me I was doing something wrong.

Hurt, and keenly aware that we were not meant to be, I texted Simon later that night (because he said he "hated" talking to people on the phone), explaining that while I had loved getting to know him, I didn't see much of a future for us because we were just too different. He agreed and we decided to part ways as friends. But the moment he conceded I felt pinpricks in my ears. *Why wasn't he fighting for me more?*

"Wait," I texted him. "What if we just casually hook up? We know that part works!" I wrote, my throat constricting. "That's tempting but you're right, we fundamentally don't work, ya know? What's the point?" he shot back. I felt tears rise. "But maybe we're supposed to date. I know that you see the world dif-

---

* If you think this is very close to what Charles said to me in the journaling chapter about my having only one dad and needing to mend that relationship—you win a special prize! The prize is the sucky feeling of being condescended to and mansplained about something deeply personal by someone who has NO FUCKING IDEA what they are talking about. Not much of a prize, huh? I'm sorry for both of us.

ferently than I do, but I could love you if you'd just open up a little bit," I desperately texted him. "Listen, you're a bright, shiny personality, you see the glass as half full and I think the glass doesn't exist," he rationally explained. "But maybe if we just hook up and treat this casually, we'll both relax and find out we are into each other?" I ~~almost~~ begged. "I'm so confused, you texted me to break up, I agreed, and now you're trying to get me to change my mind?" he wanted to know.

He was right. We were not compatible in the least, which is why *I had broken up with him*. But now, only a few messages later, I felt a profuse sense of panic. I started sobbing, pathetically, sitting on my bed, baffled by my own behavior. My vision becoming cloudy, I went to my medicine cabinet and kicked back a fairly heavy benzo. And then another.

When I woke up groggy the next morning, it was to a melancholy matched with a panic that blasted through my body as if my life was being threatened *right that second,* like those jaguars from Brazil were lying at the foot of my bed. I was safe, in my own home, but my nervous system responded as if Simon had left me stranded at the bottom of Iguazú and I was paddling as hard as I could.

After three days in a purgatory between horror and depression, which felt physically exhausting and gut wrenching, I began to think about how much better it would be if I were dead. That seemed like my best option. I had spent years healing myself, and in fact, I was, up until this moment, the most mentally healthy I had ever been. But what had it all been for? I was still a fucking mess. What did that say about my future? Nothing good. The discomfort of feeling so rotten was becoming intolerable, my depression and fear clawing at my mind with no end in sight. I felt trapped and so, so guilty.

Who could I talk to about my suicidal thoughts? I had written a book about self-care, had spoken at conferences about ways to love yourself, and now I wanted to do something considered hateful and irrational by just about the whole wide world? *I am such a fraud,* I thought. I couldn't turn to my friends because I had leaned on them too much in the past and for sure at this point I was a burden to them. And my therapist? She was probably working with people more important than me, people who had "real" problems, and wouldn't I let her down by being in such shambles?

Not knowing what else to do, I decided to go on a walk on my favorite nature trail where, even if I was totally miserable, at least I was miserable among my favorite living beings—trees. Still crying, I set off in the dust. It was a weekday, so there was no one there to see me trudge down the trail wailing aloud, "Why, God, why?" and "Please help me." From a bird's-eye view, it was probably funny (or offensive?)—a privileged white girl in high-waisted, cutout Lululemon spandex, in one of the safest neighborhoods on planet Earth, in no immediate danger, cry-walking and calling out to the sky like her life was in danger. But. My life *was* in danger.

It's very hard to explain this if you've never experienced severe depression or suicidal ideation but it can make you feel full-body sick, like your insides are going to leap out of your skin or, sometimes, like every muscle is paralyzed. It's an excruciating kind of agony that you want to end at all costs. And you *believe in your bones* that you will feel like this forever. You forget what it is like to feel good, or even okay, and you lose all hope that the future will be any better. As I continued down the path, I approached a cliff and looked down, to the bottom of the canyon below me. *What if I just . . . ran forward?* I thought. *What if I jumped? Would I die or just be paralyzed?* If it was "just" being paralyzed, then I wanted no part. If the fall could kill me, though, wouldn't that make all this agony go away?

I edged closer to the rim of the cliff, and then a little closer, my hiking shoes now hovering just over the ridge. As I started to play with shifting my weight forward, a different part of me came online, a part that cried out, with all the force she had, *Danger! Step back! Stop! No!* This voice startled me into taking one giant step backward, after which I fell to the ground. Sitting in the dirt with tears streaming, I pulled out my phone, left a message for my therapist, and texted my close friends Fisch and Julia, "Guys, I'm not good. I'm having really dark thoughts. I'm scared for my safety, and I need help."

Fisch called me right away. "Schustey, what's the matter?" she asked. "Fisch, I'm so desperate and scared. I want to die and I'm afraid I'll never *not* want to die and I'm in so much pain and I'm so humiliated," I moaned. "I'm so sorry, I'm so, *so* sorry, what can I do?" she asked, alarmed but reassuring me in her tone that she was there and wouldn't leave me. "I just feel like . . . I'm so unneeded and alone and in so much pain. I'm sorry, I'm ashamed to call you like this. I shouldn't need you so much." "Schustey, are you kidding me? *I* need *you.* You are the sister I never had and the aunt to my children and you get me, you *get* me, and you've always been there for me. I've never once thought that you're a burden; you're a *blessing,* you make my life BETTER." She began to cry a little. "I don't want to know what a life without you would be like. I wouldn't be me if there was no you."

I had always looked at Fisch as the model of a good human being: endlessly kind, REAL—never one to fake an emotion or pretend things were any different than they were, but also *so down to have fun,* always while wearing some fabulous outfit because her taste was iconic. She had been my rock for fifteen years and I had always felt like the deal was uneven, like I was on the winning side, getting so much more from her than I could ever give, but in this moment, hearing that someone I intensely loved and *needed* needed ME gave me enough purpose to walk off that trail, get into my car, and drive home.

I started going to therapy twice a week and instead of working on my wounds, we created a safety plan that could help me when I plunged into anguish so severe it seemed death was the only way out. Dr. Candace gave me a tool to use when experiencing suicidal ideation, and I found it so helpful that I would like to share it with you. It's a systematic approach to managing big, overwhelming feelings, especially when one is thinking about self-harming, developed by Lisa Ferentz, a clinical psychologist and expert in the de-pathologized treatment of trauma. It's called CARESS.

CA: Communicate Alternatively

For ten minutes, find a new way to communicate your pain and emotions. This could be through journaling, drawing, painting, stream-of-consciousness writing—any form of communication.

RE: Release Endorphins

Raise your heart rate. Run in place, do jumping jacks, dance, do anything that gets you a little breathless for a few minutes. When I am in a dark place, or even just a shitty mood, I do burpees and push-ups for *immediate* relief, even if it's minor and temporary. I know it sounds ridiculous, but it helps get you back into your body (i.e., out of your head) and into reality.

SS: Self-Soothe

Indulge in any soothing activity. Rock your body, sway back and forth, wrap yourself in a blanket, hug a pet, take a bubble bath. My friend Sarah (the one who gave me the term LadyGod) sent me a stuffed animal I named Baby the Bear to hug and I use it to this day when I need to give myself some solace. Is it silly for a grown woman to clutch a stuffed animal? No, it's lifesaving.

After you follow these steps, rate your danger level on a scale of one to ten. If you're starting to steady and relax your emotions, keep repeating CARESS until you've calmed yourself to a tolerable level. If you're feeling the same or worse, it's time to call a mental health professional.*

* * *

As I worked in therapy to wrench myself out of depression's tight grip, Fisch, Julia, Sarah, and my sister, who I finally told the truth of my feelings to, checked in on me daily for over a month. We developed a code word for if I was really in a terrible place so that they could immediately know to come grab my hand and pull me up from the underworld. I didn't have to explain myself, or feel embarrassed, I just needed to text them a single word and they would snap into action.

Looking back, I see now what I couldn't see then—my downward spiral was not about the Hot Rabbi, or dating, or about me being weak or unhealthy. Ironically, it happened *because* I was healing. For years, I had made every effort to bring my emotional wounds to the surface so that I could tend to and alleviate them, and in so doing, find freedom from my trauma. But it wasn't until recently, through my soul work, that I finally had the resilience and wisdom to reach down to the little abandoned five-year-old who lived inside of me and grab her hand. She had been alone for thirty years, with no one to comfort or even witness her, but now that I—a safe adult whom she could trust—had shown up, she could let loose the torrent of emotions within her and whisper to me her darkest, but totally rational, secret: She wanted to end her agony.

---

* If you are having thoughts of harming yourself, there are many free resources available to you. Dial 988 for the National Suicide Prevention Hotline (available 24/7). If you want to talk to someone who specializes in the LGBTQ community, call the Trevor Project (866-488-7386) or text them by sending START to 678-678. Help for the Day offers resources for people around the world at https://www.hftd.org/find-help, and https://nowmattersnow.org/skills offers videos to help you.

We often think that suicidal thoughts or actions are the byproducts of severe, lifelong, unsurmountable mental health issues, or that someone has to be irrational or selfish in order to contemplate ending their life. But that's not me, and I have been to this dark place more than once. We don't like to believe it, but there are some things in life that feel so unbearably bad—abuse, neglect, enduring extreme physical pain or disease—that we would do *anything* to end the suffering they cause. That's what we want to end— that suffering. It's not irrational to want to end suffering. And the more we admit this—that suicidal ideation is not something reserved for one kind of person, that it can strike *anyone* given a certain set of circumstances—the more lives we can save because we take away the *shame*. Think about it—if you've heard your whole life that people who consider suicide are profoundly "crazy" and self-absorbed, how likely are you to tell someone if you are having thoughts of disappearing? While I in no way advocate that we glamorize suicide, I do think, for the sake of the people we love the most, it would be a great service if we put ourselves in their shoes instead of looking at them as other. And if you are lucky enough to be in my shoes, today they are size nine-and-a-half gold Salvatore Ferragamos, so you're welcome.

I can also say that when my friends asked questions instead of barraging me with advice and solutions, or told me how much better I'd feel in the future (something I couldn't imagine would exist), I felt a lot of relief. When Fisch asked, "How is right now for you?" or when Dr. Candace asked, "Can you describe to me the pain in your body?" or when Sarah boldly asked, "Are you thinking of killing yourself anymore?" I felt like they were truly connected to me, not embarrassed for me, not desperately wanting me to be different, not running away from me. And connection to other people, well, isn't that always a part of what saves us?

So what am I trying to tell you with all this? First off, don't fuck your rabbi. Second, clichés and well-meaning phrases like "It will get better" and "I can't imagine" are not particularly useful to anyone, including yourself. *Try* to imagine, try to imagine what it would take to think about ending your own life before giving someone else advice. Even if all you have to say is, "That sounds so hard and I'm so sorry," that's a fuckton better than, "Look on the bright side!" Like, please. *No one* wants to hear that. As I write this, I feel fat, hot tears pooling in my eyes because I have such compassion for my own torment and for the torment of anyone who has experienced this. This is why we *must* touch and comfort our own sorrow if we are going to help anyone else, because if we don't, how can we ever truly empathize? So, can you see how your healing is my healing and how much I need you? And I bet that other people need you pretty badly too. We might even fight over you, cuz we know you're a big deal, full of potential love, and deserving of so much. But I'll leave all that for another day. For now, will you join me in fighting for us all?

A Letter to Anyone Contemplating Suicide

Hi there,

How are you? Well, I probably already know the answer to that question—NOT GREAT, to say the least? I, too, have been "not great," and those times were, without a doubt, the loneliest, most soul-crushing experiences of my life (and I've been getting Brazilians since I was sixteen so I know a thing or two about pain). I know we haven't technically met (Sidebar: Don't you think the fact that you are currently physically close to me in some form is pretty damn intimate?), but I do know that you aren't bad, or worthless, or irredeemably damaged. If I were with you right now, I would hold you so close to my skin that you would get a nose full of my amber-scented perfume, and feel a little uncomfortable because you'd be wondering why this stranger has you in a death-grip hug. I would ask questions like, "How is this moment for you?" "How does this feel in your body?" "Are you thinking of harming yourself?" Maybe you could write about it in the pages of this book, so I can share what you're thinking and feeling right now. I'm not ashamed of you in any way, I'm with you, right next to you, and I'm not scared of your darkest thoughts. Can you hand them over to me? Can I carry the weight with you?

Your feelings are valid. How could they not be? I think it's brave that you are even willing to admit your mood given the fact that most of us LIE ALL DAY LONG about how we feel, including myself. Today, when I went to the pharmacy to pick up my antidepressant (Wellbutrin) and the pharmacist forgot to fill it for the *second day in a row,* I wasn't angry-bordering-on-furious-bordering-on-murderous because *I desperately need my fucking meds.* Nope, not me. I was "fine."

Look, I don't know that your life will get immeasurably better and that all the pain you've endured will be healed. But here is what I do know: *You are needed and you are loved.* Please listen carefully as I say that: *You are needed and you are loved.* Even if you don't feel that way right now, even if you think you don't have anyone in your life who loves you—let me burst your bubble: *I* love you. *I* need you. I don't need to know you to know that you and I are connected by that weird animating force of the universe, by our stardust. My fate is tied up with yours, we are lucky enough to walk this earth at the same time, and given that the place is such a shit show, we really need all players on deck right now. And you might just be the MVP.

I also know that tomorrow will be different. You know that, too, even if you feel that things will always be the same. So, all I would ask is: Can you hang on until tomorrow? And if you can't, can you call someone to be with until you can hang on until tomorrow? Because you are needed and you are loved and while today might be a total piece of shit garbage nightmare that any reasonable person would want to excuse themselves from, you have no fucking clue what tomorrow might bring.

And that's all I'm trying to say—you don't know shit. SORRY, I love you, but you really don't. You don't know what you'll be like in a week, or who you'll meet this month, or what new adventure you could go on next year, or who is going to come into your life. You just don't know, and since you don't know, since you don't have enough information to make a final choice, can we wait this out a little?

I love you and I'm grateful you're here. And, again, you don't know shit. That's a good thing, because the mystery of your life is still *unfolding* and it would be a real shame if you ducked out and missed out on what could be.

Your friend and part-time lover,

Jara

A Little Thing That Helps

The time to work on depression is when you're in a good place: Go to therapy and research online resources, they exist. Create the game plan for how to help yourself when you are well, not when you are depressed. Working on tools for depression when you are depressed is like learning to swim as you drown. Not easily done.

III.

GLOW

She Cute

Reconnect to Your Essential Self (You Do Have One)

I'M SWAYING MY HIPS FROM side to side and throwing my arms in the air like I'm doing a solo version of "the wave" while singing my heart out to Saint Britney Spears's "Toxic" (which is tied with "I'm a Slave 4 U" as one of my favorite songs of the millennium).* My outfit is *on point*: white Converse sneakers adorned with red hearts, cutoff jean shorts, a pink rhinestone-and-sequin tank top that looks like woven, shimmering cotton candy, and, of course, hot-orange kneepads. Can't forget the kneepads. You see, I am letting *loose* at a guided, all-female dance party in downtown LA. I'm attempting to have more "fun" in my life and my friend Milana suggested that I check this out.

Without any dudes around, there is no chance someone will creepily sidle up and try to grind on me. WHAT A RELIEF THAT IS! I had never fully realized how omnipresent freaking was, how I subconsciously braced myself for random bros to rub against me every time I went out dancing.† This new understanding comes to

---

* Another contender is Timbaland's "The Way I Are"—which, when played at max volume and bass, is a perfect piece of music. Don't you agree?

† Sidenote: How strange are freak trains? How odd to be in a line, legit humping another human being while one humps you. Stranger still, in my day this dance move was broken out most fre-

me now because I feel their absence profoundly. AND THAT AB-SENCE FEELS GOOOOD.

I feel . . . *free*. Free to take up space, to move my body any which way, and at this very second, free to drop to the ground and start doing a dance-slash-crawl move, slithering my limbs as if they were snakes, really making sure I get a return on my kneepad investment. The music shifts and hundreds of women are ushered to the back of the cavernous hall. As soon as we are settled, an actual, professional dance squad, some decked out in neon blue leggings, some in hot-pink leotards, some wearing a thong-thing *over* their leggings (which I'm oddly into), burst into a choreographed dance number to Ciara's "Goodies." Another classic.

They stomp, spin, and jump to the beat in perfect alignment, their bodies pulsing with joy and health. The dancers are so solid and alive and in sync with one another—it truly is a sight to behold. I'm transfixed with just how spectacular bodies in motion are and how much skill it takes to dance. *Woo-wee,* these women are hitting their marks in unison, their perfectly articulated movements blending into this vibrant light of YES. The deeper I get into watching the dance, the more I feel connected, alive, and just flat-out *good*. I suppose this is "fun." Mission accomplished.

A few days later, at the office, in my work attire of a silk blouse, black jeans, and no kneepads or outside-the-pants-thong-thing (tho I am considering it), I see I have a DM from Milana on Instagram. It's a video from the party, of me watching the big dance number. Everyone else is standing still, noticeably frozen in place as they watch the routine in motionless respect. But there I am, in the back of the line, bending my knees, bouncing up and down, moving my head to the music, snapping my fingers to punctuate

---

quently at bar and bat mitzvahs in front of parents, grandparents, and . . . God. What were we thinking? We weren't, we were *way* too horny to think.

the beat. Milana has literally caught me dancing like no one is watching. I see myself in my purest form—glittery, enthusiastic, and . . . *trusting*. I trust the world—or, this environment—to let me be me. *All* of me is free to shimmy and to shake. Milana messages, "I can see your inner child and she cute!" As I rewatch the video and think about the words "glittery," "enthusiastic," and "trusting," I know Milana is right. She has captured some essential part of me on video and I have to agree—*she cute*.

Many of us believe that we have lost our most authentic selves. Some of us think we never had them to begin with—we might believe that our trauma happened so early that we never even had the chance to meet the people we were born to be. Others think, *Maybe I HAD an essential self, but the world, my parents, my circumstances, my inability to deal with my circumstances, all of these things screwed it up too much and I won't ever be able to recover it!* We think we no longer know the self that desired nothing more than to chase butterflies and tell adults what unicorns are made of (*ice cream and hugs, obvi*). For a long time, I, too, thought that I didn't have a fundamental self. Or, even if I did have one, she was super fucked-up and not to be trusted.

I couldn't discern the critical, damaged parts of me from the healthy, vibrant me underneath all the BS. But after a lot of healing and growing I've had the space and ability to meet my pure, unharmed, shiny, beautiful, vital self. *Can you believe that? I mostly can't.* I even know how to get back to her when I go astray. And the more I've talked to others on this journey, the more I've guided workshops, the more I've seen that we ALL, every single one of us, no matter our situation, have that very same stardust spirit inside of us. Google did not lie to me under that star field in Arizona. We might feel a little disconnected from the magic within, we might not even trust it (yet), but that doesn't mean that it isn't deep within us, totally pure and already shining, even if we can't currently see it. The best part of all is that we don't have to make that part up, there is nothing we have to fix, improve, or spend money on to create—*it is already here.*

If you are having trouble finding faith in yourself, if you often find it impossible to make and trust your decisions, if you regularly feel like there's just *something wrong* and you aren't living the life you want but you thirst to, then brava, my friend, brava! The first step in finding yourself is noticing you've lost your bearings to begin with *and* feeling compelled to do something about it.

That's *you*. I mean, there's no way you would have read this book this far if that wasn't true. So, let me whisper something to you that kind of blows my mind. Come a little closer, will ya? Here goes: You know what all of that discomfort is, right? It's the vital spark within you, flickering brightly, trying to get your attention, shouting, "Um, *hello*? Let's get moving! We don't have all day." That restless pull is cautioning you that it's time to change course, and I don't know about you but I couldn't be more grateful that we have a "don't waste your life" early detection warning system embedded within us.

Together, with practical tools, we are going to rediscover ourselves, find our passions, learn how to draw beautiful boundaries; we are going to meet our future selves who can guide us along the way, we are going to channel some of our greatest hurts into our power and energy, and we are going to glow, oh baby, are we going to glow. If that sounds way too ambitious to you, please know that you can trust me as your guide. My qualifications are unparalleled for this journey. I can successfully do one pull-up AND I can operate a pressure cooker without inadvertently blowing up my apartment. You see? *I know what I'm talking about.*

I think of the self within us as a lamp that someone threw a heavy blanket over. When I look at it, it makes me nervous and uneasy, worried because I know it's dangerously hot and could erupt into flames. I inch up to it, scared but knowing I need to take the initiative. I muster all my courage, whip the blanket off, and am blinded by the light of a shine that was there the whole time, exquisite, not dangerous. The *blanket* was the dangerous part. Together, we're going to unleash your incandescence so that you can weather any storm, from the resurgence of trucker hats (*why, God, why?*) to losing someone you thought could not be lost. We are going to find a place in our selves where it's possible to stay grounded even when the details of our lives—our relationships, our jobs, our health—are very much up in the air. Because I love you, but things are *always, always* up in the air; we don't get life breaks where things feel "chill" except in retrospect. If you're counting the days until everything calmly falls into place, you'll be waiting on the sidelines of your life for a long time and I don't want that for you. Do you? Together, we're going to help you uncover the person who makes an active decision as to how they react to all circumstances beyond their control (so everything) because *that* person is very much you.

So let's find our quintessential selves and bring them out to dance so wildly and live so fully that everything we touch turns to glow.

A List of Ways to Catch a Glimpse of Your Essential Self

These are the questions I ask myself to get in touch with my soul, and yes, I did just write that sentence. I try to incorporate my answers into my daily life to revive and sustain myself.

1. Describe a scene of yourself as a little kid that exemplifies *you*. If you can't think of one for whatever reason, what were you like as a child more generally? Cheerful, stubborn, nosy? Enthusiastic? Bookish? Joyous? Shy? Just try to

remember what being yourself *felt* like, when you had no reason to pretend to be anything else. (If you're really stumped—don't worry, I got you, just give me a minute!)

2. Think back to as far as you can remember. Did you have any special clothing as a kid? Was there one thing you just LOVED? For me, it was *always* handbags. What about a toy? Think back to what young you adored.

3. What did you want to be when you grew up? Even a *hint* of an answer is good.

4. When I was a child, I was weirdly obsessed with _____. (For me: dinosaurs, Beanie Babies, crystals, Batman.)

5. If you are having trouble remembering your younger self, can you find a recent moment where you felt at ease and content? Or like things were going *right*? Describe it— what the energy was like, how your body felt, the activity, every single detail.

6. If you can't think of a recent "yes" moment, what do you *think* would make you feel at ease and content? Just guess!

7. How would you describe your most essential self? Again, you can guess! Let's not take this so seriously and need to be "correct."

8. Next, ask your nearest and dearest how they would describe your essential self. What resonates? What are you surprised by? Did it match up with how you described yourself?

9. Where do you feel most at peace? In a forest? By the beach? On your couch? For me it's walking among the aspen and ponderosa pine trees, on my way to a rambling stream on the Borrego Trail in Santa Fe. I could live on that trail. I think part of my soul does.

10. Is there anything in your life that feels wrong or misaligned? Something that dims your light? A job? A boss? A friend? Living arrangement? Romantic partner? A conflict you want to resolve but have avoided? Write about it until you can get to a truth of why you are engaged in something that suppresses your potential. No judgment, BTW. If your job sucks but you need the income, that's real, and I don't expect you to quit, but still write about it. *See* it for what it is. There's power in seeing and acknowledging, even if you can't change *the whole thing* today.

11. In the above, do you recognize *anything,* even a baby step, you could take to help yourself?

12. Why haven't you yet? No shade, just asking. What's getting in the way?

13. What are you too afraid to know about yourself? What are you trying not to feel? Why? Now that you wrote it down, is it really that scary?

A Little Thing That Helps

I keep a framed photo of glittering, enthusiastic, trusting, five-year-old me on my desk, both to remind me of my true self and to let that little girl in me know she is not alone and now has a (pretty dope) thirty-five-year-old protector. Have you hung out with your true self lately? They're so excited to see you.

What You Really, Really Want (Zigazig Ah)

You Can't Get What You Don't Ask For

I THINK YOU WOULD BE annoyed with me if we worked together. No need to placate me or tell me differently, I'm pretty positive that would be the case. Here's why: When I was unceremoniously ousted from an office and moved to an open-floor-plan cubicle during a company-wide move, I never—not one time—worked from my new cubicle. Instead, I saw that there was a small conference room right next to the president's office, and I grabbed it. I had my phone line forwarded to it and set up shop. Many times, our facilities department told me that this was not "allowed," but what were they going to do? Confiscate my whiteboard and rose-gold stapler under cover of night? Well, let me tell you. *They did,* and it turns out I don't really staple shit. Within a few months, tired of my proclamations that I had "squatter's rights" to the conference room, they gave in. The grave injustice I had suffered by being moved to a cubicle was rectified and I was given a real office. I was clear about what I wanted and what I would accept and eventually, it all worked out in my favor. *WAHBAM, Facilities, in your face! But also: Thank you for all of the unsung work you do—our offices would be legit disgusting without you.*

Why was I so adamant about that conference room? Because I knew I had done the work to deserve it, and that no one was going to give it to me unless I was clear about what I wanted. End of story. There has never been one promotion, salary increase, or stolen conference room office I have *ever* received that I did not ask for and then tenaciously pursue. No one invited me to write a book, guide a workshop, or engage in my creativity. And I certainly didn't come out of childhood generous, compassionate, or embedded in a strong, loving community. Those were all things I had to actively seek out and bring into my life because I *wanted* them. I know this sounds girl-boss-y and braggy so I'm really wracking my brain to see if it is entirely true, and really, I can't think of one time someone asked me to do the thing I wanted to do or just freely gave it to me. The one exception, of course, is my very existence, a gift I did not ask for, but which has been sort of a big deal to me.

My point is not that I am an insufferable squeaky wheel (*your words, not mine*), my point is that we can't get what we don't ask for. Of ourselves, at work, in relationships, you name it. I am sorry but your boss, partner, friend, or even foe is not a mind reader. I get it—we want people in our lives to just *know* what we want, but the truth is, we are all sad little human beings who are so wrapped up in our own concerns and problems that we don't have the mental capacity to guess what anyone else wants. We think (mistakenly) that it's self-absorbed to ask for what we want, but as long as we are not being egomaniacs, that couldn't be further from the truth. How many of your conflicts and miscommunications emerge from someone not knowing what you wanted, or from *you* not knowing what they wanted? SO MANY, right? Most? So let's do each other a solid and make life easier by simply asking for what we need.*

I am not suggesting that we be entitled pieces of shit who ask for privileges without doing any work to deserve those things. (*Be nice, Boomers, I think we Millennials and Gen Zers are doing FANTAS-TICALLY well for inheriting a world that's in the shape it's in.*) My office shenanigans would have never turned out well had I not been of actual value to the company. But if you are showing up for your life, doing a pretty good job of it, and are not unbearably aggravating to the people around you, then my advice is to be bold and to clearly ask for what you want, *and* listen for what others around you want.

But here is where we fall into one of the greatest pitfalls of all: What *exactly* do we want? Do *you* know what you want? For SO MUCH GODDAMN time I had no idea what I wanted or even what I *didn't* want. In my mid-twenties, I was awash in a sea of "Meh . . . what do you think?" Polling just about anyone I could to make decisions about every little thing in my life: clothing, boyfriends, career, you name it. You'd think with time and age it would have gotten better but just like I was, you would be wrong. The older I got, the more overwhelmed I became by the feeling I had to make the BEST choice or . . . something . . . bad was going to happen? I actually didn't even know what I was afraid of, but I *knew* it would be terrible.

Finally I came up with a solution: Decision Immersion Therapy. I would force myself to make small choices, quickly. At a restaurant, say, or even cooking at home, I'd give myself only one minute to choose what I wanted to eat. Sushi or veggie curry?

---

* Just so you are aware, this one is particularly hard for me with dudes. There's something romantic or magical in my mind about my partner just *knowing* what I want. As if that somehow demonstrates how close we are. But that is bullshit because frankly, sometimes *I* don't even know what I want! Help your partner, be clear. I am talking to myself right now.

TIME'S UP—pick one, bitch!* I did this for months and finally realized a huge whopping life truth: None of these decisions mattered in the least. One dinner basically meant nothing. I could always go back to the restaurant and try something else the next time or make something different at home. Turns out, there were almost no stakes to something I thought was so serious.

Forcing myself to make quicker, not overly thought-out decisions on small things made me see that you can go back on *most* choices. If you order the brick chicken and don't like it, you don't have to eat brick chicken forever. And the same goes with your career, where you live, even your partner. You almost *always* have the potential to change your mind. It might be difficult with weightier decisions, but I still believe that it's possible. The more I've glimpsed the flexibility available to me, the more I've been able to boldly make bigger choices because, again, I understand that they don't necessarily seal my fate.

I think this fear of making "bad" choices is why we very often end up on our "Good Enough Plateaus," where it's safe and comfy and there's a Starbucks around the corner and we know exactly what we can get (a tall caramel macchiato with almond milk and an extra shot, please and thanks!). It's sheltered on the Good Enough Plateau with our Crocs on, in an athleisure suit, kicking back and watching the latest turd of a reality dating show, and perhaps more important, it's *predictable* in a world where so little ever is. Now, I don't mean to knock your Good Enough Plateau, you know I sometimes chill there myself, but we get into real trouble when we start believing *that's it,* when we stop expanding, growing, and shoving off on new adventures. Then we deprive ourselves of the opportunity not only to mature and taste a richer life but also to deepen our experience by knowing what it means

---

* How do we feel about the use of "bitch" right now? Am I reclaiming it here, or falling victim to it? I just thought it sounded funny.

to come up short. So if you have been lingering on the Good Enough Plateau for a minute now, it's not that you're doing anything bad or wrong, it's just that you're losing out on fully inhabiting your singular life and all of the possibilities available to you. Just that.

And there's another reason many of us don't know what we want—because we've been taught that it's unacceptable to long for more. Even as I write this, I'm thinking, *Fuck,* am I really saying to people that they should cry out for more? Isn't that kind of grandiose? It is. WHAT IS MORE GRANDIOSE THAN YOUR LIFE?! I'm not talking about more *stuff,* here, *God am I not talking about more stuff,* but more abundant, genuine, wholehearted experiences—more love, more curiosity, more thrills, more adventure, more of that ineffable thing when you laugh with someone and lose track of all time. That's the kind of hungering for more I am talking about here—*more life,* like the prophet Drake so eloquently crooned about.* And far from being some egocentric or terrible thing to want to eke every last drop out of your moment on earth, if you truly appreciate the unbelievably precious gift of your being, you will do everything to live it to its very fullest. That's how we show gratitude for our existence, damn it! By showing the fuck up! By choosing the brick chicken on a whim! You do this not just for yourself, but for the health of us all. Right now, I'm looking out my window at a climate in crisis, mass injustice, war, an actual plague disease that is spreading like wildfire (oh, and since it's California—*actual* wildfires too) . . . and I feel like . . . there's just *got* to be a better reality we can all help build. But if we can't *imagine* an existence better than this one *for ourselves,* how in the hell are we going to do it for the *planet?* How can we build a more healthy and kind world if we've lost all hope in our individual wherewithal to do that for ourselves?

---

* Of course I am referring to our blessed Drake's 2017 banger of an album, *More Life.*

So, how do we figure out what we want, what we really, really want? Well, get out your journal and let's try a little something, shall we?

A List of Questions to Find Our Deepest Desires Even If We Think We Don't Know or Have Them

1. What do you *want*? More connection, more love, more joy? Sometimes we know the answer to this question but don't *want* to know it because we assume it will be too difficult to get or we think we don't deserve it. Forget all of that for now, just tell me: What do you *want*?

2. Go through the past few months and ask: *When did I feel the most YES in my life?* When were you doing something that just felt right and clear and aligned? What were you doing? Who were you with? How did it make you feel, in your body and in your mind? Is there a way to bring this YES feeling into your life more? How? Make an actual plan for how you will do this thing more often.

3. What are your priorities? What really matters to YOU? Learning? Travel? Love? Friendship? Community? Kindness? Write down at least five things that are important to you. Not to anyone else!

4. Write out a typical day in your life—get granular. Seven A.M.: Wake up with children, rush around. Eight A.M.: Feel exhausted, drink more coffee, imagine going back to sleep. Etc. Now: How much room do you have for your priorities in your day? Are the things you profess to cherish even in your day-to-day life? If not, can you course-correct so

that your days contain a *little* bit—even just fifteen or thirty minutes—of the things you hold dear?

5. Why are you here on this planet? What's your purpose? Don't know? Make an educated guess. Don't get stuck here or overthink, just write! Anything!

6. If there is something material you want—a new job, for instance—get to the root of it—ask yourself WHY you want it until you get to something that feels true.
    For example: *I want a promotion.*
    a. Why do you want the promotion? *So I'll make more money.*
    b. Why do you want more money? *So I'll be safe.*
    c. Why do you want to be safe? *So that nothing bad will happen to me.*
    d. Why do you want nothing bad to happen to you? *Because I want to feel loved and taken care of.*

    PAY DIRT!! You want to feel loved and taken care of, how BEAUTIFUL! Are there other ways to get what you want instead of using something material (a promotion) to mend something emotional (a want for love)?

7. If today was your last day on earth, would it be well spent? How might you adjust tomorrow to reflect more of what's important to you?

As you look at your answers, I hope you can see that you do, indeed, want *something* more. Knowing what you wish for is not indulgent, it's not the icing on your life cake—it's the actual cake. And in my case, it's carrot because obviously carrot cake beats all other cakes. When we have the wisdom to understand what we care about, we end up living in a way that is more *us*. I hate the word "authentic" because I feel like it's reached peak "let's write this on a mug" status, but to me that's what authenticity is all about—allowing yourself to know what *you*—singular *you*—want to do with the time you have.

Okay, now you have a clue of what you might want, but how do you know when your desires are aligned with your actions? Well, let me tell you. I know you've heard of hustle, I know you've heard of flow, but have you heard of a Full-Body YES?* A Full-Body YES is when I can feel every cell in me scream, "YES, WOMAN, YES, *THIS! MORE!*" These moments can be small (eating fresh farmers market blueberries), they can be gigantic (a career change), they can be accidental (discovering I love running by forcing myself to run), they can even happen when I am *not doing* something that used to cause me pain (when I decided to stop dating wishy-washy guys cuz I ain't got time for that anymore—what a RELIEF!). The key is to pay attention, to notice these moments, savor them, feel them, relax into them, so that you pinpoint what makes you come alive.

As the Spice Girls once wisely sang: "So tell me what you want, what you really, really want." When you know the answer, the real, root answer to this question, you will know the direction in which you want your life to go and you will feel like you are truly living it, because you are. This is not theoretical. You must *choose* every day if you are going to live the life you want, or something else. Your desires might change over time, you might realize that something you thought you wanted no longer sounds good to you, and that's okay. What's not okay is to live without investigating what you crave, a life fulfilling someone *else's* desires—and if

---

* There is a book I haven't read called *The Full Body Yes: Change Your Work and Your World from Inside Out* by Scott Shute (Page Two Books, 2021), which is about how to make your work a part of your life. It looks good! If I didn't have five thousand books on trauma to read—I would read it!

you don't know your own, how are you going to tell the difference? You won't be able to and that's not what *I* want for you. And this is all about what I want, right?

A Little Thing That Helps

When you can't figure out what you want, simply ask, "What is the best choice I can make for myself *right now*?" What's the first thing that comes to mind? Even if it ends up being a mistake, you're getting it SO right because you're building your ability to hear yourself clearly.

Emmy Un-Nominated
Stop with the External Validation

EMMY SEASON IS MY LEAST favorite Hollywood season. It predictably brings out the worst in people: the naked need for recognition, the myopic focus on individual achievement, and so much Botox that it seems as if the people of Hollywood are frozen in time, which they kind of are. Then of course there is the actual Emmy ceremony, which is often referred to as "TV prom," when you and your colleagues put on gowns in the ninety-five-degree heat, waddle down a red carpet where no one cares about you (unless you are talent), only to be ushered into an auditorium to sit for three hours oohing and ahhing over things you've never heard of before, like "Outstanding Derivative Interactive Program," which sounds more like a financial term than something that could or should be applied to entertainment. In summation: I hated Emmy season.

Until, of course, I was nominated for an Emmy. And then all of a sudden: YES, YES, YES, YES, YES, YES, YES, EMMYS ARE THE BEST!! I was THRILLED, elated, on an Emmy-induced ego high. You see, I had been working the previous four years on a Web series (yes, you can be nominated for that). While it received little attention from anyone else, it was my utter pride and joy. We had a shoestring budget so we filmed the episodes in the common area of a TV show office, after their workday had ended. There was no set. We taped a poster to the wall and used a sofa that was already there. The comedians involved, however. Oh boy. They were the funniest, smartest, kindest people I had ever met and because our budget was so meager, I got to do *everything*.

What does "everything" entail? Not only was I in charge of the shoots, I would also help create the ideas for each episode and the arc of the season. When the director wanted to shelve the project entirely, I convinced the team to continue. Late at night, after we wrapped, I would take the film and drive it to the offices of the editor in Santa Monica. Then, the next day, I would sit in on the edit and ~~help decide~~ steamroll the editor on where to make cuts and how to shape the episode. I came up with the title for the last season. And perhaps my shining achievement, the thing I was the proudest of, was how the comedians responded to my work.

In Hollywood, creators get "notes" on their projects that they then address either by using the feedback to improve the idea or ignoring it with a "thanks, but no thanks, it's good as it is." Since I was overseeing the Web episodes, I received notes from the comedians themselves. Eventually, I had honed my skills to sync with their sensibilities so well that their notes began to say, "No notes." That is the highest compliment you can receive, FYI, and I taped those emails to the walls of my office. I had never been prouder of myself because I knew I was working at the top of my ability and it was being recognized by people I deeply respected.

Which is why the Emmy nomination meant so much to me. Because in a town where sometimes you have to erect a thirty-thousand-dollar billboard of a celebrity on Sunset Boulevard not for advertising purposes, but just so said celeb can take a selfie with their face blown up to cinematic proportions, I felt like I had *earned* this approval and was ready to let myself enjoy it. I fantasized about the perfect dress to wear to the event, nothing too "gown-y" but definitely not casual, maybe something with a little rock-and-roll flair? *Could I get Zoë Kravitz's stylist on the line, please?* I realized that now and forever "Emmy Nominated" would go next to my name, like I had earned my PhD in entertainment. Friends, colleagues, and people from my past texted me well wishes. And then, like most things, I forgot all about it. The Emmy nominations and the Emmy ceremony are two months apart, leaving my digitally ravaged brain ample time to move on to other concerns, like what is the best brand and type of sunscreen? An odyssey of mind and spirit that I have been on for the past ten years. And like all great mysteries in life—I still don't have the final answer.

One night, not thinking about the Emmys, I was at an out-of-town work dinner with my colleagues, waiting for my grilled sea bass with cauliflower rice, no sauce, and a steamed veggies sub for cream of spinach because I guess I like to punish myself at dinner. I saw on my phone that my boss's boss's boss was calling me. *Hmm. Weird.* I picked up. "Hey there, how's the trip going?" he nonchalantly asked as my nerves began to sizzle like a hot pan you've just thrown a piece of garlic into and you know it's either going to add a rich flavor or be burnt to a crisp. "Everything is great! How can I help you?" I replied. "Well, are you in a place where you can talk?" *OH GOD NO. WE ALL KNOW NOTHING GOOD COMES FROM THAT QUESTION.* I was not in a place where I could talk, but when the boss's boss's boss calls, you make it work. I left the table, exited the restaurant, and sat on the curb outside. "So, the Emmys . . . I'm calling because it's not a great idea for executives to be on nominations." The world got fuzzy and all I could hear was his voice. "It's not a good look, you know? We aren't the talent, we shouldn't be nominated. We didn't do the work." I protested, "But I *was* the producer on it, I actually *did* the work, for *years*."* "That might be true, but again, it's just not a

---

* Let me back up and explain something. I had just switched roles from producer (someone who makes things) to executive (someone who oversees the making of things) which meant, of course, that I was now sort of doing both jobs. What I was calling out was that even if my title had changed, the work I was doing largely had not—except that now I had even more responsibility.

good look. Things like this happen, I'm sorry to say. I'm not telling you what to do, but you have a choice to make. Call me and let me know what you decide."[*]

I could not move. I could not cry. I sat on the curb, in the actual gutter, shocked by the news and embarrassed by how distressed I felt. What had just happened? I replayed the events in my head. For years, I had worked on a project that no one gave a fuck about. That project was now nominated for an Emmy. I had not entered myself as a nominee, the company had, and the entire thing had been a pleasant surprise. But now, I couldn't be on the nomination because it looked bad for someone who *did the work* to receive credit for the work?

I didn't want my colleagues to see the rush of tears that I knew were about to explode from my eyes so I hailed a cab (yes, a real cab), and left, my sea bass uneaten because who would have wanted to eat that anyway? I never had. I returned to my hotel room and in a daze called my boss's boss's boss back and gave him the only possible answer I could: Please Emmy un-nominate me.

Was having a nomination I formerly didn't even care about taken away from me a big deal in the grand scheme of the world? No. But the nomination had unexpectedly made me feel like I was a real person, someone who was verifiably contributing to the world and doing it well. And now, what did it mean that my company was going through the trouble of withdrawing my name from the already announced nomination? I was Full-Body Embarrassed (the ignoble second cousin of Full-Body YES), feeling stupid for caring this much about something so self-conceited. But at

---

[*] P.S. I know my boss's boss's boss is coming off . . . not great right about now but you should know, in most other ways he championed me, helped me climb the ranks, gave me excellent advice, and was a wonderful mentor and friend. I give him the benefit of the doubt that he thought he was doing the right thing at the time and was not intentionally hurtful. No reason to hate the player; hate the game.

the same time, I felt hurt and sad, like something important was being ripped away from me. And what about all the people who had wished me well? What about when they watched the Emmys and saw that my name was very clearly not there? Should I get ahead of that moment and pre-emptively explain it to them?

Sitting in my hotel room, my ego pierced, deflated, and currently writhing on the floor, I made a promise to myself: I would never again let something external validate me. Never, ever, ever. I had learned this pivotal lesson much earlier in my career when I was "the digital girl" for TV shows (ugggggh, please feel Full-Body Revolted with me because I used that term in professional conversations). It was my job to look at and analyze the likes, shares, and comments of videos we posted on the Internet and my main takeaway had been "NEVER READ THE COMMENTS." First, because I saw so many genius-level comedians focus EX-CLUSIVELY on the bad comments—never the thousands of good ones—which drove them crazier than they already were (jk, jk, jk, but also not jk), and second, because WOW were people weird and mean when they were anonymous online. It finally registered that if I continued to tie myself to awards or reviews or achievements, I would always be the passenger to someone else's opinions, my stomach lurching as they made hairpin turns on the road that was my self-esteem, getting whiplash every time they slammed on the brakes to question my talent.

If any of us are to lead lives free from external validation, we have to figure out a way to value *ourselves,* to acknowledge and see all the kick-ass work we are doing because, I'm sorry to tell you this, but maybe no one else ever will. I know your supervisor sucks and you're working overtime to meet his demands and you wish he would say *one* kind thing to you, but why would you hold out hope that he ever would? He's a dick, ergo his dickish behavior. That's not gonna change, sweetie, so can we just give up on wanting and waiting for his approval? As gently as I can, I would like to say: Quit wasting time wishing someone else would value your work and value it yourself.

I'm not gonna sugarcoat this: Self-esteem re-framing is so fucking hard. Even after my doomed date with an Emmy, *in this very moment* I'm feeling a flare-up of needing praise. The only difference is that now, post–Emmy incident, I am totally aware of what's going on inside my little head AND I have a tool to help me through it. When I feel myself fiending for the sweet hit of someone telling me, "Good job!" I remind myself, "*I* am the only person who can validate me and I'm doing the best I can." BECAUSE IT'S TRUE. Because every SINGLE time I've looked for a compliment or flattery to make me feel good—it hasn't worked! The nice words don't stick—they feel hollow, I don't believe them, and I am so bad at remembering them that I have to write them down. This might be some deeper psychological issue I need to look into and if so, thank God, because it gives me more material to write about. But until I figure that out, before I email someone to ask if I did a "good job" on something, I say these words to myself on repeat.

Instead of focusing on validation and outcomes, I've started paying attention to the thing that I really loved all along—the process. After all, it was making those webisodes that lit me up with motivation, inspiration, and glee. It was working with other artists and gaining their respect (not approval) that felt like a real win. Had the whole Emmy thing never gone down, I would have been happy as a clam, basking in the glory of a job well done. So these days I (again, *mostly*) focus on making my creative process as fulfilling, and fun, and *me* as I possibly can.

This means I preserve time in my day to actually do creative work! Mostly in the early morning, with a cup of delicious coconut-milk-infused coffee and a rose-scented candle burning at my desk with my "Wall of Saints," a corkboard with images of Glennon Doyle, Dolly Parton, George Saunders, and Lil' Kim,

among other heroes, which hangs on the wall behind my desk.*
These icons join and bless me every time I sit down to write. I'm
mostly ~~obsessed~~ in love with my process but it's not always "fun."
It was not pleasant to wake up an hour before everyone else on a
bachelorette trip to Austin when I'd spent the previous day dancing wildly in a bikini and flannel shirt while connected to a "flo-
tilla" of other party boats. It didn't feel "awesome" to write with
that next level of a hangover, but it did feel *right*.

Process can also save our ass when we are struggling with a big
decision, like "Should I leave my job?" or "Should I leave my partner?" or "Should I move?" I have a different question for you—
what are your days like? Are they aligned with who you are and
what you want most in the world? Are they built to be good for
you? And if not, could you try out whatever new job you were
thinking of during your lunches? Could you see if what's really
plaguing you is your relationship or is it the fact you haven't had a
good night's sleep in two years? Do you really need to move or is
your self-doubt going to follow you to your new zip code? Maybe
you will quit, maybe you will leave someone, maybe you will
move, *you do you, boo,* but by adjusting the very process of your life
to work for you and by putting as little pressure as possible on the
big choice, I guarantee it will be easier to figure out what you
really want. And I know you're busy with kids and work and the
minutiae of being a person, but still—this is the *only* time we ever
get here, so what are you going to do about it? Complain that
there isn't enough time? If you want something to be different
you're going to have to be the one to do things differently. My
systems have ensured that I enjoy nearly every single day of my
life, and what bigger dream could I have than that?

I'm not saying anything new. We've all heard it a million times

---

* OG *Lilies* readers: It's not *the* desk. After more than a decade of honorable service, I had to re-
tire the desk for a bigger one. No need to grieve, however. She's gone to a better place, to the
room of a young woman in middle school who wants to be a writer.

before: The journey is the destination. *Ugh, yes, we know, we don't need it etched into a paperweight, thank you very much.* But how many of us actually buy that? COME ON, do *you*? Do you seriously believe that the process of how you get somewhere is the payoff? Be honest, how often do you live your life as a series of if/then statements. Like, *If I find a romantic partner, then I'll be fulfilled. If I get into that school, then I'll be happy. If I lose a few pounds, then I'll be pretty.* Any of these sound familiar? They sure do to me. They had set the course for a good chunk of my life. But now I know why they are so deeply problematic and damaging: They rely on an outcome. No outcome, no contentment. And since we know we can't control outcomes, we are . . . what's the polite way to say it? Fucked.

While I have never been nominated for an Emmy again, after I told the story of being un-nominated while teaching a workshop this past winter (a process I ~~love so much I want to make out with~~ enjoy), my workshop participants gave me a much greater gift than I could have ever hoped for: "The Un-Emmy Award of 2022: In Honor of Changing the Lives of Gorgeous Lilies Everywhere." It's a plastic trophy in the shape of two shooting stars filled with golden glitter and just about the most *me* thing I could ever imagine. This award means more to me than any Emmy ever could because it's not about any one outcome. It's not about how many books I've sold, or if anyone thinks I'm the "best," it's recognition that I'm on a path, in a process, that is helpful to other people. I'm healing and growing with *you* and oh my fucking lord has this been fun and meaningful and just a total gift in and of itself. You didn't have to throw in a trophy but you did, cuz you're generous like that.

A Little Thing That Helps

Celebrate your wins! Get the good ice cream, buy yourself the fucking lilies (had to get that in somewhere), open the nice champagne or sparkling seltzer. You know it's not *about* the wins, but when they happen, take them in. You earned it!

Orbiting Stars
My Current Thoughts on Romance

A LITTLE PERSONAL NEWS, AS they say: For the past ten months and five days (not like I'm counting) I haven't been on a single date! *Thank you, thank you, no need to applaud. Just a regular American hero over here.* I have neither contacted an ex-boyfriend for a little flirtation with a side of bad decisions nor sought male attention when out on the town. (Okay, well, I have a *little,* but it's not my fault I look so good in the highlighter-yellow, curve-hugging dress I just bought.) All dating apps have been deleted from my phone, and instead of swiping, I've been spending my nights writing or hanging out with friends. Now, this might seem unremarkable to you, but it's a big deal for me. You see, for the past fifteen years, I have ricocheted from dude to dude to dude, never going longer than one month without dating someone.

When I was breaking up with a guy (which was often) I was almost always simultaneously setting up someone new in the wings. I know there is a term called "love addict," but I'm not quite ready to use it because *oh my God, I can't label myself one more thing.* Still, I do think I was caught in a painful pattern that I couldn't seem to escape on my own. And although I had a sense of what the pattern could be about (my childhood—duh), there was something underneath it all, something deeper that I just couldn't figure out. So I decided to take a pause from dating and really get curious about my dating history.

The thing that pushed me to take this hiatus was my breakup with the Great Gatsby IRL. (Remember him? Liam? Self-professed millionaire borrowing money from me?) That relationship had just been so *obviously* fucked-up, and yet I had stayed in it, trying to convince myself he was "the one." But "the one" for what? Feeling terrible about myself? Even as I dated him, I *knew* we weren't going to be forever partners, so why did I put up with the bad treatment? Why did I try so hard to soothe his whims and feelings if I knew it wasn't going anywhere? And why had I dated so many men *just like him* even if what I told my friends was that I wanted to meet my life partner? I knew I would never know the answer until I could "stop the bleeding," as I told Fisch one night on the phone. It was time to get still, time to figure out where I was going wrong if ever I wanted to get it right.

My romances have not always been so . . . *dramatic*. I have not always dated raging narcissists (see above) and former sex cult members (Slow Burn Charles). I assure you, there was at least one healthy, kind, non-horrifying, book-chapter-worthy man in my past. My very first college boyfriend, Jack, the first person I ever fell in love with. I hadn't thought about Jack in a while, like a decade-while, but during this step-back-from-dating-dudes-who-are-oh-so-wrong-for-me time, I hadn't been able to get him off my mind.

We met freshman year of college, in the year of our Lord and Savior Martha Stewart's conviction—2004. I was studying in a Starbucks, pounding a chai latte and those madeleines in the plastic shrink-wrap (*how good are those?*). I looked out the window to see on the other side of the street a tall, lean guy with 1950s-style black glasses, wearing a bright red, vintage sweater. He was just about to cross the sidewalk in front of an alleyway in his Chelsea boots and green corduroys (wow, I was really paying attention). I didn't even notice I was staring at him until he looked back, directly into the window of Starbucks and right at me. We locked eyes for a flash of a second. I definitely had madeleine crumbs all over my shirt. Had he even seen me, though? From that moment on, I couldn't stop thinking about Red Sweater Guy, wondering when I might see him and his 1950s glasses again.

A few weeks later, a little dejected by the thought that I might not see him again, my friends took me to see a short student film for which I had *low* expectations, but ultimately, it blew me away. It was a shot-for-shot parody of the opening scene of *Apocalypse Now,* but done entirely using toys and puppets. . . . It was brilliant and hilarious and just felt so *alive,* like it was bursting with creative energy. *Holy fuck,* I thought, *who made that and how?! College is so cool!* At the end of the screening, the director came onstage for a Q and A and—*ta-da!*—of course—blessedly—it was Red Sweater Guy!

Afterward, I loitered in his general vicinity, trying to catch his eye as he talked to audience members, and just when I mustered enough courage to finally introduce myself, another girl cut in front of me and started chatting with him. I chickened out and decided to leave, but as I turned to walk away, I felt a hand on my shoulder. "Hey, wait a minute, hi, I'm Jack. I . . . wanted to introduce myself." We made eye contact for the second time, only now, from the way he smiled at me and from the electricity that surged between us when he shook my hand, I was *sure* he saw me.

We started dating almost immediately. For our first date, he drove me—*drove*—(a big deal to a freshman who was not allowed to have a car on campus) to eat Italian food on Federal Hill, a neighborhood in Providence, Rhode Island, famed for both its cannoli and its deep ties to the Mafia. Leading up to the date, I worried about what to wear to impress him (What did college girls wear?! I had just started!) or what I should say to make him like me (Talk about Francis Ford Coppola? Puppets? Red sweaters?

WHAT?!). Unfortunately I couldn't envision what kind of clothes he would like best so I settled on the coolest outfit to *me,* a black-and-red horizontally striped sweater with embroidered cats, a black vest from the three-piece suit I wore to my sweet-sixteen, and ripped-up jeans. I figured I would have plenty to say once I was actually on the date but studied Francis Ford Coppola's IMDb page just in case.

I was nervous, but the moment we sat down he relieved any tension. "So tell me everything about yourself, Business Bangs?" he asked. I laughed. *What did he mean by "business bangs"??* "Your haircut, you've got bangs that could run the world! They could be a CEO! If they ran for president they'd have my vote." I giggled. I *GIGGLED!* We spent the entire night laughing and sharing our passions, and when, at the end of the date, he kissed me good night, his stubble rubbing against my face, the skin on my neck and arms breaking out into the most tantalizing goose bumps, for one magnetic moment I felt . . . perfectly at peace and good and vibrant. For the first time in my romantic life, I had the feeling that it was okay for me to be fully myself, cat-embroidered sweater and all.

I never questioned where I stood with Jack, never felt insecure or worried about our relationship, because he unabashedly showed me how much he cared. As we dated, Jack would leave little love notes in my dorm room for no reason, he would take me on adventures to the big city—Boston—and we would spend hours in bed laughing about God-knows-what. It felt like neither of us ever wanted our dates to end.

Before then, it had never felt safe enough for me to be totally vulnerable and affectionate with someone. I had grown up in such harsh circumstances that I sometimes worried I didn't know how to love. But I did, and I loved Jack. I made gifts for him. A mixtape here, a flip-book of Polaroid photos of the Pacific Ocean there. During Christmas break, he sent me a ludicrous photo he had taken at the mall, all six feet of him spilling out of "Santa's" lap. He took it simply to make me smile.

We were inseparable. My friends loved him, and raved that I had met my match. As stupid as it sounds, I thought that with Jack, I had found the safety I had always been after and maybe even . . . *wholeness*? We often took long walks on campus together and on one of the last days of fall, a year and a half into dating, when the yellow and red leaves on the ground shone in the gray New England evening, he asked if I wanted to get some fresh air. We walked hand in hand until he found a redbrick stoop and asked me to sit down. "Tara, I need to tell you something." I looked up at him and those 1950s glasses I loved. "I want to break up, things aren't working, and I'm about to go abroad, and . . . I just think it's for the best if we stop seeing each other."

At first, the words didn't even register. A few days ago, he had been fantasizing about what our first house together might look like. "Wait, what? Wha-why?" I stammered. "Well, I'm going abroad and that's going to be hard . . . ," he explained. Everything started to spin, and I felt like I might throw up. I have no recollection of what I said, or how I got back to my dorm room that night.

The rest of that semester was a blur. I was in such bad shape that my friends forced me to go to psychiatric services, where I was given an antidepressant and a note instructing my professors to let me have an extension on my finals, a lame party favor for heartache if ever there was one. Had I been a stable, well-adjusted sophomore, this might have all been a painful but manageable event. But as you well know, my life up to that point had been a series of disappointments, largely centered around feelings of abandonment. Now I had opened myself up to someone, believed I could be loved, and of course, the inevitable had happened, I had been left. And since I really had been *myself*, since I had held nothing back from Jack, it was devastating. He had rejected the real me.

I don't remember how long it was after that breakup that Jack spotted me on the main green and asked if we could talk. Part of me didn't want to, but the other part just couldn't resist him. We walked across the grass slowly as he rolled his Bianchi bike by his side. Finally, he said, "I've really missed you. I made a terrible mistake. I freaked out because I'm going abroad but I love you and I can't believe how stupid I was. Can you forgive me? Can we get back together?" he asked with tears in his eyes. I agreed, but there was no excitement to it, no sense of relief. Jack had broken something very fundamental in me that felt beyond repair, and my blood ran cold.

We dated for six months after that, but I felt distant, so distant that I started cheating on him (something I had never done or thought I was capable of doing).[*] The cheating felt like an out-of-body experience beyond my control, almost like a compulsion. I didn't feel good doing it, I didn't even *want* to do it, but . . . I felt driven to find someone who wanted me so badly they were willing to do something wrong. Jack knew something was awry (I'm pretty sure he knew I was cheating) but he still tried to get me to stay. Toward the end of our relationship, he took me on an elaborate beach date where he set up a picnic in the bed of his pickup truck complete with candlelight, wine, and one of my favorite things in the whole wide world—a charcuterie and cheese board. But as we sat close to each other in the truck, I couldn't have felt farther away or less in love. That night, I broke up with him for good.

For years, I laughed off our relationship. Sure, Jack had been my "first love," but who knows what real love is when you're that young? And yeah, he broke my heart, but again, we were just kids! Doesn't everyone get their heart broken? But in the past ten months and five days, I've been doing a post-mort of all my relationships (*it's a long-ass document*) and it's revealed something I never

---

[*] OG *Lilies* readers: This is how I met Keats in all his theatRE glory.

saw coming—it was clear that my whole love life took a left turn after Jack, as if it had affected every relationship thereafter.

Since Jack, I had exclusively dated people who made me feel panicked and scared. *I knew this*. And yet I would fall into the same pattern over and over again: I sought out dudes who were in rough shape themselves, I'd feel . . . unsafe and uncomfortable with them in some way but move forward anyway, I'd become *anyone* I thought they would like in a bid to get their attention. I'd try to "fix" them, then I'd grow exhausted and resentful, and then I'd break up with them. I was *always* the one to leave.

My relationship autopsies further showed me that all of these men had something else in common that I'm not proud to admit. I perceived each to have status, money, and respectability—things I thought I lacked and wanted. In college, I hadn't given a shit about Jack's social status, but since him I had been almost obsessed with finding someone who would give me his bona fides, his shine, who would make me look important to the world. I cared way more about things looking good than actually being good.

While that might not be my most flattering trait, it's true. I am so grateful that I stopped dating because otherwise I'm not sure when I would have been able to see my patterns so clearly. This sabbatical has been one of the most beautiful times in my life. Now that I'm not subject to some boy drama, I've felt more PEACE than I knew existed. I've spent weeks on end feeling at ease, content, and even joyful. Instead of catering to a guy's needs, I've catered to mine, doing whatever I want to do: making deep new friends, staying up late reading the books I'm interested in by candlelight, and walking around my apartment naked FAR more than I ever knew I wanted to. *To my neighbors across the way: You're welcome*. I've even been able to indulge in dumb stuff like eating exactly what I want when I want without ever having to compromise on restaurant or recipe.

And as I've done more of what I want, I've seen that it's okay and even healthy for me to have non-negotiables in my dating life—things I can't compromise on without compromising myself. It's okay that my partner will need, first and foremost, to be kind. It's totally acceptable that he should enjoy physical activities like I do, so I have someone to talk to aside from LadyGod on my hikes. And given all that I've been through, it's even all right that I need this fella to be *stable*—emotionally, financially, relationally, in all of the ways. I see now that when I bargain away these things, I'm ignoring the kind of life I want to lead. I'd rather never date than settle like that again. While I used to dread being alone, now I dread ever feeling as trapped as I did in an unfulfilling relationship.

I've also been able to see my blind spots. All those times I was looking for a man to bring me money, status, and respectability . . . I couldn't recognize that *I* already had money, status, and respectability. I had my little fainting sofa of savings, but more than that, I was finally rich by my own definition—I had the love of my friends, my time was my own, and I was doing *exactly* what I wanted with my life—mainly, being with *you,* as it so happens. I think right about now is when I should quote Saint Cher of Power Ballads. When her mom suggested it was time for her to settle down and marry a rich man, she responded, "Mom, I am a rich man."* Fuck. Yeah. Me too, Cher, me too.

So what now? Well, for starters, I'm not pining over Jack. I know that he was not my person. He found his person. And I've found mine: me. I'm at home in myself and don't really worry at all about dating, even as literally every one of my friends gets married and has children, because I'm having an *excellent* time dating myself. And, I don't want to date again until I'm sure I can make decisions that are in my own best interest.

I've been asking friends about who they think I should date (when I'm ready) and I've had a major insight. One night I posed

---

* https://www.youtube.com/watch?v=dZsL5R_CR-k

the question to my dear friend Annie. She took a pause and simply replied, "You should be with someone who likes to do the same things as you." It was so simple yet so stunning. I had NEVER, not one time, considered or even looked at the "about me" section on someone's dating profile—I had always gone off of photo, job, and school—the holy trinity of status. And! I had never even put *my* interests in my profile—which meant the people I dated were also only going off my photo, job, and school! Like I said, I'm not going to date until I know I can choose differently, and this time I will be choosing to pay attention to what I put in my dating profile.

I once thought that true love was something that completed you and maybe even saved you. That if I was authentically bowled over, I would merge with another person and all of my childhood wounds would evaporate. Most important, I would finally be *whole*. But I've changed my mind on that. When I was in Flagstaff, I visited the Lowell Observatory to explore the famously dark sky. Using a super-powered telescope, an astronomer took me on a tour of the universe through his lens. We looked at the surface of the moon, which, by the way, is INSANE. It's full of craters, and tunnels, like it's an excavation site, the rocky terrain moved every which way. He showed me distant nebulae and stars and then stopped at one particular luminescent ray of light. "You see this star? It's named Albireo, it's the brightest one in the sky tonight. Beautiful, right?" he asked as he made room for me to look. I peered into the viewfinder, and yes, the star was shockingly beautiful. It pulsed with clarity, like one brilliant, faceted gemstone scattering its light. I stepped back and he adjusted the telescope again. "But on closer inspection, what do you notice?" he asked. I focused my eyes. "It's two," I replied, as I saw that what had originally been one bright burning star was actually one golden star and one blue star. They were completely separate and each remarkably distinctive, but their shine blended and complemented each other to make a new and beautiful glow, and the *contrast* of the blue and gold made it one of the most extraordinary sights I had ever seen.

This is now how I like to think of love, not as one person merging into another, but as two stars who have been through their own pressures and turmoils and triumphs, coming together to shine side by side, no matter how long it takes to get there, each giving light to the other and then to us all.

I'm looking for my blue star (obviously I'm gold). I know you're out there and I can't wait to shine with you.

A Little Thing That Helps

I was embarrassed by how long it was taking me to find my mate, until a friend said something that completely blew me away: "You've invested so much time into healing, growing, adventuring. Don't you think it's possible your person has been doing the same? You've both been busy!" Isn't it nice to think that right now, your future partner is having an epic journey of their own, and because of that, it will be all the more sublime when you finally meet?

Eggies on Ice
Make Decisions for Future You

I HAVE ALWAYS BEEN AMBIVALENT about whether I want to have kids. I think this is because my own childhood left me with the apprehension that getting married and having offspring were cataclysmic disasters that destroyed your happiness. My dad often referred to his marriage to my mother as "the fight of [his] life," and described it as "terrifying." When I asked him why he married my mom, someone he described as "scary," his answer was always the same: "The only reason I married her was because she was pregnant with you. I barely knew the lady, but I wanted to do the right thing." He also said, "The only reason I stayed married was because of you girls." I don't think my dad ever thought about how I might interpret his words: His life was demolished by my mom and the only reason he ever got married, and then stayed in a disastrous union, was because of his kids. Ergo, I ruined my dad's life. And so, I came to believe that just as marriage and kids impoverished my dad's existence, they would be sure to wreck mine. Family was something dangerous, a trap you had to escape by the skin of your teeth.

What has always puzzled me about my dad's version of events, however, is that I know he loves me. I have never questioned that, and he has regularly said that me and my sister were "the best thing that ever happened" to him. I've always wondered: Could it really be both? Could a distressing marriage he (wrongly) stayed in also have yielded one of the greatest things in his life? Could my sister and I, just by being alive, redeem the decades-long black hole that was his merging with my mother?

A few years ago, I finally asked him, "Dad, do you regret having kids? I know it was such a burden to you. If you could go back, would you do it over?" It didn't even cross my mind that I was asking if he regretted my existence. "How could you ask that?" he said with a look of genuine surprise (and slight horror) on his face. "Of course not! You and your sister are the greatest blessing to me, the only thing I've done right in my life, you've never been a burden to me, not once, not ever. Why would you think that?" *Um. Maybe because that's what you've told me implicitly and explicitly for my entire life?* I almost didn't know what to say to his answer, it was not what I expected AT ALL and a slightly astonished smile filled my face in place of words. *Huh. If I wasn't a burden after all, could it be true that I really was a blessing?*

This conversation threw everything I knew into question. It challenged my core belief that I was a costly, lamented affliction to my parents. And if I was indeed a blessing, something good in their lives, then was it possible for family as a whole to be a *beneficial* thing and not a stressful mistake? As silly as it sounds, that's really what I thought family was—something that could make your time on earth miserable.

Still, I worried that because my childhood was so tumultuous, there was no way I'd be able to avoid screwing up my kids. I am extremely sensitive to children in pain—I can't watch a TV show where a child is mistreated (even in the most minor of possible ways) and if I see someone yelling at a kid in public, I become physically ill. Having no example of what it meant to be a "good parent," I felt doomed to be a *terrible* parent and I would rather die than hurt a child. That sounds extreme, but please know I have tears in my eyes right now for how true that is to me.

A few weeks after the conversation with my dad, my BFF-soulmate, Fisch, called me and asked if I could come down to Orange County, where she lived, and help with her three young children. She was drowning and needed support. I had never in my life taken care of children, and wasn't sure I was up to the task, but I thought that, if she trusted me with her kids, this might be an opportunity to find out what the big fuss about family might be.

Fisch, as you know, is one of the most important people in my life. She is deeply kind and good. I have never one time seen her act in a way that is not grounded, appropriate, and fair, and her husband and I often lament that she is usually right about everything. *Fucking Fischy.* The first time I met her, at a gathering for incoming college freshmen that was held at her parents' house, I clocked her cool-girl clothes and her athletic frame, decided she looked like a cast member from *The O.C.,* and assumed she must be a total nightmare bitch who I would steer clear of. But alas, from the moment an Art History 101 study group forced us into meeting (believe me, I was not a willing participant), she has been my BFF-soulmate. She has always been there for me, no matter what state of mind I am in, which as you know, can be all over the fucking map, and so, in the midst of Covid, after she had a new baby and was now in charge of three children under the age of four, when she asked me if I could help her, I *leapt* at the opportunity. FINALLY! I could at least *try* to pay her back for the millions of times she had come to my rescue.

I rented an apartment close to her house and for the next month and a half poured myself into a project I called "Family Immersion Therapy." In the mornings, I'd do my rituals at my place (meditating, journaling, working out) and then I'd go over to Fisch's house to cook treats; rock the newborn, Hannah, to sleep; play a game with the eldest, Maya, in which we pretended she was a fish and I was there to eat her unless she escaped by morphing into an inedible mound of trash (her imaginative getaway, not mine); and watch in wonder as Fisch's middle child, Lily, a chill toddler, told the adults that while she appreciated an invitation to play, she would prefer "lonely time," her version of a meditative moment to herself. Fisch bought me a giant black leather bag, and from it I would pull treats and toys and games for the girls, including my own stuffed animal that they had chosen for me, a King Charles spaniel I named Charlie Boy.* I fashioned myself a twenty-first-century Mary Poppins, tho there would be no spoonfuls of sugar because who would want to be around three bouncing-off-the-walls, sugar-high kids? Not this Mary.

What struck me the most about my time with Fisch and her family was how she and her husband made their daughters the priority of their lives and never looked despondent about it. In fact, they seemed kinda happy! They would laugh as their little girls danced to Doja Cat and they would delight in reading them bedtime stories. That's not to say there weren't moments of anarchy and stress—even with three adults for three children bedtime remained chaos incarnate—a true test of patience and courage that often left us so exhausted that all we could do was collapse on the couch and watch *The Bachelorette* in complete silence. But in time, I found myself doing without a second thought things that, at first blush, seemed like they would genuinely suck: I organized the kids' toys after play time, I cleaned up the truly shocking amount of food that fell to the floor during meal time (like, was *anything* getting into their mouths?), I made them snacks that I ~~occasionally~~ often pilfered, I even changed a few diapers, and when I found that Maya was mad at me because despite having not eaten *any* of the crackers with Laughing Cow cheese I had just prepared for her she was afraid she didn't have *enough,* and broke into a level-ten meltdown, I didn't take her crying personally. That might surprise you

---

* Hannah, the baby, fell in love with Charlie Boy and now has her own version. I have a stuffed animal twin with a one-year-old, I am extremely proud to say.

that I ever would, but up until that point I was kinda afraid of children in general, and scared they wouldn't like me. But very quickly I saw that Maya was just a kid, a smart, wise, beautiful kid, but a kid nevertheless. She could not regulate her emotions. It was on *me* to be the adult who could handle her feelings and make her see that she was safe, no matter how she felt. It struck me that—*oh my God*—I really could handle this. With time, I came to understand something I never had realized before about kids—I would have sacrificed anything for them *gladly,* with pleasure, because they were young and helpless and lovely and deserved everything, that was just their birthright. That is every child's birthright. Nothing I did for them ever felt like a sacrifice. It felt like love. And these weren't even my kids!

As I watched Maya, the eldest, navigate her days in her pink-and-red tie-dyed "twirling" dress, I started to imagine her in my shoes as a little kid. What if Maya lived in a falling-apart house that she was afraid of? What if her parents filled her head with the idea that the entire world was out to get her and that their family was financially doomed? What if she felt scared and alone most days and didn't have anyone to comfort her when she was hurt? Thinking of Maya in those circumstances broke my heart open. It broke for how fragile and vulnerable Maya was, and for everything young me had endured. However hard I imagined life with my parents would have been on Maya, it must have been just as hard for me. As I thought about Maya stepping into my shoes, I had a rushing urge to protect her, to shield her from things she couldn't handle and help her grow into who she was born to be. I could feel that these were healthy adult instincts, to want to take care of the precious joy muffin that is a little girl. If my parents hadn't felt those impulses to nurture and protect, that wasn't a reflection on *me,* it was a reflection on them and their own limitations. Maya had never once been a burden; she was a glorious, playful expression of life. Finally, I could see that I had not been a burden either.

At the end of a month and a half, it was time for me to return to Los Angeles and I was surprised that I really didn't want to. It was *nice* to be a part of a family and surrounded by love and not calamity, stress, and screaming. It felt *amazing* to be needed, and I became aware that even though Present Me still had no idea if she wanted children, my thoughts were ever so subtly shifting, and Future Me, the person I was becoming, might have a different opinion.

I have always used the idea of Future Me to guide me when I'm not sure what to do. For as much as I trust myself, there are still some things I don't know how to handle. How do you navigate a serious health problem? Or what about a death you never saw coming? When these difficulties come up, I turn to Future Me, who in my mind is Anjelica Huston sitting on a cloud, wearing flowing white linen and PILES of beaded necklaces. She is calm, wise, has been on every possible adventure, and has some stories about Jack Nicholson back in the day that would make you blush. Future Me is the highest version of myself, both the purest expression of the essential me I have already met and the version of myself I'm glowing into. For example, when I'm in a conflict with a friend and tempted to start declaring how right I am, I can call on Future Me to remind me relationships are the most important thing in my life, so maybe press pause on sending that snide email. Future Me can hold my hand, look me in the eye, and say, "You know, I get why you think being petty would feel good, I do. But, darling, I'm really not into that and you won't be either. Now shall we jet to Saint Tropez? Valentino has two spots on his yacht calling our names." Twist my arm, Anjelica Huston Future Me. *Twist my arm.*

When it came to my evolving thoughts on whether to have children, Present Me was currently in therapy and very much trying to heal herself so that Future Me could make a decision that was her own and not a clapback to trauma. The only problem was, as a thirty-five-year-old without a partner I knew that my body might not give me the healing time my spirit so desperately needed. So what should I do? I decided that while I couldn't make a decision right then and there, it was the job of Present Me to give Future Me as many options as possible.

I'd long heard about freezing eggs as a way to beat the biological clock, but had never looked into it. To be honest, it always sounded like a scam to me. The first time I heard about it was when I was in college, in the cafeteria with Fisch, feasting on a ritzy lunch of chicken tenders and Nutella sandwiches, when I saw an advertisement in the campus newspaper: EGG DONOR NEEDED, UP TO $15,000 FOR YOUR IVY LEAGUE EGGS. *What did that mean?* I wondered. As I read on I realized (a) that I *had* eggs in my body (news flash), and (b) that apparently people really wanted them.* As I thought about the loans my dad and I had taken out for me to attend Brown, I thought this might be a viable answer to help me get out of debt, but was immediately turned off when I realized it meant I would be giving up a part of myself that could be my child. That was too weighty of a decision for Chicken Tender Nutella Me to make.

Since then, I had always thought the procedure was probably unnecessary. What even was a biological clock? It sounded like a scheme for men to make women feel bad about themselves like so many other things in life and something I could for sure dodge because I'm special like that. I was also suspicious that it was a plot to keep women at their desks, working at demanding, probably tech jobs with the promise that they could have kids "someday." Even as increasing numbers of my circle underwent the procedure and the older women in my life (Thirty-six! Shriek!) told me that it was time to consider freezing mine, I didn't really think about it.

---

* I don't know where my education went SO wrong, but it wasn't until considering egg freezing that the whole "sperm fertilizes the egg" BASIC biology of reproduction made any sense to me. Thank you, the complicated union between American education and women's general lack of knowledge about their bodies! What a cute couple!

But shortly after my Family Immersion Therapy, I realized I actually had an egg-freezing benefit as part of my old job's health insurance and that it would soon be expiring. I needed to use it or lose it.

This prompted me to finally google "egg retrieval" and learn that it was a procedure in which a doctor would coax my body into producing viable eggs that could be frozen and then saved for future use. That was what the biological clock was all about. My uterus would stay youngish for a while to come, but there was a finite number of eggs in me and as they aged, their quality diminished, and so, too, did my chances of carrying a child. I bristled to think my eggs were "geriatric" (the actual term for eggs of women over thirty-five that we ALL need to protest and ban because genuinely—what the fuck?). I thought ALL of me was in the prime of her life, especially because I was the sanest and most grounded I had *ever* been. It wasn't fair, I thought, for my body to be so "old" when I had just figured out how to actually live. Then, I just about lost my mind when I found out that without insurance, the procedure could cost anywhere between ten to twenty thousand dollars in Los Angeles. WHO HAD THAT KIND OF MONEY!? I decided I couldn't pass up the bargain of my soon-to-expire insurance benefit, and without a ton of thought started making the necessary appointments for the procedure. This way, I would be giving Future Me more options and allowing Present Me to indulge in my favorite pastime of all—getting a deal.

When I asked my friends who had done egg retrievals about the experience, the typical response was that it was "no big deal." Someone said it was like "getting your wisdom teeth removed." I'm not sure what kind of horrific, multi-week, hormone-infused, orthodontic procedures that person has experienced, but I soon found the entire process to be more like a root canal. Of all of your teeth. At the same time.

First, I had to buy specialty drugs, worth a small fortune, that were so sensitive they had to be refrigerated the moment they arrived at my home. Then, I had to somehow become both a chemist and a nurse with the ability to mix these drugs (some of which were powders) and then get them in syringes without *any* air bubbles (which I worried would kill me and worried even more when I couldn't find any information to the contrary) and then inject them into my body.* I would need to do this two to three times a day for two weeks, all the while going to a fertility center, a half an hour away, every other day to have my blood drawn and to have a vaginal ultrasound so that my doctor could monitor the progress of my eggs. I'm pointing out that this is a *vaginal* ultrasound, and not a wand with goop on it passing over your lower belly, because the more your eggs grow, the more uncomfortable the exam becomes. All told, in the course of two weeks, I would be stuck with a needle around *seventy* times before the final needle that, in a surgery, would be put up my vagina to puncture my ovaries and then suck out my eggs. If you're queasy right now, I'm right there with you. Can you imagine saying to a dude, "Hey, we are going to poke you with needles seventy times and then knock you out and stick a needle up your dick to vacuum out your sperm, but don't worry, it's 'no big deal.'" Any man in his right mind would consider that a very big deal and so did I.

Since I didn't have a long-term partner (I had actually just started dating the Great Gatsby IRL), and was squeamish about needles, I hired a nurse to come to my apartment every night and mix and administer the injections to me. I did this because I was, after all, saving an exorbitant amount of money with my discount shopping insurance scheme and because I had neither the talent nor the ability to do any of the mixing or actual administering of the drugs myself, and frankly, to this day, I don't understand how

---

* Obviously, do not take ANY of this as health advice. I have my degree in being Emmy Un-Nominated, not in medicine. I did the bare minimum of research and don't recommend that way of making health decisions AT ALL!

anyone does. My sister is a doctor and when she took a look at the drugs and the syringes, she decided she would need an hour of watching YouTube videos to *maybe* be able to administer the drugs. Just about the only pleasant part of the process was my nurse, Savannah, a sweet Southern belle with a big laugh, who would stick me right as the beat dropped to Taylor Swift's "Ready for It?"* The process was difficult, but after the procedure, with hopefully enough eggs to give Future Me more choices (not a guaranteed outcome—I know people who have gotten zero eggs after *all that,* and also, not all eggs survive being "thawed out" later), I felt proud of myself. I had made a mature, reasonable decision for Future Me and it had worked out! YAY ME!

If that had been the end of the story, I would recommend egg freezing to you now. But *hoooooooo boy,* unfortunately for me, it was not. There are risks to the procedure and one of those is ovarian hyperstimulation syndrome (OHSS), a condition in which all of the hormones you have been shooting into yourself for weeks cause the ovaries to swell and leak liquid into the rest of the body. It feels just about as good as it sounds. When I had the procedure, I was in little danger of this complication because my hormone levels didn't indicate anything was wrong. Typically, if the doctor detects that you are in danger of OHSS, they will sometimes "cancel" the procedure because it can be excruciatingly painful and potentially dangerous.

A few days after the surgery, as I was recovering at home, I noticed I was feeling worse and not any better. I called my doctor to ask if this was normal and she reassured me. "I can say *for sure* you don't have OHSS, you have none of the warning signs for it. You're fine, this is just an uncomfortable experience, hang in there!" she cheerily replied while dismissing my symptoms.

---

* BTW, this marked the one and only time I have had a neighbor lodge a noise complaint against me. I would like to see if they would have preferred the alternative: me screaming and crying in agony as I attempted to administer the shots myself.

Shortly after, however, after gaining eight pounds of weight and having trouble breathing, I knew there was no way this was "fine" and a friend rushed me to the doctor to figure out what was happening. In the ultrasound chair, I heard my doc say something you never want to hear: "Well, I haven't seen anything like this before." Apparently, though it had not seemed I would have been a candidate for this condition, I had an unknown genetic predisposition for OHSS. *Cool, cool, great,* I thought as I lay on my back cursing the grainy images of the ultrasound.

The following two weeks were by far the most physically grueling, most physically painful period I have ever suffered through. There was so much liquid in my ovaries that I couldn't lie down at night and had to sleep sitting upright, for fear that the liquid would push up against my lungs and make it impossible to breathe when horizontal. I felt extreme cramping at all times of the day and night. A friend of mine, who had recently given birth *without* an epidural and who had also experienced OHSS herself, told me, between the two, "OHSS is way worse; if you can get through this, you can have a baby with no drugs, easily." There's no world in which I want having a baby without ALL OF THE DRUGS to seem "easy," ya know? I was in such all-consuming discomfort that it felt like I would never get any better and I would always be sick. And I was one of the lucky ones!

Many people with OHSS require IVs and follow-up surgeries, but blessedly, mine passed naturally, if you could consider pumping your body full of drugs to turn both of your ovaries "on" when normally only one is active, then cultivating as many eggs as possible in ovaries designed to hold only *one* egg total, then farming those out through surgery, then having your ovaries swell in reaction to all of this, then taking additional drugs to try to calm your ovaries, then not walking for two weeks "natural."

I made it through the procedure and the OHSS and now my eggies live on ice in a penthouse in Beverly Hills. I pay for them to live the high life in a building with many, many backup generators. What can I say? My babies have expensive taste, just like their mama. And though I found the process excruciating I also learned something—women's bodies are actual miracles. It's phenomenal that our bodies can hold babies and then birth them and that *any* of us can endure labor. Any woman who has been through IVF, endometriosis, miscarriage, birth, or just had a period for twenty years is a FUCKING WARRIOR BECAUSE OMG are those things hard and excruciating and scary. Motherhood is often looked at as something completely natural, but in my brush with mothering eggs, the process was anything but natural, and I'm not talking about the hormones I was taking. It was weird to have anything grow inside of me and I can't imagine that having a full-blown human stew in there for nine months before I squeezed it out through my vagina would feel anything other than downright alien. BECAUSE DID YOU READ THAT LAST SENTENCE? That's what childbirth is and it's a *giant* fucking deal. And to do *all of this* while also holding a job, or taking care of other children, or without the support of an *army* of partners, I'm not sure how that would even be possible except that women do it every day with no acknowledgment of their bravery.

It is often said that "women are born to do this," and because of that, it can't really be that extraordinary. But my experience navigating the world of insurance, having my body poked and prodded at with little regard for *how much that sucks,* advocating for myself with doctors, having the procedure, and then having complications that severely impeded my ability to do anything and forced me to take weeks off of work, showed me that women are nothing short of remarkable; each pregnancy that occurs is a spectacular and unique revelation. Women's bodies are magical machines of unfathomable complexity and power that somehow CREATE NEW HUMAN BEINGS. The next time you feel powerless just remember that between your legs lies the very future of the world.

Looking back, I'm not sure if I would do the egg retrieval again. The process was so agonizing and upsetting that I might rather take my chances getting pregnant the old-fashioned way and if that didn't work, I've *always* thought about adopting kids. When I think of all the children who are neglected and abandoned, and think of how I myself felt growing up, I know now that I could give tenderness and love to a child who had no one else. And maybe for me, that would be a good option. But on the other hand, the whole reason I went through the procedure is because there are things about myself that still need healing if I am to be truly unencumbered of my childhood. Given that I understand how much change is possible for me, and that I have faith in my ability to transform, I am sure there is a future version of me who will know what she wants to do and I want her to have as many options as possible.

Future Me is one of the most powerful tools I have in my arsenal to help myself. If Present Me is lost or unsure, all I need to do is sit down, get quiet, and ask Anjelica Huston Future Me what she would do in my current position. The first thing she usually says is, "Breathe, darling, breathe. No need for rash decisions, let's just take our time." When I'm not sure if I should go on some adventure, she'll usually cajole me, saying, "Darling, we have the whole world to see, grab your hat, we're going on an adventure!" And when I am deciding whether or not to get rid of all my handbags from high school in a misguided attempt to become "minimalist" in my style, Future Me will scream, "What are you possibly thinking? Everything that's old will come back again, you are going to want that mini Vuitton more than you are going to want thirty dollars from the secondhand store." Whether or not I listen to her is my choice. I didn't during my clothing purge and let me tell you, she was right. When mini handbags and bucket hats came back in 2022 I had to tell Future Me she was absolutely correct and vow to never, ever again be taken in by the myth of minimalism. It's not a fun way to live.

I think the best part about Future You is that when you ask her for advice and follow it, you are actually allowing yourself to evolve *right now*. You are bringing Future You into existence and accessing the deepest wisdom within you. How can I tell my future voice from my present? It's easy. Future Me is not frantic and overburdened, she never rushes, she doesn't try to force me into anything, her words are clear and slow, and she takes as much time as necessary to deliver her message. I, in my day-to-day life, tend to be scattered and quick to make decisions (unless I am agonizing over them, of course) so it's pretty easy to discern whose counsel I am following.

What does *your* Future You look like? Does she have serious, Greta Thunberg, punk rock vibes? Or the courage of Malala Yousafzai? Or maybe she's got more of a Trixie Mattel thing going on? Or maybe it's a sleek black panther, about to claim her prey. Maybe Future You is your long-deceased, wise Himalayan cat (RIP, Coco). Choose whatever feels like a powerful, comforting symbol for your future. Let's find out who or what your Future You is made of.

A List of Ways to Conjure Future You, but You Can't Have Anjelica Huston Because She Is Mine

Seriously. She's mine. Step off. These are the questions I use to evoke Future Me. Sometimes I'll meditate intensely on one question. Sometimes I'll be running errands and I'll babble about them to Future Me under my breath. I suggest you set aside time to really build Future You using the questions below AND revisit these questions as frequently as you can. Maybe

this is a Post-it-Notes-around-your-room situation? I believe
in the power of Post-it Notes as much as I believe in the power
of Future You. Which is to say I am a woman of faith.

1. Choose a person you admire who might exemplify Future You. I find it helps to have an image of someone else (Anjelica Huston) so there's no chance I'll start picking her apart like I can do with myself. What do you admire about this person? Why did you choose them?

2. What does Future You look like? Where do they live? What do they enjoy in life? Get granular and really describe what they wear, how they move, how they present themselves to the world. For example, Anjelica Huston Future Me lives on a cloud. I don't know why, but she does. She only wears flowing white linen and her skin glows (I need to ask her about her products). Describe your Future You.

3. Does Future You wear something you are obsessed with in particular? Or do they give themselves a special treat? Or keep fresh flowers (lilies, duh) in their home (or cloud, in my case)? Or do they have one physical attribute you think is *just amazing*? What is one thing that totally delights Future You? How can you try to bring whatever that is into your life today?

4. What makes Future You smile?

5. How does Future You spend their days?

6. How does Future You make other people feel when they are in the same room?

7. What are the top five priorities and amazing qualities of Future You?

8. What is Future You most proud of Present You for?

9. What does Future You understand is difficult for Present You, and how are they compassionate about that?

10. What kind, soothing words do you need to hear more often? What would your ideal parent say to you right now? Can Future You remind you of the same thing?

Future You is your hope for what is to come, but the best part about it is that it's not some fanciful delusion, it's not some societally enforced preference, it's *yours,* purely and utterly yours, and you have the power to bring your highest future to your present today.

Future You is standing here with you, on this path, holding a flashlight, illuminating exactly where you need to go next and ready to whisper helpful tips into your receptive ear. And how about this? While you can't have Anjelica Huston Future Me, we *will* go on a double date with you and your Future You. Pick an Italian place, because few people know this but Anjelica LOVES spaghetti and meatballs. I know, I know, basic as can be but doesn't it seem chic for her? Like OF COURSE she has iconoclastic taste. We'll stay up too late, probably drink too much wine, but we'll all feel good knowing that we are working toward a better, more radiant, totally possible Future You.

A Little Thing That Helps

Cull a one-page description of Future You from your answers above. Post it somewhere you will see it. It's soothing to know this being is already here, in a way, and it's helpful to be reminded daily of where YOU want to go.

Grief and Gratitude
The Bittersweet Blessing of Boundaries

DID YOU KNOW I HATE my first name? First off, no one can pronounce it. *Can you pronounce it?* Mostly people say "tair-uh," but it's pronounced "tahr-uh." Those are straight-up different names! People I have known for *years* continue to call me "tair-uh" even after I purposely and repeatedly say my name in front of them in an anguished bid to train them. I do play a part in this pronunciation butchering because I never actually correct anyone (I'm afraid of confrontation!). So, hearing my name said aloud is pretty much always a bummer, which, after thirty-five years, can really grate on a person. Another reason I hate my name is because it sounds hippieish and woo-woo and faux-spiritual. Who has even ever heard of "Tara"? It doesn't come from anyone in my family and has no special significance to the Schusters. I think what probably happened was that my mom read one spiritual book, one time, and then chose my name based off her lukewarm interest in 1980s mysticism.* This is why for years I've asked people to call me T$ (T-Money, for the uninitiated), or T, or Schustey, or anything other than my first name—BECAUSE THEY ARE GOING TO FUCK IT UP! And if right now, you're beginning to think that

---

* My dad recently confirmed this. "Your name came from a book of Greek goddesses because your mother liked it. She said yours was the goddess and tamer of men and wild animals." A lot to put on a newborn, no?

this chapter, and potentially this entire book, might be a passive-aggressive ruse to get people to say my name correctly—you're not entirely wrong.

While I have always disliked my name, I had never actually investigated what it meant until I was in Flagstaff. You'd think that somewhere in the preceding thirty-four years I might have *once* questioned its significance, but I had no curiosity about my name whatsoever. Like if I ignored it, it would just go away. It came up for me in 2020 when I needed to drive to Sedona to pick up campaign literature for the local races I was volunteering for, bring it back to Flagstaff, and then litter unsuspecting voters' front doors with pamphlets they would surely never read because *who reads pamphlets?* I'll admit to you now: I am the person who papered your front door for Coral Evans and Felicia French in 2020 and had you heeded my advice, you would have had two very fine women in office, one of whom knows how to land an Apache helicopter on water, which I think qualifies a person to do just about anything.

ANYWAY. I needed to go to Sedona to pick up the leaflets and because I can't let anything be simple in my life, I polled every local I knew in Arizona about how I could make this errand into a fun day trip. Friends suggested hikes with epic names—the Devil's Bridge, Cathedral Rock, the Birthing Cave—and over and over again I was told I HAD to visit an outdoor, thirty-six-foot statue of the Buddha and a smaller, though still beautiful, statue of the goddess "Tara." *AHA! She WAS a goddess! I KNEW it was some woo-woo hippie shit, Mom!* I said to myself. Some light Web research revealed that Tara means "star" in Sanskrit! And not just any old star—the kind of star that radiates so brightly it can guide the path for all people on their spiritual journeys (!). Tara is also a (mother-fucking) goddess in Buddhism, where she is considered the mother of liberation, and is known for her endless compassion and fierce wisdom. She is maternal, loving, nurturing, and her greatest power is to see suffering in the world and help relieve it. In one legend, she began as a devout princess who stayed in a state of meditation for ten million years so that she could help countless souls reach their full potential. Knowing how excruciating *ten* minutes of meditation could be, I had to admit she was a lot more patient than I am. As I sat there at my computer, learning that my namesake was way more intriguing than I had previously imagined, I was struck by how these descriptions were *everything* I had ever aspired to be.

Since I hadn't meditated yet that day, I decided to meditate on my name (tho for less than ten million years) and what I had read about "Tara." I closed my eyes and brought an image of Green Tara to mind (there are twenty-one versions of her, each a different color to represent a different attribute) because she was associated with a lotus that blooms in the moonlight and given the option, I will always choose floral. I held that image of Green Tara sitting on her lotus throne with regal ease in the dark, extending one hand toward me and all of humanity, bearing witness to how hard life can be, and offering us all her wisdom and a loving embrace.

Flagstaff is the highest point in Arizona, and maybe it was altitude sickness, or maybe it was genuine revelation, but as I sat there contemplating a god who had the wisdom to help others transform and the compassion to hold them with love when they were lost, I was struck by a vision of my mother, who had chosen to bestow the name Tara upon me. For the first time, I considered the idea that maybe naming me Tara was a sign of *her* deepest wish and longing. Maybe my mom had always yearned for compassionate, maternal, and wise love in her life.

I never knew much about my mom's life. I knew next to nothing about her early childhood other than the fact that her father was a horse jockey, which meant her family moved frequently, following races. I knew that she was named "Miss Orange Bowl" in her teens and that she was academically brilliant—the brightest student in her high school class—which allowed her to get scholarships for college and eventually enter the male-dominated world of gynecology (which, why?). And then I knew that when I was a child, she had made me feel scared and violated. That as I grew older, her attacks on me became stronger and to this day I have a fear of listening to voicemail because as a teenager, I would receive vicious messages from her in which she would say things like, "You are a pathological liar and obsessed with money just like your father who is scum. Call me, it's your mom," or "Your grandmother killed your grandfather and I tried to save him and your father is EVIL and I have the documents to prove it! The *Today* show had a deal on purses. I'll buy you one." Sort of the mother of all non sequiturs that last one, right? I knew that in my early twenties, after a lifetime of enduring her psychological abuse, I had to make the extremely difficult decision to cut off contact with her. It was a choice I never wanted to make, but I didn't know how to live if I was going to be constantly torn down by the woman who gave me life.

But I also knew that, when I was younger, my mom told me time and time again how much she wanted me. How much she dreamed of me and hoped she would have a little girl and that she loved me more than anything. She once illustrated a book for me called *The Magic Ponytail,* which featured me as the plucky protagonist, using my ponytail to whip me into different points in history.* I also have a memory of lying on her chest as she drew circles with her hand on my back and told me how wanted I was. This message was of course sullied by how, in her next breath, she said that my dad wanted to abort me, but still. I have never for one minute doubted my mom's sincerity, and in that meditation in Flagstaff, thinking about the promise of my name and what she

---

* The construction of King Tut's tomb, the American Revolution, Marie Curie discovering radium—I was there for all of that thanks to a well-chosen accessory.

might have hoped for, I was flooded by compassion for how hard my mother's life must have been.

At this point, I had taken care of Fisch's kids (not to mention my own eggs) and understood that the instinct to protect the young was just something natural. That any healthy adult would go out of their way *not* to harm a vulnerable child. If my mom's instincts had been to isolate me, to make me feel like she was the only one who loved me, and then harm me emotionally, what must it have been like to live in her body and mind? How tortured must she have been? And how utterly, completely sad was it that the thing she wanted the most—my love—was the thing she guaranteed she would never receive by the way she treated me? For so long, I had held my mom at arm's length, but now I felt close to her. She had suffered through something and wanted so deeply to be loved, protected, and taken care of. I knew exactly how she felt.

It was as if some wall I had built between me and my mother, some barricade that protected me from her, came tumbling down and I was flooded with great waves of empathy for whatever it was that she had been through and how difficult it had made her life. My mom had very few friends, and as I thought about how important the love and support of my Friend Family had been in my life, how many times Fisch's words, Julia's embrace, or even the kindness of an acquaintance on a rough day had saved me, I realized how much my mom had missed out on, and it broke my heart. As frayed as my feelings might be from time to time, I would never be a stray thread, I would always be woven into a community much larger than myself because I recognized that I knew how to love and be loved. My mom, because of whatever trauma she had been through, was trapped in her own devastating patterns and never really got to live, or at least she didn't live a life *I* would have wanted. She didn't need my condemnation, she needed the kindest part of me—the part that is good and pure and only wants love—to simply see her pain and bear witness to how truly difficult and tragic it can be to live on earth.

I forgave and forgive my mother. For all that she did. I can't even be that mad about any of it when I think about how much it must have hurt her to hurt me. I did not come to this conclusion lightly. For years, I wished my mother dead. I wished I didn't have to deal with her. I wished I could have been born to someone else, someone who loved me, someone who took care of me, but now I saw that I had done a pretty good job filling in for her. And the upshot of her abuse was that it helped build me into someone who could truly relate to others in distress, people who felt alone, or those who yearned to be loved. I adore my life, I love my friends, I even *like* who I am. Would I have any of that had I not gone down this path? And who set me on that path if not my mother?

In an instant (that I had been building toward for thirty years), I felt completely clear: I had finally forgiven my mother, and maybe I'd even lived up to my namesake just a little. This does not mean I swung the door open to having her in my life by any means. We have still not spoken in years, but it does mean the door is open a crack and that even if we never speak again, I feel close to her, I feel compassion for her.

But for some reason, just as I felt the boundary between my mother and me dissolving, I increasingly felt like I needed to construct a stronger one between me and my dad. For most of my life, my dad had been the only adult around for me, and he had not always taken that responsibility seriously. There were all the things you know about: his addiction to weed that led to my addiction to weed, his inability to show up sober for me, the way he never protected me, the way he scared me into thinking I would be doomed in my career and finances, and on and on. But there was something even more glaringly wrong about our relationship. I was increasingly realizing that he didn't really *know* me. Conversations with him rarely contained any questions about me, more often they were rants from him about how the DVR machine didn't work, or about a new article of clothing he was obsessed with. During the Covid pandemic, he never once asked how I was doing, if I had enough masks, if I felt safe, or if I was anxious. He expressed no concern for my health whatsoever.

Meanwhile, I worried incessantly about him, concerned that his age left him vulnerable to sickness, and for some reason still hoping and praying that one day he would be curious about who I was. This was a time of tremendous healing for me! I felt like daily I was liberating my own soul from the complex trauma she had endured, and so all my conversations with my dad just struck me as thin, superficial, and unpleasant. When one night he confessed that he might have been exposed to Covid in a meeting with "forty-eight other people that you don't want to know about," I was outraged. Here was yet again, some shady-ass thing my dad had done and he was talking to me about it like he was *my* kid, provoking me to reprimand him. I couldn't take it anymore. I decided I needed a break from my dad because what little esteem I had left for him seemed to be grated down by every new and unsatisfying conversation. So, in the middle of a global pandemic that was bringing into clear view how important family was to everyone, I decided to stop speaking to my dad.

I had never once in my life drawn a boundary this stark with him. If you read my last book, you know that I came to a peace with my dad after his brush with death. I wish I could tell you that after those dramatic, lifesaving surgeries to stop the bleeding in his brain (that had only been caught because *I* had noticed something was horribly wrong with him and rushed him to the hospital) we had a perfect, happy ending and that he finally realized I was a good daughter and made me feel valued and cherished. But that would be far from the truth.

Instead of growing closer together, we became increasingly contentious with each other after I asked him to create a will that might make life easier on me and my sister should the very real possibility of his death come to pass. One day, during his recovery, I excitedly drove him to buy me hiking shoes, the thank-you he wanted to get me for all the help I had given him. As I drove, I brought up the will as gently as I could, reminding him that my sister and I didn't give a damn what he had—in fact, I assumed it was nothing—we just didn't want to be inundated with paper-work while also grieving his passing. I asked one more time if he could create one, and he became apoplectic. "STOP THE CAR," he shouted. "PULL OVER!" I abruptly turned to the soft shoul-der. "You're just like your mother! *You ARE your mother!* You're moneygrubbing and selfish!" he roared at me as he flung open his car door to get out. "Dad, wait! It's not safe for you to walk alone!" I called after him before immediately breaking down into tears. The whole moment was so *out of nowhere* and strange and just had this hateful energy that my dad had rarely directed at me. He spoke to me as if *I* were my mom, the woman he hated. I sat in the driver's seat contemplating what to do. I was afraid he might fall if he walked alone, but I was paralyzed by how hurt I felt. He kept on walking and I drove to the North Face store, wearing sunglasses to hide my tears. It may have been the saddest shoe purchase in the history of Beverly Hills, California.

That experience had been wounding to me, but I never told him that, nor had I demanded he apologize or treat me better in the future. We just acted like nothing had happened. I'd never said anything because what was the point? My whole life, there had never been a single consequence of my dad's behavior (for him, at least). He could be mean to me, degrade my dreams, raise me in a household of constant threat and anxiety, and yet, I always came back to him, playing the part of dutiful daughter and also some kind of weird mother. *Enough,* I thought. Finally, *enough.*

* * *

I stopped speaking to him outright and it was agonizing for my dad; my sister told me that he cried to her about how upset he was, how he felt alone and abandoned—a feeling I knew well. I didn't have any ill will for my dad, I just couldn't handle him any longer, and in the two years I didn't speak to him, I found that, just as I predicted, without him taking up a major portion of my brain space, I was free to better figure out who I was and what mattered to me. Without needing to defend myself from him in the present, it was far easier to heal my wounds from the past. I was also free to spend more time with the families of my friends and learn from them without worrying if it would hurt my dad's feelings, as I always had. The entire reason I was able to invest so fully in Family Immersion Therapy was that I had the double excuse of Covid and this break in communication to not see my family. I think that was the key—for the first time ever, I didn't worry about my dad or think about how I needed to protect or help him, and that lack of responsibility gave me space to take care of myself.

I might have continued the pause in communication with my dad for years to come, but in the winter of 2022, my sister texted me, "I know you're not speaking to him, and he's doing fine right now, but you should know Dad contracted Covid." My entire being went into high alert. I worried that his age and previous brain injuries might make him susceptible to death, and in that instant, any issue I had with him evaporated. I sprung into action, calling his doctor, asking a million questions to make sure I was as informed as I could possibly be. My brilliant doctor-sister came up with a treatment plan and every day I did a FaceTime wellness check with him, insisting that he do specialized exercises that protected his lungs and making sure he was eating. Being forced to be in contact with him in such a dramatic fashion thawed the mountain of ice that had grown between us. And I learned something startling: My dad had been in therapy the entirety of the preceding two years.

My dad had never really been to "a shrink," as he called them, or if he had, he hadn't taken them seriously and complained that they were a waste of money. But apparently, when I stopped speaking to him, he was so rattled that he started therapy to try to better cope with his new reality. I had begged my dad to go to therapy for years; in fact, for my last two birthdays before our break I told him that I didn't want any gifts, I just wanted him to go to therapy. Now he had, and as he healed from Covid, I noticed something peculiar— he in almost no way resembled the dad I had known. It was now like I had two dads: pre-therapy Dad 1, and post-therapy Dad 2.

Dad 2 did strange things—he *thanked* me for aiding him. "I'm so grateful to you and your sister for your help with Covid, I've never felt so loved or cared for in my life," he told me with tears in his eyes over Zoom. He let me know he was proud of me. "I'm so proud of all the work you're doing, I'm in awe. You're doing amazing, you're unstoppable, go, Tara!" he enthusiastically cheered. He told me that he now saw that my childhood had been traumatic and that he wanted to help heal it. "I know it must have been hard, but I don't totally understand it. I know I was there, but I don't remember much. Would you tell me, please? If you are up for it? I want to hear it, all of it, and take responsibility for it because I'm sure it happened," he insisted on a video chat one day. "I'm in therapy because I want to be a better father to you. I realize I didn't protect you. Frankly, I wasn't thinking about you when you were growing up. And I never thought about what it really meant to be a father," he confided. For the first time ever, my dad wasn't defensive; rather, he seemed genuinely interested in sharing the burden of my childhood with me, in bearing some of the weight of it in order to help me heal. He even invited me to do family therapy with him, saying, "I'm still learning how to communicate, how to ask questions. . . . I feel like I'm half a person and finally I'm learning how to become a whole human."

These conversations, some with the assistance of his therapist, were incredibly difficult. As much as I knew I had been neglected growing up, it was still hard to hear how right I had been in my perceptions and I could tell that it was painful for my dad to admit that he had not protected me. After these calls, I'd often spend the rest of the day on my sofa, gut-crying and grieving the childhood I never had and the person I didn't grow into. Because as much as I can spin anything into spiritual lemonade, there is a loss, no matter what I do, that will always exist. I will forever wonder who I could have become if none of this had happened. Would I have my own family by now? Would I be doing something completely different? I'll never get to meet that person, and that death of a different version of me is something worth grieving. I bet she would have been something special.

Just as my dad and I began our healing process, I myself contracted Covid, and though I had heard *all* of the warnings and bleak predictions, I was in no way prepared for how it would affect me. In addition to having a sore throat that felt like a hot knife was being shoved down it, I had brain fog so thick I was afraid to leave my apartment because I thought I would get lost. One night, I left my front door wide open, and on another, as I spoke to my sister on the phone, I became distracted by "how weird voices are," and couldn't continue speaking. My hands were violently shaking, and to this day I don't know if it was my imagination. It was frightening and I wondered if I would be afflicted by cognitive problems long term. Add to this the fact that I was still single and lived alone and didn't have anyone to help me.* To my total astonishment, my dad stepped in. "I always thought you were so strong and powerful and didn't need my help," he explained to me. I laughed and quickly regretted doing so as it caused my entire body to ache. "I have never thought of myself that way, not one time." "Well,

---

* P.S. I know others had Covid FAR WORSE, but for me it was nowhere near the "mild cold" many people spoke of at the time. I've yet to have a cold where I hallucinated.

that's what I thought, but now I realize you're my little girl, and you need help. I'm here for you. What can I do?" he asked. I was gobsmacked. "Well, I don't have any food, not that I'm hungry . . . ," I admitted. "Say no more, I'm on it," he replied.

For the next week my dad sent me meals: matzo ball soup, lox and bagels, dim sum, and acai bowls, which I don't know how he even knew was a thing. And every few hours he texted me to ask how I was feeling. It was the first time I felt taken care of by my dad, or really anyone, when I was sick, and I had a glimmer of what it would have been like if I'd had supportive parents growing up. How much less afraid I might be, how much more confident. It made me realize that maybe, just maybe, now that I'd felt that, I could hang on to it, carry it with me, and bolster it with the confidence I had found in myself. Maybe I could see how it felt to live with the freedom safety provides you.

My dad is seventy-eight, which makes me incredibly sad. I have lost so much time with him. The years when he was at his most active and adventurous are gone and now he lives in a different state, which means we don't get much time together. But. I might get to have a few years with a real dad. It's not perfect, the loss is still present, and yet, wow. *I might have a few years with a real dad.* With Dad 2. Even if all I ever get are the past six months, they have made me feel more loved than I knew was possible. I never thought that was in the cards for me, and my appreciation for this new fact of my life is never-ending.

I'm not saying that if you lay down a boundary with someone, they will change. That is rarely the case. But, when you do make a boundary, it means there are consequences to their actions. They are forced to consider living in a different way if they want you in their life. Even if it was painful, Dad 2 would admit to you now that my not speaking to him for two years was "one of the best things" I could have done. "I didn't like it, but I'm not sure I would have gone to therapy if you hadn't," he admitted. "And, I feel like

I'm getting my life back. I feel like I finally have a shot at actually living." None of that would have happened for him had I not put my own health first.

I grieve the person I never became, the lost time with my parents, the experiences I will never have. And I am endlessly grateful that I was given a life to begin with, that for some odd reason my mom and dad met. I'm grateful for the person I have become, the adventures I have been on, and that I have the possibility to create something real with my dad. Everything is on the table now. There is no truth too sad or too hard to exist. At the intersection of grief and gratitude, in the space we have carved out for honesty, I have found my own salvation.

We often think that if we don't admit the truth, maybe it won't exist. We believe that if we put ourselves first, we're putting others last. That if we draw a boundary, it will hurt someone, even if we know it could save ourselves. These lies keep us captive to the past, running the same, tired, limited patterns over and over again until they are the faded, uninspired blueprint for our lives. They are deadening for you *and* the person you are supposedly protecting. I love you very much, but if you are not setting a boundary, you're impeding others from their own growth. If you never speak up for yourself, if you accept what is unacceptable to placate others, you deny *them* the opportunity to show up for you and to change.

If you believe you are an integral part of your community (Yes, you are! If you can't trust yourself with this fact, trust me: You are an integral part of MY community), if you believe you are made of the same star stuff as the rest of us, then your healing matters just as much as anyone else's, and in fact, your healing becomes the healing of everyone else as you show others that they have a responsibility for their actions. And until you set the boundaries that are necessary to heal, until you take yourself seriously, the rest of us won't know it's safe enough to follow your lead.

Glow On

I HAVE A NEW RITUAL these days. Every night, instead of letting another day just pass me by, I go outside and I look up at the stars. Sometimes there is nothing to see through the LA smog, but I *always* look, in case I can catch something magical. And after, when I crawl into bed, I ask myself three questions:

1. Was I kind today?

2. Was someone kind to me?

3. Did I live this day the way I wanted to?

My answers can be all over the map, but the more I am intentional about my life, the more nights in a row I whisper, "Yes, yes, HELL YES."

I don't know you, or at least I probably don't, and yet, I absolutely do. As corny and cliché as it is, I know *you* because now I know *me,* and we are all the same—different bodies, same spirit. And look, if you really chafe at all my ethereal talk, then how about, different bodies, same science? You can't deny *that*. We all arrive here made of the same stardust, we all suffer, we all feel joy, we all have the potential to lead lives so meaningful and so deeply *us* that we wake up in the morning ready to cry out, "Another day!

YES!" But the thing I've learned is that leading a glittering, liberated, bountiful life is a choice you have to make for yourself, *daily*. It's not something that you just stumble upon, when you're older, or when you finally have the time, unfortch.

Let's be real, though: In this world, it's a goddamn struggle to be yourself and insist on your right to lead the life you actually want. First, you have to be aware enough to see that's even possible. *Wow, is that hard.* Second, there are so many distractions and restrictions placed on us: our jobs, the roles we are supposed to play, our fears, all the trauma and bullshit and tragedy we have been through and will go through, the unstable, unfair, dangerous world we live in—*all* of those factors can hold us stuck in place or even worse, pull us into the comfort of the past, even if that past was wildly uncomfortable. If you are starting to feel like the world is not set up for our success, you're not wrong. And to top it all off, we are made to feel it's downright selfish to choose how we want to live. But I'd like to tell you what I now know: It's wrong *not* to live your own life. It's a giant "fuck you" to the stardust within yourself, and the stardust within *everyone else,* and the lights of others that were extinguished too early. And if you say, "But I don't know who or how I want to be . . . ," *that's amazing*! You now have a worthy challenge I know you can meet. And hopefully, a whole book to help you and encourage you and hold you close, forever, as you return to your sparkling essential self.

You are here one time. I know you know that, *but do you really*? There is only one version of you that will ever exist. HOW FUCKING COOL IS THAT? THERE IS ONLY ONE YOU, *EVER*! What will you do with that *stunning miracle*? That stardust in you, all it wants to do is show itself in its perfectly unique way. It doesn't want to be suppressed or hidden, it yearns for freedom. So, the moment you rip off the lid that has been placed upon you, you will feel fully aligned because you're finally letting your inner, truest self do the only thing it wants to do—glow.

* * *

I like to think that, in a way, my name was a prediction. Because I wasn't treated with compassion, because I was not properly cared for, because I felt (and at times was) abandoned, I yearned for a different life that would somehow give me all that I lacked. I saw my parents in pain on their chaotic, winding roads, and I knew I had to walk in the opposite direction if I ever wanted something better. I didn't know where I was headed and I didn't see much light in front of me, but I learned pretty quickly that there was another way: I could hold my own candle and illuminate my own world of possibility. I would have to be *Tara*—my own shining star.

As my life has increasingly become in sync with who I am at my core, I've learned something I never expected. The only way to guarantee I receive the things I've always wanted the most—love, comfort, safety, understanding, help—is to give them to others. I can't control if my mother will ever love me in a healthy way or if I'll ever heal enough to be a mother myself (if that's even what I end up wanting), but I *can* give the best maternal love I have in me to my sister, to children, to anyone I know who had a hard day. I cannot go back in time and give myself safety, but I can cultivate it in the pages of my journal and try to provide it for my Friend Family. I cannot erase decades of "moneysick," but I can share my newfound knowledge as widely as possible. No one has to give me these things for me to feel them, make them my own, and offer them freely. And this is why self-care is always community care. The only way we can find the world we yearn for is by *being* it now. This world *needs* you to give what you never received.

I want to feel seen, to know that I matter and that my life has value, and that's why I see you. And, oh my friend, do I see you in all your glory. I see the shine you sometimes lose sight of, I see how hard life can be, and I see how fucking courageous you are in showing up and standing up, even as you get knocked down.

Will you do me a favor? (Aside from reading this million-page book, *show-off*.) Will you go on a walk with me back by the side of the road in the Mojave? It's chilly out on a cloudless desert night, we've both forgotten our jackets (again!), so we gotta stay close to keep warm. I grab your hand because it can be scary to be in the dark and to have no idea where you are headed or how long it will take to get there (if you can *ever* get "there"). The moment our fingers intertwine, we feel in our bodies the fizzy warmth of the truth we have always known—we've always belonged to each other. We belong to all the people who came before us and to all the people who will come after us. We are *made* to give our glow. That's the reason we're here. We can offer our love, our under-standing, our humor, our mercy, our justice. And we can make meaning of all the tragedies and shortcomings and failures we've endured if we tend to them and share the lessons we've learned, and the people we've become, with one another.

As we look out, we see that the night is dark, there's no denying that. But we continue to walk, and others join us, adding their lights to our own, and suddenly the ground is illuminated by our collective brightness. We can see where we're going now, one step at a time, not sure of what the future holds, but not worried, ei-ther, because we know we can handle and outshine it all, as long as we're together.

We glow on.

ACKNOWLEDGMENTS

THANK YOU, MY FRIEND, FOR sticking around when things got tough, for laughing at my ~~somewhat~~ dark jokes, for opening your heart and showing me that I'm not alone. So many of the topics in this book (intense journaling, dealing with anxiety, not feeling like we're enough, imposter syndrome, money . . . I mean . . . I guess *every* topic in this book) started with suggestions you gave me in person or on the Internet. I dove in on your behalf and I only hope I did your questions a tiny bit of justice. Thank you for giving me the opportunity to write this book, thank you for giving me meaning, and most important—thank you for making T$ a thing. No one likes when someone else says they have their "dream job." It's annoying, so I won't say it, but I will thank you.

If you appeared in this book in any form, then I owe you a thank-you for being my teacher. Some lessons were more painful than others, but they were all ~~ultimately, after a lot of therapy~~ helpful. Thank you to my editor and birthing partner, Annie Chagnot, for your brain, your soul, your ability to take the (overwhelming) jumble of ideas I have and edit them into something coherent and maybe even good (thanks to you), and for the stardust energy that bursts from you every time I'm lucky enough to be in your orbit. Our meet-cute was one of the luckiest and most important moments in my life. It's impossible to write you enough thank-you notes, so all I want you to know is that you gave shine to every word in this book. There would be no books and possibly no sanity without my agent, Monika Verma. Thank you for always being game to talk about my soup of ideas and pulling the meatiest nuggets out. That sounds way grosser than I imagined it would but you know what I mean. Thank you not only for your excellent suggestions and encouragement but also for tempering my "doom-spiral-everyone-is-against me" tendencies. I don't think people would like me half as much as they do if you weren't there running interference.

To my literary home, Dial Press, *merci beaucoup*. In particular, Whitney Frick, for being my champion and pushing for me in ways I won't ever even know or see. Avideh Bashirrad, thank you for believing in me and for your expert guidance since we first met for *Lilies*. Thank you to Andy Ward for saying "hi" that one time I was in Whit's office—you made me feel like the real thing. Thank you to the stellar marketing and publicity team at Random House, in particular Debbie Aroff (why do you always look so effortlessly good on Zoom?), Madison Dettlinger, Lindsey Kennedy, and Maria Braeckel. Thank you to Alison Rich for your savvy and vision and to your entire team: Rachael Perriello, Zehra Kayi, and especially to Stephanie Bowen for being the most radiant and helpful cheerleader and collaborator I could ever imagine. Thank you for answering my texts, I swear I won't bother you anymore. *For today*. Thank you, Donna Cheng, for the approximately ten million versions you made of this cover and Diane Hobbing for making the inside look as good as the outside. Thank you to Katy Nishimoto for just being the best. Did you know you have a great smile? A round of applause is in order for Nancee Adams and Barb Jatkola for your brilliant proofreading. I actually didn't know how many times I use the word "actually," until you came along. Kelly Chian and Ada Yonenaka, I am grateful for the care you gave this book all through the production process.

Thank you to the early readers of this book who lent their expertise and deepened my education: Khe Hy, Dr. Ellen Vora, Dr. Richard Schwartz, Rabbi Dr. James Jacobson-Maisels, and Coral Compagnoni, LMTF, in particular. I'm grateful to those who have supported me on this book odyssey and lent me a part of their glow: Glennon Doyle, Melissa Urban, Catt Sadler, Linda Phan, and Bonnie Donaghy. Special thanks are in order to Adam Grant for being the first person to vouch for me and then sticking around with guidance every step of the way. Your example has made me a better giver. I hope that *somewhat* makes up for the sheer volume of questions I've asked you. Sarah Hurwitz, you deserve every delightful treat known to mankind. Thank you for sharing your mind and heart with me, and for the sage and rigorous notes that made this book significantly better. THANK YOU for being such a force for good in this world and for enveloping me in your love in my darkest moments.

Thank you to my lawyer Matthew Levy for being so thoughtful and protective of my career at every step of the way and for spending way more time on me than is reasonable, and thank you to Nancy Josephson, Sanjana Seelam, and the team at WME for your help in making my Hollywood dreams come true. I am grateful for Emily Hessel who helped get the word out there with such passion and savvy. Many thanks are in order to Drew Sullivan for believing in me and giving me the chance to share my ideas IRL.

Thank you to my Lady Harem (and now Lady/Partner/Child Harem), past, present, and future. You've had my back when I didn't have my own and have always reminded me of myself when I get lost. Also: thank you for peer pressuring me into having fun.

Dr. Candace, you helped me regain my soul and find my freedom. Thank you for creating a safe place where I could finally unburden myself. Thank you for bearing witness, for guiding my recovery, and for your brilliance. Thank you for your kind wisdom and for never getting annoyed when I insist that we should book an extra appointment so I can heal "faster." I now believe you, "the slower we go, the faster we'll get there." That said, if you have an extra slot next week, I'll take it.

Thank you to my sister for your support, for loving me, for the way only you can make me laugh, for all of the work you have done on yourself and for others, and for being proud of me even when it's complicated because so much of this is your story too. That is never lost on me and I am grateful that you are still speaking to me. Thank you to your fiancé for helping to form our new family and for being the best brother I could ever hope for. He even lets me third-wheel your vacations . . . who does that? I'll meet you both at the Harbor Hut.

Thank you to my mom for giving me life. I'm sorry for all the pain you've been through. I wish it hadn't been that way and I hope that one day I'll meet your stardust self.

Thank you to my dad. Dad, I am so proud of all the work you have done to show up as a truer, kinder, more generous version of yourself. RIP Dad 1. Long live Dad 2. Your hard work has made my life better and has given me a taste of safety and support that I never dreamed I would have. . . . I am grateful to have finally met you. You're wonderful and the dad I always longed for.

A JOURNAL
SO YOU HAVE NO EXCUSE
NOT TO JOURNAL

Time to Glow

A journal to help you find your inner shine so you radiate
strength, bravery, and joy in any situation. Yes. Any situation.

My dearest, darling reader,

So, how'd we do? You must have at least *liked* the book if you've stuck around to the end and for that, I have to say: THANK YOU for coming with me on this journey*; thank you for opening your heart to me; and most important, thank you for sharing the most precious resource of all with me, your time.

In case the previous *hundreds* of pages were not enough info for you, I want you to know that I am the kind of person who arrives at a party early and stays late (hosts *love me*). I don't want to miss out on *any* of the revelry (what if something funny happens and I'm not there?) and it's with that sense of ~~thirst~~ zeal that I just couldn't end the book at the end. Instead, I want to share with you a journal I wrote to help you integrate what you've learned from my story into your life. (Though I do recommend skipping the whole "dates a former sex cult member" situation. No one needs to integrate that into anything aside from a trash can.)

Here's something I haven't told anyone about how this book came to be, so I hope you feel special (mostly because you just are). During my "free-fall time" (remember that cheery ride to Arizona, the dissociative episode, and the ensuing months of suffering? *I sure do!*), I was voraciously writing. I felt compelled to document all of my ups, downs, and every last question I was asking myself, almost as if I were a witness to my own life. I also knew I wanted to write a follow-up book to *Buy Yourself the F*cking Lilies* and hoped that maybe *somewhere* within the brain gunk, I'd find usable material. But when I looked at my heap of pages I was stumped.

Who would want to hear about a supposed "self-help expert"† whose life was an actual painful mess (again)? Didn't that make me a fraud? Didn't it make everything I said in my last book pointless?

---

* I am deeply uncomfortable with that word, it's kind of cheesy, no?
† No one has ever called me this.

In a Hail Mary,* I sent partial essays and ideas to my editor to see if she could discern anything in my swamp of pages. I titled the loose collection *Grow Your Own F*cking Lilies,* because I am a very creative person. My editor, God bless her soul, read and highlighted one little passage that stuck out to her:

> What I've found is that confronting your life as it really is and committing to learning and expanding beyond what feels "safe" and "good enough" is the next step we must take after finding stability. It lights your soul up with phosphorescence so that you can glow even in the darkest of situations. Let's glow in the fucking dark together, shall we?

I hadn't even remembered that I had written that! But once it was pointed out to me, my whole body filled with the good chills, tears came to my eyes, and I felt waves of truth surging through my blood (much like I feel right now—rereading). Suddenly my mess of writing, my current bleak headspace, and possibly my entire "expedition of the mind"† of giving myself the nurturing I never received made sense. There was something within me that had been dimmed for so long, and that something yearned for light. That something yearned to see a path toward emotional and spiritual freedom. That something had big plans, I could tell.

I CAN SAY THIS WITH a straight face: *Buy Yourself the F*cking Lilies* is the book I was put on earth to write. I know that. That is my purpose—to share with others an essential truth I have discovered: I am allowed to nurture myself. I have permission to re-parent myself in the exact way I wish I had been growing up. In fact, when I

---

* I believe this to be a "sports" reference.
† Do we like this phrase better than the word "journey"?

treat myself as if I'm worth taking care of, I grow into a better, stronger version of myself and member of my community. Self-care is not silly nor indulgent; instead, it's one of the only things that can lead to a beautiful, stable life. *Glow in the F*cking Dark,* on the other hand, is the book that wrote me.

Let me explain: If you are going to be so ridiculously bold as to suggest you can get right with your own soul and *then* have the chutzpah to tell other people you can help them find their own souls, then you *really* have to walk the walk. Ya know? You can't choose a title like that and then make weak decisions that don't honor your glow. Almost every choice I've made for the past three years, I've had to ask myself, "Is this a soulful, beautiful, worthy decision that *glows*? Or am I settling and making a choice out of fear and desperation?" "If I knew I had an inner light given to me by the universe, would I act the way I am currently acting?" It's been a long-ass three years. I didn't always succeed, OBVIOUSLY, I still made plenty of dim decisions where I did not value myself or repeated old limiting decisions.

And! And, and, and, I made more *glow* decisions than I ever thought possible. My life, pushed off the plateau, has so much more soul, so much more strength, so much more "OMG, it's a new day for me!" I know, feel, and can never lose the truth—no matter how many mistakes I make—that I have stardust at my core. I am pure light, pure goodness, and all the rest is kinda dumb. I also know that *everyone else* is made of the same pure stardust so that if I hurt someone, I'm always hurting myself. But! When I heal myself? Welp. I'm healing everyone else too. And when I say, "we are made of stardust," I hope you know by now that I'm not trying to make you feel good, or use a cutesy term. There's no line of Etsy mugs with that slogan to sell. (Although, if I were smart, maybe I would do that? Anyone want to partner with me?) If you *still* don't trust me, trust astrophysicist Carl Sagan who said based on science, yes, science, "The cosmos is also within us. We're made of star-stuff. We are a way for the cosmos to know itself." What he's saying is that most of the elements found in our bodies were created inside *stars* over the course of billions of years. The carbon in our muscles, the iron in our blood, every atom of oxygen in our lungs, *all* of those came directly from stars. And what do we say about stars? Has anyone ever said, "Those stars are not good enough," or "Those stars aren't worthy of love because they can't finish a to-do list?" NEVER ONCE HAS ANYONE SAID THIS! We all agree, stars are gorgeous, mystical, miraculous orbs of light with whom we all have the *pleasure* of co-existing.

Once you know that to be the truth, that not only are you made of stardust but so, too, is *everyone else,* doesn't that dramatically alter how you show up in the world? Doesn't that shift not only how you treat (and hopefully honor) yourself but how you behave toward (and hopefully honor) all the other stardust-filled bodies on our planet?

By this point, I've been leading a life full of glow for years and I have to report to you, rather than this being a difficult expectation I've placed on myself, my days are filled with so much more ease than I ever thought possible because I am no longer beholden to bullshit, limiting, mean thoughts. I found the freedom to shine and to relate to and cultivate the shine of everyone else in my life. If you think this is not possible for you, just remember, you and I are full of the same stardust. There is no reason in the cosmos that you can't find the light you are looking for.

WITH GRATEFUL TEARS IN MY EYES THAT WE'VE MET AT ALL, ALWAYS AND FOREVER YOURS,

TARA

"RAMBLING-ABOUT-STAR-STUFF-AND-FEELING-REALLY-GOOD-ABOUT-IT" SCHUSTER

How to Use This Journal

You can use this journal however you want. You can pick and choose your prompts at random—I don't care. Though, actually, I vastly prefer if you go in order with me. . . . So, I guess . . . actually I do *really* care so please don't do this however you want. I spent a lot of time and thought on the order and progression, and I only said "I don't care" because I want you to think I'm "super chill" but SPOILER: I'm made of flames. I think you probz are too.

I'm giving you four weeks of prompts in the hopes that you might pick up the journaling habit! I would love you to complete all of them, taking fifteen to twenty minutes to answer each question. This isn't arbitrary. From all the studies I've read on the scientific benefits of journaling for anxiety, depression, emotional regulation, and even healing things like *legit* wounds and medical conditions, this cadence of journaling seems to be essential. Though that is the last time I will talk about science because . . . have you met me? I'm just not that kind of gal.

When you sit down to journal, I'd also like you to ask yourself, "What am I feeling?" and then label your emotions using my handy-dandy emotion wheel (see page 38) to help you get specific about your mood. The more we practice figuring out how we *actually* feel (not how we want to feel, nor how we want others to think we feel) the quicker we can start making new choices about how we react to the world. Capice? If this confuses you—don't worry—it will all make sense shortly. Ready? LET'S F*CKING GLOW!

Week 1: Heal

Today I feel:

- How do you feel *right now*? Do you know? Cuz most of us don't. And the less aware we are of our emotions, the less we are able to do anything about them, be it to savor them or to get help! Please use the emotion wheel on page 38 to describe your mood.* You can start from the center and work your way outward or start from the outer circle and work your way inward. If you are currently as gloomy as can be, you might identify: sad-despair-desperate. If you have pep in your step, you might identify: joy-interested-free. However, if the category of "joy," for example, is too big of a concept for you (sometimes it is for me), you could also identify "curious" in the outer ring and work yourself backward to interested-joy. Maybe you are not skipping-down-the-street joyful, BUT it's important to identify, even if vaguely, that you have a little inkling of joy in order to cultivate more of it.

- Now, what led to this mood you are in? Any ideas? Is there a way you would rather feel? No judging, no doing allowed, just labeling and investigating. Moving forward, you'll write down your emotions every day at the top of the page.

Today I feel:

- Is there any itty-bitty voice within you that wants to be heard? Maybe you've noticed fleeting moments where you think, *This isn't the right job, This isn't the right partner, I need to escape, I feel numb to my life,* or maybe you feel, *This is the thing I love to do, Wow, I have incredible friends,* or *I feel super hopeful about my own power.*

---

* There is no way to do this wrong. You don't have to do this perfectly. Don't think too much, just go with the emotions that feel most present to you.

- If you haven't heard this voice, can you imagine what your true inner self needs you to hear? Don't worry—we aren't going to take any actions (i.e., if our voice wants us to quit our job, we are not obligated to do so). Just: Is there something in you that wants to be heard? List every single thing you hear.

Today I feel:
- List twenty things, people, or experiences that make you feel good and happy and light. Do you see any common themes? For example, is your list mostly made up of people, adventures, moments in nature? See any patterns?
- Now list twenty things, people, or experiences that make you feel . . . well, not great . . . to bad . . . to awful. Do you see any common themes? For example, is your list made up of tricky relationships, work concerns, or things you feel guilty about?
- Looking at both lists: What would you like to bring more of into your life and what would you like less of? Again—you will not need to take *any* actions, just write it down.

Today I feel:
- All week you have been working on recognizing your emotions and now I have a question: Have your emotions killed you? Did writing them down drive you mad and into the attic, *Jane Eyre* style? Did your words leap off the page with tiny paper knives and leave you with thousands of microscopic paper cuts? Which, *wow,* that sounds painful. How did the experience of paying attention to how you feel affect you? If you felt *nothing,* cool, cool, I still have ten more prompts with you. I'm not worried.

Week 2: Grow

Today I feel:

- Please list the circumstances in your life where you feel powerless—locally and globally. Examples: the illness of a loved one, your own illness, hating a job, being unable to develop a habit you want, the multiple raging wars, environmental degradation, etc. What are you powerless over?
- Now, looking at your list, are you actually, for real, 100 percent, without any doubt, utterly *powerless* over these situations? List one thing you could do to reclaim your agency and exert your autonomy for each item.
- Bonus points: DO ONE OF THESE THINGS!

Today I feel:

- Is there one habit you really want to develop in your life? Why do you want to? What's holding you back? Can you experiment with setting aside actual real time in your actual real schedule to do it? Can you make it more pleasurable so you'll look forward to it? CAN YOU BRIBE YOURSELF INTO THIS HABIT? Let's get creative, how can you actually *do* it instead of merely think about it?

Today I feel:

- Here is the scariest question in this journal: Can you describe your relationship to money? AGH! SO HARD! What words and emotions come up for you immediately? What do you believe the purpose of money is? Do you believe you're allowed to have money? Do you think there is such a thing as "enough" money? Do you have any clue what would be "enough" for you? What is one thing you wish you knew about money? Spend some time answering these questions.

Today I feel:

- Do you or does anyone you know suffer from depression? Can you describe how depression feels to you (or how you think it feels to another)? Do you or a loved one have a *goddamn plan* for what to do when depression strikes? Most of us don't (I didn't for the first thirty years of my life). Spend time describing how depression feels and how you can help yourself or someone you love when that darkness sets in. Have no f*cking clue what to do? Well, the book has a bunch of ideas you can flip back to but for now, GOOGLE IT! Ask a friend who struggles as you do if they have any strategies. Just start getting curious.

Today I feel:

- Oh man, I think you might hate this one . . . but . . . I'm going to ask it anyway. List twenty things about your body for which you are grateful. For example: I'm grateful that today I don't have any major health issues; I'm grateful that my lungs work and that I sucked in air to wake myself today; I'm grateful for sleep even tho I have insomnia—some sleep is better than none—and on and on.
- Now look at this list and instead of judging yourself or trying to change, can you just be grateful to have a body?

Week 3: Glow

Today I feel:

- Think back on a favorite memory, or a photo of you as a child, and answer the following questions: What are three words to describe this version of you? What did you love most in the world? What was your favorite item of clothing or toy? What were you curious about at that age? What was your favorite food? What was your favorite song, movie, or book? Recover just a small piece of Little You! And if nothing comes to mind, imagine the perfect Little You and answer all of the questions above.
- Now, is there anything from Little You that you'd like to bring into your current life?

Today I feel:

- What's an object you've desired recently? It could be something small, like a new face serum (clearly speaking about myself here). Is there anything behind your desire? For example: If I ask myself, "Why do I want the face serum?" The answer is: "Because I want to look pretty, to be attractive, to find love." AHA! Will face serum bring me love? ~~Maybe~~ Hell no! So, I can have compassion for myself for being so lusty for a material object *and I can work on what I actually want—love.*

Today I feel:

- When have you felt a "Full Body Yes"? It's a moment when you feel clear and easy and you know you're doing the right thing. Examples: hiking, giving a presentation, playing with your kids. Write at least ten things that give you a Full Body Yes. Can't come up with five, much less ten? GUESS! What do you think might make you feel like you are in the zone

and totally aligned? Now look at your list; is there any way
to bring one of these things more into your current life?

Today I feel:
- If you were to look back at Current You from the vantage
  point of the future, what would you have wanted to accomplish? What would have actually been meaningful to you? Is
  there a Future You you're working toward? What do they
  look like? What are they most proud of? What do they want
  you to know?

Today I feel:
- I ask myself this every night before I go to bed and I'd like you
  to try it with me: Was someone kind to me today? Was I kind
  to someone today? Did I act like the person I want to be? The
  more you practice that one prompt, the more you can change
  the direction of your life in a way that is full of more *glow* than
  you ever thought possible.

Week 4: Shine Your Light

Today I feel:

- In week 1 I asked you to list twenty things, people, or experiences that make you feel good and happy and light. Have you incorporated any of the twenty delightful things into your life? Why or why not? How did it feel to bring more joy into your life?
- I also asked you to list twenty things that make you feel not great . . . to bad . . . to awful. Have you reduced the twenty "not great" things in your life? Why or why not? How does it feel to take things out of your life that you know suck? Or if you haven't reduced the known painful things, what's holding you back? Do you have the power to break free and help yourself? If you know what brings you down there's no reason on earth why you can't lessen it!

Today I feel:

- What are you struggling with? What burden weighs heavily on your shoulders? What hurts the most? What situation would you most like to change in your life? I *promise* if you write it down it won't kill you. And . . . in fact . . . I'll bet you $1,005* it makes you feel better.
- Now that you know you're made of stardust and that you have the power and ability to radiate light, what's one thing you can do to help yourself with the burden you just described?

Today I feel:

- What are ten small luxuries that bring you joy? Blueberries from the farmers market? Seven-dollar lilies from the grocery

---

* Why have I chosen this *very* specific number? Your guess is as good as mine.

store?* A drawer of socks without holes in any of them? A walk with a friend on the beach? List any you can!

- Can you schedule time this week to do at least one of the above? Part of glowing is treating yourself the like the precious, stardust-filled self you are.

Today I feel:

- Over the course of the past four weeks, have you learned anything new about yourself? If so, what would you like to do with that knowledge? Bolster it? Heal it? Stuff it in the basement? In which case, please don't do that! How will you bring the lessons you are gaining into your everyday life?

Today I feel:

- What do you wish I had covered in this journaling section? Questions about your goals? Physical health? Relationships? Write a list of anything that occurs to you. Now, look at your list and pick one thing you want to work on.
- Can you commit to helping yourself work on this one thing? What's the first step? This is what you're going to journal on moving forward. And if you find it helpful, you can continue to work your way down the list, crossing off each situation as you go. You can change your whole life (if you want to!) by taking on one thing you know is not right at a time.

This isn't a prompt, just a note from me: I love you an unreasonable amount. Even if we've never met my stardust is connected to your stardust and your healing is my healing is the world's healing. So please, keep on going, evolving, growing, questioning, and enjoying on behalf of all of us.

---

* This one goes out to all my readers of *Buy Yourself the F*cking Lilies*—I see you! And I thank you for taking on not one but two of my books!

Tara Schuster is the author of *Buy Yourself the F*cking Lilies,* a finalist for Goodreads' Best Nonfiction Book of 2020 and selected by *Cosmopolitan, Real Simple, Goop, Publishers Weekly,* and many more as one of the year's best books on mental health and self-care.

Previously, Schuster served as vice president of talent and development at Comedy Central, where she was the executive in charge of such critically acclaimed shows as the Emmy and Peabody Award–winning *Key & Peele.* A contributor to *InStyle, The New Yorker,* and *Forbes,* among others, Tara Schuster lives in Los Angeles.

taraschuster.com/newsletter
Instagram: @taraschuster
TikTok: @taraschuster

Tara Schuster shares more brutally honest, often hilarious, hard-won lessons in learning to love and care for yourself.

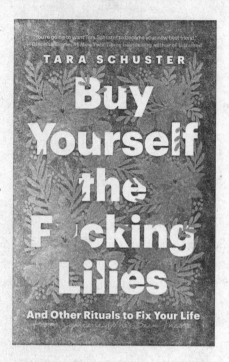

"You're going to want Tara Schuster to become your new best friend."

—GLENNON DOYLE,
#1 *New York Times* bestselling author of *Untamed*

"Compelling, persuasive, and useful no matter where you are in your life."

—CHELSEA HANDLER,
#1 *New York Times* bestselling author of *Life Will Be the Death of Me*

**Sign up for Tara's self-care newsletter at
taraschuster.com/newsletter**

Follow Tara on social media

@taraschuster   @taraschuster   @taraschustar

Available wherever books are sold